BETWEEN A ROCK
AND A HARD RACE

Published by Robert Deaves

First Edition 2017

Copyright © Robert Deaves, 2017

Photos © Robert Deaves, 2016

ISBN: 978-1-912724-07-9

BETWEEN A ROCK
AND A HARD RACE

ROBERT DEAVES

Contents

Preface

A Rock and a Story

In August 2016, 23 of the world's best Finn sailors gathered in Rio de Janeiro to fight an epic battle to win an Olympic medal. For many, the gold medal had been a foregone conclusion for much of the previous four years, as Giles Scott, after a shaky start, got the job done early and with confidence, to enjoy the medal race, with the gold medal secure. However, the silver and bronze medals were considered anyone's with most of the fleet capable of winning races and even taking a medal. The winners, Vasilij Žbogar of Slovenia and Caleb Paine of the USA were not unexpected medalists but not among the most likely candidates, many of whom, as so often happens at the Olympic Games, failed to live up to expectation.

The racing was hard with a huge contrast of conditions on the various course areas chosen by the organisers, from the big wave open ocean courses, to the flat water, shifty, harbour courses. However, one feature of Rio figured in every race either as a wind barrier or as a landmark.

Sugarloaf Mountain, the rock in the title of this book, played a larger than life role in many of the sailor's strategies, as well as being more significant in the actual race outcomes, than perhaps any geographical feature in any previous Olympic regatta. If it wasn't Sugarloaf, then another rock was prevalent. There were a lot of monolithic landmarks overlooking the race areas to choose from.

This book represents four years work by the author and the sailors on the long road to Rio. It is based on the hundreds of interviews and press releases over the years from 2012 to 2016, much of which is included unaltered in these pages to provide some context amid the immediacy of the time they were carried out, to add perspective of the campaign trail to the developing story and to our understanding of how the sailor's thoughts and mindsets developed as the Olympics loomed ever closer, as well as the struggles they faced and the many challenges they had to overcome.

It took far longer than intended to bring this book together so without further ado…our story begins on a hill four years earlier…

PART 1

OVERTURE

1

Shadow on the Hill

A Score to be Settled

On the perilous race course below hearts were pumping at maximum capacity, every nerve was strained and every muscle working hard for the final supreme effort. Thousands upon thousands of expectant faces gazed down at 10 sailors as they performed the final brief ritual of an extraordinary competition that had begun in the same amphitheatre seven days before.

On that day, and in that final race, destiny played into the hands of one man to rewrite history one more time, to leave his mark in way that no one would ever likely do again, to exceed his own incredible achievements. It would be his final performance in this arena, a finale to 16 years of Olympic success and Olympic medals. There was only one inevitable outcome and even though the man himself didn't know it, the majority of the hopeful crowd expected nothing less from their day out on the hill.

Above on the hill, the shadow of another man was lost in the crowd, enduring a kind of terrible torture, a personal battle with himself because he knew it could have very easily been him down on the water below, instead of being just a spectator. He knew he could have been in a position to win the Olympic gold. He had won most of the events leading up to the Games, but his peak performance had come just a little too late to win his ticket to the Olympics.

Giles Scott sat on the hill and watched but wasn't really sure he wanted to be there. He felt that it should have, or could have, been him, out in front of the crowds, instead of Ben Ainslie. But he had made some mistakes during the intense trials series and it wasn't him down there and he just had to live with it, and move on.

While Ainslie attempted to become the most successful Olympic sailor ever, Scott was perhaps a bit hesitant to engage with the battle being played out below by his teammate and fierce adversary. Instead, he just watched, waiting for it all to be over, so he could begin the process to return in four years time to claim the same glory as Ainslie.

Despite the intense rivalry on the water they had remained friends and they met up several times during the 2012 Olympics, but Ainslie's victory would still be a bittersweet moment for Scott. However, his failure to achieve his goals in 2012, was perhaps the single biggest driver that led to Scott not only winning gold in four years time in Rio, but also doing so in a manner that would exceed the achievements of his predecessor and rival.

The drama on the secluded racing area between the Nothe promontory and Portland Harbour walls was a dramatic conclusion to an epic battle that had played out in Weymouth Bay over the previous week during the 2012 Olympic Sailing Competition. At stake was Ainslie's fourth Olympic gold medal, and fifth in total to become the most decorated Olympic sailor of all time. Challenging him were Jonas Høgh-Christensen of Denmark and Pieter-Jan Postma of the Netherlands.

Perhaps it was destiny or perhaps it was just a great story waiting to be told. If it were fiction, then it would have been a little far-fetched. Ainslie was one of the best dinghy sailors the world had ever seen. Høgh-Christensen, the Danish pretender, was fighting to defend a record held by one of his countrymen for 52 years. He saw himself as the protector of the record held by Paul Elvstrøm, of four Olympic gold medals won between 1948 and 1960, a record that had stood unrivalled across generations of sailors. Elvstrøm was the most respected and accomplished racing sailor in history and Høgh-Christensen certainly didn't want that accolade to be passed to Ainslie, when it was in his power to stop him. But one more gold medal for Ainslie would mean he would surpass Elvstrøm's record. Høgh-Christensen felt it was his destiny to stop that happening.

The Games had started where it would end, on the Nothe course. First blood went to Høgh-Christensen, claiming two race wins on the opening day. Many commentators were happy that Ainslie hadn't made his traditional mess of the first day. He came out with two second-places, and that was a good start for him.

The Dane continued to dominate on the second day with Ainslie dropping to third in the overall table. Ainslie came ashore saying he was angry and normally that was enough for him to find some extra inspiration. But it didn't quite work and Høgh-Christensen notched up two more victories over Ainslie before the mid-competition break.

Høgh-Christensen seemed unstoppable, even coming back in Race 4 to finish seventh after a huge mistake at the start where he hit the pin end boat and started last out of the 24 boats. Even after this, he still beat Ainslie across the finish line. In fact Ainslie hadn't beaten him in any of the six races before the break and the British camp was starting to get a little worried.

It then developed into a fascinating and fierce battle of wits between two sailors, both at the top of their game. Dubbed by TV commentators as the 'battle of the bay', the epic struggle between Ainslie and Høgh-Christensen made headlines around the world, and for a variety of reasons. Both were vilified and glorified for their actions and their alleged conduct out on Weymouth Bay. But as often in sailing, to win the war you have to win the final battle. It doesn't matter how you start, it matters how you finish.

Ainslie had of course been expected to dominate on home waters, but a combination of over training, recurring injuries, the intense pressure of a home crowd and the ever expectant and demanding media, all conspired to drain him of the answers he needed to respond to the Danish onslaught. At the mid way stage in the regatta, no one was betting against Høgh-Christensen sealing the gold medal. But then not many we're betting against Ainslie to produce a comeback finale to beat them all. After all, he was very good at comebacks.

AINSLIE BEGAN TO turn it around in the second half of the week and his inevitable fight back into contention gradually gathered momentum. The mid regatta break saved him in many ways, allowing valuable recovery time and some time to reflect on the closing races, while he drew inspiration from the success of other British athletes in the Games.

The break also introduced a new set of tidal conditions on Weymouth bay with shorter upwind legs, where Høgh-Christensen had been so dominant in the early races, and long offwind legs, where Ainslie knew he could excel more than any other sailor out there. With a different set of racing conditions, it seems unlikely that Ainslie would have reeled in the Dane as he did. But because of the change, race-by-race, leg-by-leg, reel him in is what he did. Four races later, including two race wins for Ainslie and a few mistakes from Høgh-Christensen, and the scorecard was level. In terms of races it was still 7-3 to the Dane but it was heading for a thrilling conclusion with a winner takes all medal race finale on the unpredictable Nothe course area. Only one point separated them, and with the medal race being double points and non-discardable, it would come down to who beat whom across the line.

The 30-minute medal race at the end of a week-long battle remains a contentious way to settle an Olympic gold medal. It brings elements of randomness and luck into a sport that has historically always been about performing consistently across of variety of different conditions.

The medal race in Weymouth was held on the course area where the racing had begun a week before when Høgh-Christensen shocked the sailing world by notching up two race wins on what had been widely criticised as the most difficult race course the sailors ever had to contend with. Stuck under the striking Nothe headland, and with the predominantly south-easterly wind coming off Portland Harbour, it produced a plethora of wind shifts and pressure changes than would catch out both the wary and the unwary.

Both had trained extensively on that course area in the preceding three years. Both knew it could be random at times, and both knew the percentages. Høgh-Christensen estimated that he had done around 300 races on the Nothe course area during training. Eighty per cent of the time, the left side would pay.

As the final deciding race unfolded, Høgh-Christensen had the advantage in the pre-start leading Ainslie on a dance around the committee boat, keeping his formidable rival at arms length and controlling the situation perfectly. At exactly the right time, the Dane escaped and hit the line at speed with Ainslie slightly late and behind. But he had made too perfect a job of it as Ainslie quickly realised he was in trouble and had to bail out to the right to clear his wind and find some space.

With Høgh-Christensen convinced the left was still good, his plan was playing out perfectly. How better to start the race with the advantage and forcing his opposition to go the wrong way behind the fleet? With hearts pumping, muscles stretched and brains working hard, Høgh-Christensen sailed towards what he thought was a clear advantage on the left: just like the opening race when he had controlled the left and led the race at every mark. It was a dead cert.

But he had let Ainslie escape to the right. Ainslie was probably the most dangerous Finn sailor in the world when backed into a corner, and to let him go that far away, and gain that much leverage, was a risk. Then, just like a work of fiction, the first shift came from the right and Ainslie found himself ahead while Høgh-Christensen struggled to get back across.

They both rounded the first mark deep but Ainslie made the best of the free pumping first downwind to move into second place at the gate at the bottom of the course, while the Dane was still at the back. As they turned to head back upwind for the second and final time, Ainslie could probably have sailed away from this position and even won the race, but he took no risks and covered Høgh-Christensen for the remainder of the race, dragging both of them further back and away from the fleet. In doing so they both ended up right at the back while the only sailor who was capable of beating either of them to the gold medal, Dutchman, Pieter-Jan Postma, was able to sail his own race, and he was getting dangerously near the front.

Postma knew he could have won the gold medal if both Ainslie and Høgh-Christensen were right at the back of the 10-boat fleet. And incredibly, that is the way it played out. Ainslie probably overdid the match race tactics, but had little choice. If Høgh-Christensen got ahead, it was all over, so the first job was to keep him behind.

In the randomness of the Nothe course area Postma then found the perfect shift to move into the top three, ironically on the left side of the course. He was now in the bronze medal position. With Ainslie and Høgh-Christensen at the back Postma was just one place away from stealing the gold from under their noses. Coming down the final leg, he was in a comfortable medal position, but as he has done so many times, before and since, he took one risk too many. Perhaps he was blinded by the thought of the gold medal, which was within his grasp, or perhaps he was too nervous to think straight, but he pushed too hard and fouled another boat during a manoeuvre while trying to move into second place just 50 metres from the finish. He had to do penalty turns. That foul gave the gold to Ainslie and cost Postma a medal. If Postma hadn't fouled the other boat, it would have been a very different story. But the gold was Ainslie's and the history books needed rewriting again.

In the run up to the 2012 Olympics, the only person who seemed to doubt that a fourth consecutive gold medal was on the way was Ainslie himself. The world put him on a pedestal and he could do no wrong. Whatever he did, whatever his results, he would always win through in the end. That was his nature. That was his destiny. And that was what [almost] everyone believed. He described it as the hardest two weeks of his life.

While Postma hung his head in his hands in sorrow as the gold, inevitably, went to Ainslie, Høgh-Christensen shed tears for the lost opportunity, and Jonathan Lobert of France celebrated his dramatic win in the medal race to take the bronze medal.

GILES SCOTT STOOD on the hill and watched the performance play out beneath him. Though he was still infuriated with himself for not winning the Olympic selection trails, he knew, he absolutely knew for sure, where he wanted to be in four years time, and he was going to make absolutely sure that he did everything within his ever growing powers to be able to achieve that goal.

From the time Scott returned to full-time Finn sailing in 2013, after a spell with America's Cup boats in the Prada Luna Rossa team, he was invincible. Rather than the rise and falls of the majority of sailors as they peak for certain events, Scott's performance was more of a flatline of gold medals, culminating in the gold medal in Rio. What he already knew he could achieve in 2012, he had to wait four more years before he could hold it in his hands.

His rise to greatness could have many starting places but for this story the starting point is undeniably the 2011 Pre-Olympic trials in Weymouth, at the 2011 Sail for Gold regatta. His defeat there at the hands of the eventual gold medalist at the 2011 Pre-Olympics and the 2012 Olympics, Ben Ainslie, affected him so deeply that it completely changed his preparation over the next five years. This was a crucial turning point in the mood of the then 25 year old. He had tasted defeat and he didn't like it one little bit.

Defeat changes a person in ways that are not often apparent. Ben Ainslie's defeat in the Laser in 1996 to Robert Scheidt was arguably the most important result of his career. It changed his way of preparation; it inspired him to be better than the best, to push himself beyond his limits if that meant gaining a miniscule advantage over his competitors. The final race of the 2000 Olympics was evidence enough of that as he clearly proved he had prepared better than Scheidt, and defeated him, in the most memorable race in Olympic history. Without that defeat in 1996, victory in 2000 may not have happened.

So Scott's defeat at the 2011 Sail for Gold was perhaps the defining moment in the making of the gold medal in Rio. Afterwards he questioned his ability to be able bring back a big one. However within the next six months he had brought home both the European and the World title, both in quite dramatic ways.

He described the European title, coming just weeks after the Weymouth defeat as an enormous relief. It was a consolation prize in many ways, however with Ainslie not attending, the victory was not absolute proof of his skill against the man who was to go onto become the most successful Olympic sailor of all time. But it was important for another reason. Though he took a 16 month gap from full-time Finn sailing between the 2012 Sail for Gold, which he won, and the autumn of 2013, the European title of 2011 was his first taste of Finn gold, a taste, which, over the coming five years he would come to know intimately.

2

A Long History
The Ultimate Challenge

Within the sport of dinghy racing the Finn class is often cited and widely regarded as the ultimate challenge. It was created from the hand of Swedish canoe designer Rickard Sarby in Uppsala, Sweden, in 1949 as his entry in a design competition to select a new monotype dinghy for the 1952 Olympics Games in Helsinki, Finland. The Finn is now the oldest class being used in the Olympic Games, but is also one of the most modern, having embraced new technology such as carbon masts and Kevlar sails. It is a modern thoroughbred that has a long and rich history, a proud heritage, a deep legacy and longstanding traditions. The class has created more sailing heroes than any other class.

The Finn was designed as an Olympic singlehanded dinghy that could be sailed worldwide and aspiring Olympic sailors could practice and develop the required skills prior to the Games. The Finn class established strict class rules and regulations and because of this proved to be a great Olympic class reflecting the Olympic spirit. The intense devotion to the Finn competition by many sailors throughout the world and a large number of former Finn sailors in other classes in the Olympics who learned their Olympic competitive spirit in the Finn class, demonstrates that the Finn class is a thoroughbred Olympic Class.

It all began back in 1948 when the Finnish Yachting Association was considering which boats to use for the 1952 Olympic Games at Helsinki. With the lack of a suitable dinghy in Scandinavia, they instigated a design competition to find a singlehanded dinghy that could be used primarily for inter-Scandinavian competition, but which could also be used at the Olympics.

Sarby entered a design into this competition and although it was not initially selected, he was invited to take part in the trial races because he had already built a prototype. Several trial series were held and on May 15, 1950, the Finnish Yachting Association adopted the boat as an Olympic dinghy. This boat was the Finn and an Olympic legend was born.

In Helsinki in 1952 the Finn made its Olympic debut, and over the following years, names such as Paul Elvstrøm, Willy Kuhweide, John Bertrand and Jochen Schümann sailed themselves into the record books. Elvstrøm won three of his four Olympic gold medals in the Finn (the other being in the Firefly), completely dominating the class in 1952, 1956 (Melbourne) and 1960 (Naples). The first Finn silver medal went to Charles Currey of Great Britain and the first Finn bronze medal went to Sarby.

AFTER THE 1952 Olympics interest in the Finn waned, but the class was kept alive because in 1953 it was reselected for the 1956 Olympics in Melbourne, Australia. Control over the administration of the Finn was handed over to the IYRU (International Yacht Racing Union – later called the International Sailing Federation and today known as World Sailing) in 1955. Then in 1956, the first ever Finn Gold Cup (the Finn World Championship) was held at Burnham-on-Crouch after F.G. Mitchell of the Royal Burnham Yacht Club was persuaded by Vernon Stratton of the British Finn Association to present the class with a Gold Cup. Until this moment there was no real basis for the International Finn Class and it is believed that the firm footing of the class started here. Also in 1956 Henri Leten, of Belgium, organised the first AGM of the class at the European Championships in The Netherlands and the International Finn Association (IFA) was born. This gave the class a strong foundation for future growth and development.

The early wooden Finns gradually gave way to experiments in GRP after the IFA decided to free up construction materials in 1961. At the Gold Cup that year, which was now an established event, the top three places were filled by GRP boats and many sailors then thought that their wooden boats were now obsolete. In fact the magically fast GRP boat that finished third in 1961 was found to have a secret distribution of lead in the hull, improving its gyration, when it was re-measured the following year. It was at this time that Richard Creagh-Osborne took over from Sarby as Chairman of the Technical Committee and he was given instructions to sort out these problems. However, wooden boats staged a comeback in 1964 when Hubert Raudaschl won the Finn Gold Cup with a home built wooden hull.

With the increasing strictness and changes in the class rules, measurement of the boats became easier to control with less manipulation of the rules taking place. Perhaps the biggest problem to overcome was controlling the weight distribution within the hull. It was soon realised that Finns with light ends were fast and, as proved by the matter of the illegal lead, the rules could be circumvented. After various attempts to control weight distribution by means of measuring the bow weight and tilting the hull on a gunwale (which were never satisfactory), a Frenchman named Gilbert Lamboley devised a pendulum test. The boat was suspended and timed over a series of oscillations. For the first time this provided an accurate method of controlling the weight distribution within the hull. It was then possible to free-up construction methods and to allow double bottoms in the hulls. The day of the 'magic Finn' was over. This 'swing test' method was introduced into the Finn class in 1972 and has since become the standard method of weight-distribution testing for many other classes.

During the 1950s, Elvstrøm gradually moved away from the stiff mast and developed a bendy rig with a full sail that was progressively flattened in strong breezes as the mast was bent through mainsheet tension. Throughout the early 1960s one of the most widespread rigs in general use was in fact Elvstrøm's mast and sail combination. But by 1968 Jörg Bruder and Hubert Raudaschl had developed rigs still further, and once again masts became stiffer with flat sails. But the tops of these masts were very flexible sideways, allowing the rig to depower for lightweight skippers. This Bruder/Raudaschl combination completely dominated the class until the early seventies. However, the seeds of change were in the wind in 1969 when Jack Knights from Great Britain turned up at the Finn Gold Cup in Bermuda with a metal mast. He was the only competitor that did not have a wooden mast, and over the next few years use of wooden masts gradually declined to be replaced by aluminium.

When aluminium masts were organised for use in the 1972 Olympics at Kiel, supplied by the organisers, as was all Finn gear for the Olympics at the time, some within the class tried to reverse this decision. However after much argument, all competitors were eventually supplied with the new aluminium mast made in the UK by Needlespar. The British did not have the advantage, as was feared by many, and the metal mast soon became commonplace. Various manufacturers built metal Finn masts over the years, but the Needlespar maintained market domination until 1993, when experiments in carbon resurfaced all the old arguments about change. By the 1980s, North had a virtual monopoly on Finn sails and it wasn't until the early 1990s that other lofts managed to break their stranglehold and produce race-winning sails.

Nowadays carbon masts have penetrated to virtually all levels of Finn sailing, and aluminium masts are mostly regarded as obsolete. Carbon construction also allowed builders to exploit the full extent of the mast dimensions and produce wing masts. These masts have an aerodynamic fore and aft section which became the standard compared to the round sections.

Following the freeing up of the construction rules, due to the revolutionary Lamboley Test, double bottoms were permitted for the first time in 1974. UK Finn builder Peter Taylor was the first to take advantage of this new rule and for a few years Taylor glassfibre hulls were frequently at the front of international fleets. In fact at the 1976 Finn Gold Cup in Brisbane, Australia, his hulls finished in first, second and fourth places.

IN 1978, A group of ex-Laser sailors from the United States took up Finn sailing and a period of American dominance began with names such as John Bertrand, Cam Lewis and Carl Buchan figuring in many International regattas. They all sailed the US built Vanguard hull, which proved to be far superior to any other boat available at the time. They dominated the Finn class until 1980, but after the US boycott of the 1980 Olympics, US interest in the Finn waned slightly and the Europeans regained their former dominance. However by now, the Europeans were also sailing the US Vanguard hulls. This hull together with a Needlespar mast and a North sail, was to be the standard equipment amongst Finn sailors right up until 1993. The Vanguard, which is an all GRP hull, has a fine bow to aid upwind performance and a broad transom to promote early planing. It is a remarkable credit to the Vanguard hull that it was used to win the Finn Gold Cup during the fifteen years up to 1992 on no less than fourteen occasions.

Today the class is very different to the one Sarby created in 1949. While the hull is exactly the same shape, with tight controls to keep the boat as one-design and as close to the original shape as possible, what has changed is the technology available to the class. The modern hulls are now all optimised GRP with carbon masts and Kevlar sails, something that in 1949 would have only been a figment of the imagination. Devoti hulls first appeared in 1994 and went on to dominate the class, though there is now a wider range of builders available across the world, perhaps more than at any time since the 1970s.

The first Finn Gold Cup (the World Championship of the Finn class) was held at Burnham-on-Crouch in 1956 and forty-five competitors from twelve countries attended. The largest fleet ever gathered was at Cascais in Portugal in 1970 where 180 boats from 34 countries competed for the cup. This event was won by the mast builder from Brazil, Jörg Bruder.

The Finn Gold Cup is the highlight of the Finn sailing calendar and is widely regarded as one of the foremost sailing events in the world. To win it is an exceptional achievement, to win it twice is remarkable, but to win it three times is quite outstanding. Until recently this had only been done on four occasions: Willy Kuhweide of Germany in 1963, 1966 and 1967, Lasse Hjortnäs from Denmark in 1982, 1984 and 1985, Fredrik Lööf from Sweden in 1994, 1997 and 1999 and Jörg Bruder of Brazil, who won it three times consecutively in 1970, 1971 and 1972. He remained unbeaten as he was tragically killed in an air crash in 1973 on route to defend his title. However since then Ben Ainslie from Great Britain has dwarfed all other accomplishments to win the trophy six times – 2002, 2003, 2004, 2005, 2008 and 2012, while Giles Scott has so far won it four times – 2011, 2014, 2015 and 2016.

IN 1952 A young Paul Elvstrøm, swept the board in Helsinki to win the first Olympic Finn gold medal by nearly 3,000 points from Charles Currey of Great Britain, who took the silver medal. Elvstrøm won four of the seven races in a fleet of 28 boats and set a standard that has never been equalled. In spite of badly injuring his hand before the sixth race, Sarby just managed to win the bronze medal.

Paul Elvstrøm won because of his hiking technique, which he had developed practising in his own boat. Most of his competitors were sitting on the sidedeck instead of hiking on the sheerguard. In addition Elvstrøm attached a sort of traveller to his boat, which was not supplied by the organiser. Most competitors considered this alteration to be illegal but the Dane got away with it. However after the fifth race, when it was already for sure that he had won the gold medal, Elvstrøm removed the device.

The 1956 Olympics were assigned to Melbourne, Australia. The Finn had proved to be such a great competitive boat in the 1952 Olympics that it was retained as the monotype and again Elvstrøm slaughtered the opposition, this time with five wins in his score. Going into the last race it looked as though the American John Marvin, who had never raced a Finn before, might topple the Belgian, Andre Nelis, since they were level on points. But Nelis pulled out all the stops and kept Marvin covered whilst notching up a second place himself.

For 1960 in Naples, there was a great increase to 35 Finns and Elvstrøm did it again. This time he only won three races and had to withdraw from the last through illness, but he was never lower than fifth in conditions that did not enable him to gain by his fantastic strength and endurance. This was the year that Russia arrived as a top sailing nation and in the Finns the silver medal was won by Alexandr Chuchelov. Nelis of Belgium took bronze.

The 1964 Olympics was assigned to Tokyo, Japan and for the first time the supplied hulls were fibreglass instead of wood. Germany was the leading nation in the Finn in 1964, and Willy Kuhweide, who was only selected at the last moment and despite a severe infection of the middle ear, led the fleet into the final race. Peter Barrett and Henning Wind stayed close to each other during that race and finished seventh and tenth, allowing Kuhweide to once again take line honours and the gold medal.

The 1968 Games were in Mexico with the sailing at Acapulco. Some picked Henning Wind, who had just won the Finn Gold Cup while others favoured Kuhweide or Jörg Bruder, the Brazilian who had won the Pan American Games. Few felt that Valentin Mankin, the veteran Russian Finn sailor and an excellent heavy weather helmsman, had much of a chance in the light weather so typical of Acapulco. But Mankin surprised everyone with a week of almost flawless tactical racing. Never below seventh at any mark, he beat Hubert Raudaschl of Austria by almost 42 points. Fabio Albarelli of Italy won the bronze medal.

For 1972, the Olympic yachting events were held at Kiel, Germany. Synonymous with strong winds and heavy weather sailing, no one was prepared for two weeks of mild weather and light winds. Before the Olympics there was a controversy about the masts supplied by the organiser. Most of the competitors favoured the old wooden masts, which they were used to, and only a few had experience with the new aluminium masts they were forced to use. The competition ended with some big names down the scoreboard. Serge Maury of France won the gold while Elias Hatzipavlis from Greece got silver and Victor Potapov, from Russia, bronze. The decisive race was the fifth, when only three boats finished within the time limit.

The 1976 sailing events were held at Kingston, Ontario. Canada furnished the hulls, while the sailors were allowed to bring their own sails and masts. Not until the weather mark of the last race was it clear where the medals would go. First around was Jochen Schümann from the German Democratic Republic with a tenacious cover on Andrei Balashov of the Soviet Union. Australian John Bertrand, the other contender for the gold was a distant 12th. Although later passed by two boats, Schümann finished ahead of the Russian and the Australian to assure his win. As striking as Schümann's excellent performance was the poor showing of the pre-race favourites, David Howlett of Great Britain and Serge Maury of France.

The 1980 Olympics in Moscow, with the yachting events in Tallinn suffered from the boycott initiated by the United States. A number of potential winners were excluded from the start. Some of those who came, felt uncomfortable within the narrow limits of the strict organisation and performed poorly. The favourites: Jochen Schümann, Mark Neeleman, Lasse Hjortnäs, and Minski Fabris failed to collect the medals. Outsiders like Esko Rechardt took gold and Wolfgang Mayrhofer the silver in front of the only successful favourite, Andrei Balashov, who won the bronze medal.

THE GAMES SUFFERED once again from a boycott at the 1984 Olympics in Los Angeles, this time initiated by the USSR. So in Long Beach the favourites from the DDR, Poland and the USSR were excluded. In the Finn class the actual Olympic sailing was preceded by an undignified controversy following the US trials. John Bertrand was declared the representative only 24 hours before the first start. In that race he had a collision with the later gold medalist Russell Coutts, from New Zealand, and was disqualified. Disregarding the mental strain of the qualification battle and the disqualification in the first race, Bertrand was leading after the fifth and sixth race. In the last race however, he lost the gold to Coutts, while Terry Neilson, from Canada, won the bronze medal.

The 1988 Olympic Regatta was held in the Bay of Pusan in Korea. The final winner, José Luis Doreste, who had competed in both the 1976 and 1980 Olympics, was disqualified in Race 4 for a collision. The silver medalist, Peter Holmberg, from the US Virgin Islands, was disqualified in Race 4 as a premature starter, and one of the favourites Lasse Hjortnäs broke his mast in Race 2 after winning the first race. These events really opened up the racing. Eventually John Cutler won the last two races to take the bronze. Larry Lemieux gave up a good position in the fifth race to rescue two Singapore 470 sailors from the water after one had lost contact with his boat, Lemieux was awarded the Pierre de Coubertin Medal for Sportsmanship for this feat. Once again the sailors had to use boats that were provided by the organisers.

The 1992 Olympic Regatta was held in Barcelona, Spain in generally light to moderate conditions. The Finn fleet was the deepest ever and it was generally agreed that anyone in the first 15 could win the gold and anyone of the first 22 could win a race. The final winner José Maria van der Ploeg, of Spain, never scored worse than sixth and didn't have to sail the final race. The two favourites Eric Mergenthaler, of Mexico, and Glenn Bourke, of Australia, performed poorly and finished 18th and 20th. Brian

Ledbetter, of the USA, was one of the few consistent sailors and won the silver medal, while Craig Monk, from New Zealand, won the last race to snatch the bronze away from Stuart Childerley, of Great Britain. Prior to the regatta, the IFA conducted a two-week training clinic for those countries desiring assistance.

When the numerically stronger Laser was bidding for Olympic status many thought that it would replace the Finn as the Olympic singlehanded dinghy for men. However this was not to be and in 1996 in Savannah there were two singlehanded dinghies for men. This worked well, as it meant that there were two boats for two different weight categories. The advance weather reports suggested a light wind regatta. However, thunderstorm activity resulted in some spectacular weather and strong winds. Poland's first ever sailing medal was won by Mateusz Kusznierewicz with a race to spare, and this in spite of losing his watch early on in the series and using the clock on the starting boat instead. Sebastien Godefroid, from Belgium, took the silver while relative Olympic veteran Roy Heiner, from The Netherlands, took the bronze on the last race.

In Sydney, Australia in 2000, Iain Percy won the first medal for Great Britain in the class since Charles Currey's silver in 1952. Sailing a very consistent series he had it all wrapped up before the final race. Luca Devoti's silver medal was one of the most unexpected medals of the Games, while Fredrik Lööf's bronze had been a long time coming. For the first time ever the sailors had been allowed to bring their own hulls as well as rigs. Also of importance to the Finn sailors of the future, Ben Ainslie won his first Olympic gold medal in the Laser class. Two years later he announced his switch to the Finn, where he dominated for the next 10 years.

Ainslie started the 2004 Olympics in Athens with a disqualification, but fought back with a string of top results to make a remarkable comeback. Sticking to silver medalist Rafael Trujillo, from Spain, in the final race assured him of his second gold medal while Kusznierewicz picked up his second Finn medal after winning the final race and taking bronze.

In 2008 in Qingdao, China, Ainslie won his third Olympic gold after winning three races in generally very light winds and very strong tides. He also won the medal race in very strong winds, the first time that format had been used at the Olympics. Zach Railey, from the USA, was the surprise silver medalist but didn't win a single race and neither did Guillaume Florent, of France, who took the bronze away from Daniel Birgmark, of Sweden, on the medal race result, both sailors ending up with the same points.

The Games returned to London in 2012, with the sailing events in Weymouth & Portland. With moderate to strong winds every day this was one of the most physically toughest Olympics ever, but it was a great showcase for sailing. Ainslie didn't produce the form that everyone expected and struggled to keep up with Jonas Høgh-Christensen, of Denmark, sailing in his third Olympics. Eventually Ainslie clawed his way back and overcame Høgh-Christensen in the medal race, while Jonathan Lobert claimed the bronze.

The Finn's appearance at Rio 2016 would be the 17th consecutive time that the class was used as equipment at the Olympic Games.

3

Faster, Higher, Stronger

The Purest Athletic Experience in World-Class Sailing

The Finn dinghy has been an Olympic singlehanded dinghy since 1952. Including Rio 2016 it has been part of the Olympic programme for 64 years, across 17 Olympic Games. There are very good reasons why it has lasted so long on the greatest sporting stage and become such an inherent part of the Summer Olympics.

In general, the Finn class perfectly embodies the Olympic motto, 'Citius, Altius, Fortius', or 'Faster, Higher, Stronger', and perhaps that is more relevant nowadays than when Pierre de Coubertin first proposed it in 1894 at the first Olympic Games. Finn sailors are stronger and taller than ever before, and Finns are certainly faster than they used to be.

The boat that began with a wooden hull, wooden spars and cotton sails, has evolved into a modern racing machine, using space age materials and raced by supreme athletes who are among the fittest athletes of any sport at the Olympic Games.

In the last decade, the Finn Class has carried out a number of surveys on its elite sailors to compare trends and accumulate data regarding the weight, height and age when they started sailing the Finn, to try and build a picture of the current fleet and to examine how these factors have changed over the years.

For the first survey in 2009, the target group was the top 50 ranked Finn sailors in the world as well as a whole group of new young sailors coming into the class. The results that followed, and its analysis, made for interesting reading.

It is a widely reported fact that many people across the world are getting taller and heavier through better diet and better standards of living and this is reflected in the results of the survey. Perhaps as a result of this, sailors are also starting in the Finn much younger than their predecessors did. In fact the average age for starting out in the Finn dropped from 24.7 for those born in the 1970s to just 17 for those born in the 1990s.

In addition, in the top 20 world ranked sailors (2009), the active age ranged from 22 to 44 years, a range of 22 years; and the height ranged from 180 to 200 cm, a range of 20 cm.

For sailors born between 1970 and 1979 the average age when they started was 24.7 years. For sailors born between 1980 and 1987 the average age when they started dropped to 20.6 years. But for sailors born between 1988 (they would have been in their last year as juniors in 2009) and 1994 the average age when they started was just 17 years old.

For the majority of the sailors surveyed, the Finn was the vital piece of equipment that kept them training and competing at the highest level. For these young, talented and extremely fit athletes who all weighed more than 85 kg and are taller than 1.8 metres, there was, and still is, no other dinghy option if they want to live their Olympic dream.

The advent of free pumping has also revolutionised the techniques of the class and the levels of fitness required to be successful.

In 2004, the Finn Class introduced free pumping downwind when the wind was stronger than 12 knots. Historically, sailors have been restricted from pumping the sail and the boat. Rules were written to allow limited physical movement of the body to move, or pump, the sail and the boat, leaving the speed of the boat dependent on the wind and on the equipment rather than the sailor's strength and stamina.

From 2004, when the wind was over 12 knots, these limits would no longer apply downwind. This revolutionised Finn sailing as the sailors not only had to learn new techniques but also tune their bodies to train for this incredibly physical skill.

This was further refined in 2010, when the limit was dropped to 10 knots. Techniques changed again, and with that, the sailors needed to get fitter and more aerobic to drive the boat as fast as possible. As a result of these techniques, combined with the physicality of sailing upwind, the Finn is perhaps the most physically demanding dinghy class of them all, and sailing the Finn is arguably the purest athletic experience in world-class sailing.

To continually pump the sail downwind, while rocking and steering the boat is comparable to an endurance sprint. Heart rates downwind in 10-12 knots are at 175-185 beats per minute. That compares to 150-165 beats per minute upwind in very strong winds. Physiologists from other sports are often shocked to see the data from Finn sailing. Rates are very person dependent, but it's pretty brutal on a three-race day.

It is crucial to synchronise the rocking and the pumping, so that both work together. Get it wrong and the boat slows. Timing and rhythm are as equally important as strength and power.

The hardest wind speed for free pumping in Finn sailing is about 9-12 knots, especially when the free pumping flag is up and the wind has dropped slightly. It's sea-state dependent, but that is generally where the rate that the sail is pumped and the power that goes into the pumps and the sailor's technique has the biggest impact on how fast the boat goes go. So it needs the hardest amount of work.

Heart rates drop as the wind increases and the sea state comes up. Then steering the boat becomes more important and the pumps become more complementary, so it becomes easier as it gets windier, until the point is reached when pumping is no longer necessary.

As a result of these techniques, downwind Finn sailing over 10 knots became an acrobatic display of skill, stamina and aerobic fitness. It is not uncommon to see Finn sailors collapsing in their boat, completely drained and exhausted, at the bottom of the final downwind to the finish, similar to rowers often seen collapsing after a 2,000 metre race.

Before the rule change, Finn sailors were allowed three pumps per wave to initiate or continue surfing or planning. Three pumps per wave is still pretty hard work and sailors could not rock and ooch (push) the boat with their bodyweight. The change in 2004 allowed sailors to pump, rock and ooch as much as they liked. With just three pumps a wave it was almost continual pumping and that was pretty hard in itself, but without rocking.

The rule change caused the sailors to start doing a one legged squat every time they pumped the sail – imagine doing one-legged lunches continually for a 15-minute leg, while pumping as well. It is very hard on the body, especially for the big guys having to get up, step across the boat and giving the sail a big lunge. If they did that in a gym for 15 minutes, their legs would be very sore. And obviously taking into account that the sailor has just worked the boat upwind for 1.4 miles, those legs are already pretty tired. The word often used to describe this extreme physical exertion is brutal.

The Finn requires enormous physical capabilities. Successful Finn sailors need to be strong and have an excellent endurance capacity. One of the reasons for that is that the hiking position (more than 50 per cent of time in the boat is spent hiking), combined with the free pumping rule, in combination with the rig, requires huge physiological demands on the sailor. This is also shown by heart rate readings during sailing with mean heart rate reaching 80 per cent of maximal heart rate over the whole race and sometimes peaking at 185 beats per minutes in certain parts of the race. Especially downwind, the Finn sailor pumps the mainsail one to one and controls the boat with dynamic actions of the whole body. In this context, Finn sailing is the hardest athletic experience in dinghy sailing and the sailors must be physically very fit.

It is this athletic and very physical nature of the boat that lends itself perfectly to the physique of elite athletes for which it caters. At Olympic level elite athletes in most disciplines are generally taller, heavier and more muscular than the general population.

THE SECOND SURVEY in 2015 took data from a smaller target group than in 2009, but still focused on the elite sailors. The average age of the group was 24, and it included about 50 per cent of the top 20 ranked sailors in the world.

The results built a fascinating picture of the class and showed the current athletes as increasingly younger, taller and heavier than their contemporaries from past Olympic cycles. Part of this can be attributed to the growing size of the world's population, but also it highlights the increasingly athletic nature of Finn sailing, with bigger sailors entering elite competition at a younger age.

The range of data included sailors from 22 to 40, an 18 years range; height from 175-198 cm, a range of 23 cm; and weight from 89-102 kg, a range of 13 kg.

The major changes between the two surveys were that the average weight had increased by 2 kg; the average height had increased by 1.1 cm; and the average starting age in Finn sailing for the group has dropped by 6 months.

Considering the boat classes used at the Olympics in Rio, it is obvious that people weighing more than 85 kg had practically no choice but the Finn if they wanted to compete at the Olympics, which meant a lot of sailors would be excluded.

Athletes participating at the Olympics are also generally taller, heavier and more muscular than the general population, except of course for some sports or disciplines such as gymnastics. Finn sailing could be compared, through height and weight characteristics, with swimming, rowing, athletics and basketball where performance is partly explained by anthropometrics: they are all tall, lean and muscular. By comparison, Finn sailors have to train physically like oarsmen (endurance and weights).

For example, previous research on the anthropometric profile has shown that elite rowers generally have a height of 1.89 to 1.95 metres and a body mass of 90 to 93 kg.

The survey also looked at fitness indictors: V02 Max varied from 5.1 to 5.68 l/min; 2 km rowing times varied from 6.17 to 6.40 minutes; and body fat index varied from 8 to 17% (average 12%).

Strength and endurance (VO2max absolute and relative values) capacity of Finn sailors are comparable with athletes from other sport disciplines such as rowing and basketball. Absolute VO2max of over 5.0 l/min means that Finn sailors, besides a needing a lot of strength, also need very good aerobic power (endurance).

The surveys also shows that Finns are sailed from an increasingly earlier age at international level and that there is an inevitable need for providing a suitable singlehanded dinghy for young men, being naturally much bigger than their parents were.

Drawing a parallel with a survey carried out on a group of elite young rowers, elite male junior rowers are 7 per cent taller and 27 per cent heavier than a reference group of the same chronological age. Within the group there were significant differences between finalists and non-finalists in body dimensions and body mass.

Data is everything and the surveys showed the evolution of the physique of young people taking up the Finn. The average age is getting younger, the weight and height are increasing, and interestingly, it shows the range is getting smaller, though it is still the widest range for any Olympic class. However, in spite of all this, sailing ability remains the key factor and the best sailor normally wins.

4

Broken Promises

Zika, Pollution, Corruption and Lost Opportunities

Every Olympic Games has its problems, but Rio 2016 had more than its fair share: from water pollution, the Zika virus, overstretched budgets, government corruption, political turmoil, public disturbances, late or inadequate construction, public safety, muggings, stray bullets…the list is endless. It was not entirely unexpected but once the problems of Rio started to dominate the headlines over and above the sporting stories it became a media free-for-all.

Stories of the dangers the athletes faced from being attacked or mugged, or taken ill from the exposure to the water and or being infected with the Zika virus eventually led to calls from many media organisations and health bodies to delay, cancel or even move the Games away from Brazil. In the months leading up to the Games the headlines were laden with messages of certain doom for anyone who ventured within 100 miles of Rio.

Supposedly responsible journalists, journals and organisations jumped on the doom bandwagon and sensationalised the bad news, and in some cases almost seemed to enjoy the negativity surrounding the Rio Games, as each week a new reason for damning the event hit the headlines.

ALMOST AS SOON as the Olympic Games were awarded to Rio de Janeiro, the waters of Guanabara Bay came under attack for being polluted and dangerous to sailors. At the time this was overlooked as the city had seven years to fulfil its pledges to clean the bay ready for the Games. As part of its Olympic bid Rio promised to increase the treatment of sewage into Guanabara Bay from around 11 per cent up to 80 percent by the time of the Games, a task which would require huge and costly infrastructural improvements.

Rio de Janeiro is home to more than six million people. The towns that lie around the rest of Guanabara Bay increase that number to around 13 million people. That is a lot of sewage to process but before the Games, only around 30 per cent was being treated before being dumped into the bay.

Sailors soon started calling the bay the biggest open sewer on earth. During early training and regattas there they also had to deal with debris on a previously unimaginable scale. Not just bags, bottles and general rubbish, but also big items such as chairs, logs and of course dead animals. No one saw any human bodies in the water, but there were enough sightings of corpses and bodyless limbs to keep the media occupied. Ebb tides were of course the worst affected. When sailing on a flood tide, water quality could be good providing certain areas and certain back eddies were avoided.

For the sailors, apart from getting sick, the biggest fear was that something as simple as a plastic bag around a centreboard or rudder could ruin a race or destroy medal chances.

Waste from the city's numerous hospitals, as well as household waste, all ends up in the storm drains and rivers across Rio. Various studies carried out in 2014 highlighted the existence of super bacteria present in Guanabara Bay and at other venues including Copacabana beach. It was classified by the US Centers for Disease Control and Prevention (CDC) as an 'urgent public health threat' and indicated that in up to 50 per cent of patients infected, the bacteria can contribute to death. One of the beaches with the greatest concentration was Flamengo beach, where the sailing spectator area was to be located.

The International Olympic Committee (IOC), backed by the World Health Organization (WHO), continually stated that the athletes were not at risk.

The situation was always worse when there had been rain. At the 2015 test event, even though the water was less dense with debris than expected, the penultimate day brought huge overnight rainstorms and the gullies and sewerage channels of Rio were full of water, bringing everything they contained down into the bay, both debris that can be seen, and the filth that can't be seen. On the following day Guanabara Bay was full of rubbish. It was so bad that one of the course areas further up the bay was closed to racing. The outgoing tide took much of it through the other courses, which remained sailable, but it was much more noticeable than the rest of the week.

The 2015 test event was a wake up call to the authorities. The raw sewage outlet into the Marina da Glória was about as good an advert as anything the Brazilians needed to start the clean up operation. For the first time the media had arrived in numbers and, shocked and physically sickened by the smell around the marina, broadcast it to the world. There was an all-pervading stink around the venue and the bay, although by the third day the smell was almost part of the experience and aroma-acclimatisation set it.

The cries for something to be done reached fever pitch towards the end of 2015 and early 2016, with media outlets up in arms on their athletes' behalf. World Sailing was even told by the IOC to stop pressurising the Rio authorities to take action because it could not be done. The money was just not there, or at least it was not available.

A report by the Rio Organising Committee in October 2015 dismissed the proposal to conduct viral tests on the waters schedule to be used for the aquatic events of the 2016 Games, which included not only the sailing venues but also where the rowing and offshore swimming would be held. This was following recommendations from the WHO.

Other pressure was also applied to the then ISAF to move the venue away from Rio, to Buzios, further along the coast, but the attraction of staying in Rio was too much to give away. Instead, ISAF issued health instructions to its officials on how to properly disinfect hands and equipment.

Many rounds of studies were carried out in the water in the year leading up to the Games and the results all concluded what everyone knew already, Guanabara Bay was polluted beyond the levels of acceptability and safety.

The results were used as ammunition for those calling for the sailing to be moved, or even cancelling the Games. The first round of tests found dangerous viruses in the bay and the near ocean up to 1.7 million times the levels that would be considered disturbing in the USA or Europe. The scare mongering from the media continued with a generalisation that sailors who ingest just three teaspoons of water from the bay had a 99 per cent chance of becoming ill. In fact, seven per cent of sailors at the 2015 test event were reported as becoming ill after the event.

Water samples were analysed for the types of viruses found in human intestinal and respiratory systems. These can cause digestive illnesses such as vomiting, diarrhoea and breathing problems, all potentially serious for an athlete during competition. In European waters a virus count of 1,000 per litre would cause extreme concern. The tests in Rio, in the middle of the racing area inside Guanabara Bay, indicated that virus levels were all 30,000 times higher than that.

Sewage linked pathogens were not just found on the inshore courses, the Sugarloaf and the Naval School course, but also on the ocean courses.

Olympic authorities continued to state that the venues would all be safe by Games time. The WHO and Olympic officials remained undecided over what, if any, testing they would carry out. Finally, In June 2016 Rio's organising committee finally ruled out conducting its own viral tests following a recommendation from the WHO. The reason for that was the lack of standard methods and the difficulty in interpreting the results.

Meanwhile the deadline for cleaning the bay, a process that began in 1992, was pushed back to 2035, instead of 2016. The promised investment of 2.5 billion reais would not go anywhere near far enough to tackle the huge problem. Estimates put the actual cost closer to 15 billion reais. The Brazilians would have to wait. The sailors would have to hope. The stink of the bay was a close friend for those training regularly in Rio.

In the meantime, the Marina da Glória underwent a 70 million reais refit in preparation for the Games, being expanded and redesigned and integrated into the Flamengo Park, one of Rio's most popular leisure areas. Whether the three to four metres of sewage sludge in the marina basin were removed is not known.

Of course nothing really happened until just before the Games when the sailors arrived to find, if not a pristine bay, certainly a vastly cleaner bay, with significant less debris and a barely noticeable smell. The authorities had failed to deliver on all their promises – perhaps due to lack of funding and corruption – but had implemented short-term measures to try and keep the bay clean for the Games.

Reports stated that a fleet of 12 rubbish collecting boats, called 'eco barcas', or 'eco boats', scoured the bay removing up to 45 tones of rubbish a month. In reality, there may have been a lot fewer boats, and their impact was allegedly less than reported. In addition, nets known as eco barriers were placed across the 17 rivers entering Guanabara Bay in an attempt to stop the rubbish entering the bay. The rivers are used by millions of people as both open sewers and as rubbish tips. The nets were cleared each day of what they had collected: tyres, bottles, plastic toys, and even household appliances; and of course more dead animals. In March 2016, the sewage that had been previously dumped into the Marina da Glória was redirected to a treatment plant.

Just before the Games, a picture was published of a bloated human body floating in the bay. Later, another body part washed up on Copacabana beach, just outside Guanabara, where the volleyball competition was scheduled to take place.

During the Games the rampant speculation that sailors were risking their health and their lives turned to nothing with few, if any complaints or protests regarding debris in the water. In the end, the water along the shore was relatively clean. Many sailors were seen jumping in the water after winning medals, while other swum off from the Flamengo beach, and did not seem overly concerned. There was only one report of a sailor becoming sick, and that passed very quickly.

Health authorities monitored the water quality daily for ISAF. Each day a helicopter scanned the bay for debris. If anything were spotted near any of the race areas, one of the 'eco boats' would be sent to remove it from the water.

For sailors, the subject was largely a side issue. Negativity has no place in an Olympic campaign so while the sailors and athletes were fully aware of the problems, and some national teams went to extreme measures to limit the potential impact on its athletes, the sailors themselves largely brushed away any questions on the pollution, annoyed that the media were focussing on matters other than the actual sporting competition.

WHEN THE 2016 Olympic Games was awarded to Rio de Janeiro in 2009, Brazil had already been awarded the football World Cup for 2014. In 2009, the then president, Luiz Inacio Lula da Silva, also announced the largest oil discovery in the nation's history, describing it at the 'passport to the future'. The good times were coming and with commodity exports booming, Brazil was building a rising international reputation and standing.

However, by 2016 it had all gone very wrong. The country was in a deep recession, allegations of corruption resulted in the impeachment of the next president, Dilma Rousseff, the Olympics were significantly over budget and there was a lack of money to finish the promised projects or even get the basic infrastructure completed.

Most of the corruption issues centred on the state-run oil company, Petrobras. A lengthy investigation, called Operation Carwash, charged both Lula and Rousseff with corruption and impropriety.

Brazil's history is one of boom and bust. It's economy is largely export based, so its prosperity, or otherwise, is dependent on exports of raw materials, such as oil. Brazil is the fifth largest country in the world by land area and population, and it has huge reserves of oil and iron ore, as well as exporting soybeans and corn. Its wealth distribution is one of the most unequal on the planet. But when commodity prices drop, recession follows.

Between 2008 and 2014 investigators uncovered a multi-billion-dollar bribery scandal at the state-run oil firm Petrobras, which was the largest company in Latin America until the scandal hit. Rousseff, who was also president of Petrobras board of directors during the time under investigation, was suspended as Brazilian president in May 2016 and was impeached on August 31 2016, between the Olympic and Paralympic Games. She was charged with criminal administrative misconduct and breaking federal budget laws.

In March 2016 an estimated three million people took part in more than 10 protests against Rousseff nationwide, in the largest political demonstrations in the country's history. Social unrest and demonstrations against the government continued up to and through the start of the Olympic Games in August.

The corruption scandal paralysed the government because the culture of bribing was endemic. It also stymied business because contracts between Petrobras and its suppliers were suspended by prosecutors, making many smaller firms, who relied on this business, bankrupt.

It was against this political and economic scandal and upheaval that in early 2014 a senior official from the IOC reported that preparations for the 2016 Olympics were the worst he had ever seen.

In spite of all this, all the Olympic venues were completed on time, and the sailing venue at the Marina da Glória was transformed from the building site that had been used at the 2015 test event. However Brazilians for the most part were disinterested in the Games with only about half of the tickets sold prior to the opening.

Just weeks before the Games started, the state of Rio de Janeiro declared a financial emergency that threatened to stop the state honouring its commitments. Many staff had not been paid for months, and the budget deficit to lay on the Games was rising each day. News outlets reported that emergency measures were needed to avoid what they called 'a total collapse in public security, health, education, transport and environmental management'. The state projected a budget deficit of $5.5 billion in 2016.

The state's revenue is largely tied to the petroleum industry, which had severely slumped in the previous two years as a result of the Petrobras scandal and the collapse in global oil prices.

While most of the funding for the Games came from the city of Rio, the state was responsible for some areas such as transport and policing. This meant that there was a serious risk to providing adequate security measures during the Games. However Interim President Michel Temer quickly promised the money would be found and the Games would not be jeopardised. Soon after, federal and local governments sorted out who would pay for the various projects, a measure that helped hurry up the work. However this did little to satisfy the nerves of already jittery visitors and media.

The biggest concerns about this financial crisis, was not just paying for the completion of the infrastructure projects that were need to handle the 500,000 visitors and 10,000 athletes expected to arrive in Rio, but also the security of the Games.

More than 400,000 people had undergone background security checks, with more than 7,000 being rejected. A huge security force of 85,000 was brought into Rio to ensure safety on the streets during Games. In addition, 250 specially trained police officers from 55 countries were brought in to support the local armed forces and police services.

Personal safety was a real concern, with several high profile muggings and attacks in the run up to the Games. The previous year a not insignificant number of sailors had been robbed at gunpoint – the security around the test event was not particularly strong. Other sports had faired worse, but then there was a gunfight at the yacht club in Niterói, the training base for several teams. Several ribs were stolen and stripped,

At the end of June, just as the first teams and visitors were starting to arrive in Rio, off duty police staged a demonstration in the arrivals hall at Rio de Janeiro's Galeao International Airport. They held up a banner with an ominous message "Welcome to Hell – Police and firefighters don't get paid, whoever comes to Rio de Janeiro will not be safe", to underline the dire state of the state's funding crisis.

And then there was the Zika virus.

IF THE POLLUTION and political problems issues weren't taking enough headlines away from the sport, matters got even worse at the start of 2016 with the WHO declaring a public health emergency over the Zika virus outbreak.

It created a saga of media interference and speculation from sports organisations, media and scientists, which did not entirely go away until well after the Games had closed.

Health officials believed there was a strong connection between the Zika virus and an increase in the number of babies born with microcephaly, a birth defect where children are born with smaller heads and brains, and which can lead to other problems such as mortality, mental disabilities and development problems. It was predicted that if the virus spread worldwide, it could cause millions of babies to be born with a life damaging disability, and become a much bigger threat to global health than the Ebola epidemic that had just killed more than 11,000 people in Africa.

Women in the region were advised not to get pregnant; and women athletes and spectators were advised not to visit the region if they were pregnant or planning a pregnancy. Even male athletes were advised of the dangers of passing on the Zika virus. Some airlines started offering refunds or rebooking. It became a maelstrom of rumour, speculation and fear that seemed to paralyse the sporting world. Several prominent athletes from other sports even announced they would not attend the Olympic Games.

A press conference by the Rio organisers in February 2016 announced that while the outbreak was causing concern they were confident that the problem would be cleared up by Games time. Others were more pessimistic.

The problem was exacerbated by the volume of standing water in the slums of Rio and the waterways leading into Guanabara Bay. This created a perfect breeding ground for the transmission of the aedes aegypti mosquitoes, whose bite was suspected of spreading the virus. Zika experts said predicting anything with any degree of certainty was impossible, but reputable media outlets engaged in huge scaremongering tactics to undermine the Games.

It was reported that Rio was more affected by the virus than any other region. This came after the IOC had declared Rio a safe zone in January 2016, something later criticised as speculation. In fact Brazil's Ministry of Health did not announce there was a problem until February, when it began counting cases. It turned out that cases in Rio were the highest of any other state. Rio, according to the media, was now not safe, but at the heart of the Zika problem.

Efforts to kill the mosquitoes and clean up their breeding grounds intensified through the beginning of the year while the media whipped up a frenzy of fear. It transformed the local problem into a real fear that travellers to Rio would spread the disease worldwide and cause a humanitarian disaster. Those who travelled to Rio were deemed irresponsible and reckless, not only for their own safety, but for the entire world.

Rio 2016 and the IOC continued to deny there was or would be a wider problem, while there were calls for everyone to face up to the reality – the Games was putting everyone in danger and should be cancelled or delayed. This, of course, was not a viable option.

In February the WHO declared that the Zika virus was a 'public health emergency of international concern', a warning that actually stayed in place until November 2016. By now more than 4,000 suspected cases of microcephaly had been reported, and Zika had already spread to 24 nations across the Americas.

However, by May, the WHO had changed its stance and stated it did not think the Olympics would significantly increase the spread of the Zika virus and cancelling the Games was not needed.

By June 2016, which in Brazil is winter, cases had fallen significantly and the organisers were forecasting no problems during the Olympics. The weather in the winter months in Rio is cooler and dryer, with average temperatures of about 21 degrees Celsius in August. Estimates now stated that perhaps only one or two tourists would contract Zika during the Games.

No cases of Zika had been reported during any of the 44 test events for both the Olympic and Paralympic Games, and many of the events took place in Rio's summer months, which is wetter and warmer, and when mosquitoes are more prevalent.

After the Games, WHO said that there had been no Zika infections reported in Brazil during the Olympics, among either athletes or visitors.

SO THE 2016 Olympic Games, the first ever in South America, opened with the host country's president fighting impeachment, a corruption scandal involving its former president in full flight, a pollution story that wouldn't go away – and continued to evolve well after the Games had closed – the uncertainty of whether a Zika endemic was really possible, as well as concerns over basic safety and infrastructure.

However once the Olympic cauldron was lit, it all became background noise and the focus switched to the athletes.

5

London to Santander

The Years of Preparation and Transition

The London 2012 Olympic Games in the Finn Class marked the end of an era. The class had been dominated by Ben Ainslie for a decade. He broke more records and won more events than really seemed possible. Along with Ainslie, a handful of others ended their Finn career in Weymouth, but 11 would be back for Rio, and five more tried and failed to qualify.

The Finn class was moving on with taller, stronger, fitter sailors than ever before. There had been a sea change in the fleet with a wave of younger athletes hoping to make their mark over the next four years.

It had already started late in 2012 with the Sailing World Cup Melbourne. Fresh from the Olympics, and in one of his last Finn events, Brendan Casey took the win, but behind him were two young Australians who were set to make headlines over the coming four years: Oliver Tweddell and Jake Lilley. Tweddell had been sailing internationally for two years, but for Lilley, it was his debut event after just eight weeks in the boat.

Into the New Year and there were more young sailors on the podium at the Sailing World Cup Miami. In a sign of things to come, Caleb Paine, from the USA, won his second World Cup event by a considerable margin from Greg Douglas, of Canada, and Jorge Zarif, from Brazil.

The approach of an Olympic Games normally has a positive influence on activities in the host country and this was already proving to be especially true of the Finn class in Brazil.

Four years previously a joint initiative between Brazil, Pata Boats of Hungary and the International Finn Association had imported a mould into Brazil to start building boats there for the first time in more than three decades.

The success story of that initiative led to an increase in boats on the water and well attended events. The strength of the class was underlined by fact that most of the boats being raced were new boats built in Brazil. While there were still some imports from Europe, the sheer cost – in terms of duties and transport charges – and complexity of this meant the unmitigated success of the home build project. The three main centres of Finn sailing in Brazil are Rio de Janeiro, São Paulo, and Brasilia.

The return of former Finn sailor and double Olympic Star medalist Bruno Prada added a new ingredient to the mix – he won the opening race at the Sailing World Cup Miami in January 2013, but was still to make a final decision on a full campaign. He had last sailed a Finn at the 2004 Finn Gold Cup in Rio. Though the numbers in Miami were low, it was a competitive week that gave Zarif the bronze, while Prada finished up in seventh. On their return to Brazil, Zarif was again dominant at the Brazilian Sailing Week in Rio, winning nine of the ten race series.

Jorge Zarif was already the top Finn sailor in Brazil. He took some time out after the 2012 Olympics for knee surgery, and for anyone with aspirations to represent Brazil in the Finn class in 2016, Zarif was the one to beat. He next took the Brazilian nationals in January from Prada. The other important development was that the 2004 Olympic Finn silver medalist Rafael Trujillo was brought in to coach Zarif, after concluding his own career with an eighth place in London.

The 2013 European season opened at the Trofeo Princesa Sofia in Palma, with the return of the man who would dominate the class over the next three years: Giles Scott. He won in Palma from Pieter-Jan Postma, from The Netherlands, and Vasilij Žbogar, from Slovenia, before coming an uncharacteristic second in Hyères a few weeks later. The winner there was his team mate Andrew Mills. In third was another newcomer to the class, Josh Junior from New Zealand.

Scott was only back for a brief period on a break from America's Cup sailing, and he would not be seen again until the end of the year.

Both those events were part of ongoing format and scoring trials, with split series and double medal races, all of which proved unpopular with the sailors. However both events attracted around 70 entries, a good turnout for a post-Olympic year.

Junior, along with double Laser Olympian, Andrew Murdoch, had recently gone full time in the Finn and with the help of coach John Cutler, the 1988 Finn bronze medalist, had fast tracked to the front of the fleet. Junior had previously sailed the 2012 Sail for Gold in Weymouth in the Finn after losing out to Murdoch in the 2012 Laser trials.

Unsurprisingly the 2013 Sail for Gold pulled a very small entry, all British boats. One of Ben Ainslie's training partners, Mark Andrews, had a good run, winning three events in a row: The Delta Lloyd Regatta in Medemblik, in The Netherlands, Sail for Gold in Weymouth, and then Kiel Week, in Germany.

The first major event of the year was the Finn Silver Cup at Malcesine, on Lake Garda, Italy. Zarif took his second Junior title, dominating the fleet of young talent. Lilley was runner up, with several others in the top ten who would be competing for places in Rio in the coming years.

The 2013 Finn European Championship returned to Warnemünde, Germany for the third time in the event's history and it attracted a record entry. The marina at Warnemünde was originally built for the first Finn Europeans there in 1961, with the second event was held shortly afterwards in 1969, so a third visit to the former East German sailing centre was long overdue.

However, the conditions didn't quite turn out as expected with only eight of the 11 races sailed. A massive entry of 103 boats from 29 nations and five continents took part, making it not only the largest entry ever for the Finn Europeans but also the largest entry for a Finn senior championship for 30 years. After placing sixth at the London Games, it was clear from the very first race that Vasilij Žbogar had an agenda in Warnemünde. He was by far the most consistent sailor and would have won by an even larger points difference but for two obscure gear failures that left him fighting for recovery. On Tuesday his halyard lock broke, dropping the sail at the windward mark and on Wednesday his mainsheet hanger broke, leaving him to sail the final beat with no purchase on the sail. He recovered to seventh and 13th in those races. But he won the final two races to take the lead, and with no wind for the medal race, took the title from Ed Wright, from Great Britain, and Murdoch. For Murdoch, it was only his third regatta in the class.

After a few weeks off, the fleet reconvened in Tallinn, Estonia for the Finn Gold Cup. For the first time ever the Finn Silver Cup and the Finn Gold Cup were won by the same sailor in the same year. Jorge Zarif's ability to read the tricky conditions in Tallinn, to make the best of the wind he was dealt and to maintain his calm composure throughout turned him into one of the youngest winners of this fabled trophy.

Estonia holds a special place in the hearts of Finn sailors and the hosting of the 58th Finn Gold Cup in Tallinn was a momentous occasion for many people. It had been 19 years since the Finn Gold Cup was last, and first, held in Estonia. In 1994 it was sailed at Pärnu, but in 2013 it was held in the country's capital and was raced from the Tallinn Olympic Yachting Centre at Pirita, which was originally built for the 1980 Olympics. Estonia has only ever hosted four Olympic discipline world championships, and two of those have now been in the Finn.

The week was plagued by light and shifty winds, with postponements every day and two days lost with no wind at all. However seven of the 10 opening series races were sailed, along with the medal race on the final day, and even that was only just managed within the time limit. Ed Wright was again second, with Pieter-Jan Postma third.

Zsombor Berecz was one of the emerging new stars and one of the major success stories coming out of Luca Devoti's Dinghy Academy in Valencia. Berecz, 27, sailed the Laser for Hungary in the 2012 Olympics, finishing in 21st place. Feeling he had unfinished business at the Olympics, and struggling to keep his weight down for the Laser, he changed to the Finn soon after. At 1.96 metres tall, he took an encouraging seventh place in the predominantly light winds of Tallinn.

The season had produced many other new faces and some great new talent entering the class. Junior and Murdoch had sent an early message to the fleet, trading places at almost every regatta and were only going to get better. Max Salminen, from Sweden, had switched to the Finn after winning the Star class gold in London crewing for Fredrik Lööf, and was now up against Björn Allansson, who would soon be World No 1, for the Swedish trails for Rio. Milan Vujasinovic, from Croatia, had impressed in Tallinn, with a fourth place finish, well ahead of the Croatian favourite Ivan Kljaković Gašpić.

After Tallinn, just six sailors ventured to Santander for the test event for the 2014 Sailing World Championships. After a ninth in Tallinn, Josh Junior ended up winning seven out of ten races to end his European season on a high point.

There was one more major event to go in Europe in 2013, which had special significance because it marked the full time return of Giles Scott. The Semaine Olympique Française in La Rochelle only attracted 12 visitors, but Scott won comfortably, even if he only won three races. It marked the start of an unbeaten run that would stretch through to March 2016.

The year ended at the Sailing World Cup Melbourne again, with a first World Cup win for Allansson. Oliver Tweddell finished one point behind, and ahead of Jake Lilley, though it wasn't going to be long before Lilley improved to be the point where he was regularly beating Tweddell.

2014 was all about the lead up to the all-important ISAF Sailing World Championships in Santander and the first qualifier for Rio.

The Sailing World Cup continued in Miami in January 2014 with a uncharacteristic narrow win for Giles Scott, probably as close as he ever got to losing an event. Trailing Tweddell all week, he finally turned it round in the medal race to take the win. Medal races are meant to be tough, but Tweddell's score for that one race was exactly double his accrued score from the previous five days. With two days lost earlier in the week through lack of wind, and only six races completed, the medal race became even more pivotal in deciding the medals. Tweddell was counting nothing worse than second going into the deciding race, so paid a high price for a poor medal race.

As the fleet moved across to Europe, Giles Scott won the Sailing World Cup event in Palma again, in a 92 boat fleet. Thomas Le Breton was the early leader after the first days were dogged by light winds. When the breeze arrived Scott dominated to win four races in a row and go into the medal race with an eight-point lead. While Andrew Mills sailed away to win the medal race, Le Breton almost turned the tables on Scott, but in a very close finish, lost a few boats to take the silver. Jonathan Lobert took bronze.

Scott and the rest of the British team skipped the next World Cup event in Hyères, to focus on preparations for the upcoming European Championships in La Rochelle.

Pieter-Jan Postma had never won a major Finn regatta in nearly 10 years in the class. He finally overcame this at Hyères in 2014 with a dominant display against the odds to produce the most popular win of the year. But it almost went wrong.

After taking the overall lead with a superlative display of speed and skills he only just survived day 4. In Race 7 his halyard broke and his sail fell down. He limped back to the finish in 57th place, and with no coach tried to fix the sail by capsizing his boat. Photographer François Richard offered to help and together they pulled the sail back up and attached it at the top, while fighting the chop and increasing wind. Finally it was fixed just one minute before the 5-minute gun and Postma made the race just in time. Two second-places the next day made the medal race a formality, with the only real interest between Ivan Kljaković Gašpić and Thomas Le Breton, of France, who took silver and bronze. Lobert retired early with a broken boat, and returned home to get it fixed in time for the European Championship.

The Europeans in La Rochelle was the final major event before the all-important Rio qualifier in Santander in August. It was no ordinary fleet, and with 101 boats from 31 countries it was the most competitive fleet so far in the quadrennium with all but a handful of the world's best Finn sailors present.

Giles Scott stamped his authority all over the championship in a week of generally moderate to strong winds apart from the first day, and he won comfortably with a day to spare. He also won the famously windy medal race to end up with a final score 50 points better than the next best sailor. His winning margin was the largest of any European title win in the recent history of the class. He was now fully into his stride and brimming with confidence ahead of Santander and the first events in Rio.

Second placed Vasilij Žbogar was the defending champion, and surprised even himself by his performance. Blisteringly fast downwind, he had untested gear and little confidence, but his conservative style and clever tactical sailing, always got him to the top mark close enough to the front to make his move downwind. Wright picked up the bronze, his fifth major championship medal in the previous four years. Lobert was again fourth.

Of the new sailors, there was a mixed bag. Murdoch and Berecz made the top ten, while Junior, Lilley and Salminen, finished in the next ten boats. There was still work to be done.

The week was hampered to a certain degree by unseasonably bad weather, but what was not in doubt was the quality of the racing and the great sailing conditions. Scott had now won every event since returning to the class and seemed to be improving event by event. Winning a major championship by 50 points in a 100-boat fleet is nothing short of phenomenal. With Scott saying there were still improvements to be made, he had set the standard everyone else needed to match. But already he was getting one hand, albeit psychologically, on that gold medal in Rio in 2016.

It was only May, and there were no more major events until August, so there was a false end to the early season, before it started up again after the summer. The other events were poorly attended. Phillip Kasüske, one of the growing number of keen German youth sailors, surprised everyone by winning the Delta Lloyd Regatta from Postma and Lilley, Scott won the six-boat Sail for Gold in Weymouth and Deniss Karpak won the first of several Kiel Weeks. Then in July Anders Pedersen, from Norway, won the Finn Silver Cup for the Junior World Championship, in Hoorn, The Netherlands.

Many sailors used the time for training at home or travelling to Rio to start their training camps there. With the first test event in August, and two boats per country allowed, a small fleet of 17 boats travelled to Brazil for the 2014 Aquece Rio Olympic Test Event.

Giles Scott once again proved to be almost unbeatable. He won six out of the 11 races, and apart from a seventh in the opening race was never out of the top five all week. In what was generally thought to be quite shifty and tricky conditions, he wrapped up the week with another dominant race win in the medal race.

The medal race may have been a formality for Scott, but crucial for the other two medals. Lobert sailed well in the breezy conditions to finish third to snatch the silver, while Wright hung onto the bronze with a fifth.

Scott said of the first Rio experience, "It's been a windy week, which was kind of unexpected in all honesty, but the week's gone great and we managed to complete a full series. For a lot of the sailors it's been a bit of a surprise as to how good the breeze has been for the two weeks we have been here. We haven't seen too much wind under 9 knots. The majority of the fleet came here expecting 7 knots tops. This week it wasn't quite like that so I think in that regard, actually knowing what the wind speed is, is a big step for learning."

Before the event the water quality was the biggest talking point, but it was not as bad as many expected. Wright said, "Sailors having to cope with the dirty, polluted water in Rio was in all the news before the racing began but I must admit it was not so bad. Yes, it was not the cleanest but where we were racing there was a good flow of water flushing it out into the ocean. It needs improvement of course. The worst was after a couple of days of rainstorms."

Silver medalist Lobert added, "The water is not crystal clear for sure but there was no problem for racing. Inside we sometimes had to avoid some plastic bags but most of the time you can see it. I really think that the Rio city is aware of the problem and is already trying to clean the bay. We saw some special boats collecting the trash on the water."

"The wind was not as light as we were told it would be. But you know that we never can predict the conditions we will have for the Games. I think we were lucky to be able to race the full schedule of races in six days but for the next test event and the Games there will be rest days so if we face some lack of wind we will be able to race the day after."

But as the sailors were finding out for themselves quite fast, "To be successful in Rio you will have to be a very complete sailor, you never know what condition you will get day after day."

Four weeks after that first event in Rio, the 2014 ISAF Sailing World Championships would begin in Santander, Spain. It was all about to get very real.

PART 2

TRIALS
& TRIBULATIONS

5

Qualification Quagmire

Selection Battles, Blind Ambition
and Rio Qualification

The qualification process for Rio 2016 was the most complicated and long drawn out qualification system ever used for the sailing events at the Olympic Games, and drew much criticism. In many ways it changed the system from sending the best athletes in the world to the Games, to sending a more global distribution of athletes. The problem with that was that sometimes, the process encouraged a possible disproportionate level of abilities and had the potential to be exploited.

It consisted of a series of events over 18 months, some of which were more significant than others. It started at the 2014 ISAF Sailing World Championships in September 2014, in Santander, Spain, where the first 12 nations would qualified and ended at the Trofeo Princesa Sofia in Palma, in March 2016.

After Santander, one place was available at the Asian Continental Qualifier in Qingdao, China; four places at the 2015 Finn Gold Cup in Takapuna, New Zealand; one place at the Oceanic Continental Qualifier at the Sailing World Cup Melbourne; two places at the North and South American Continental Qualifier at the Sailing World Cup in Miami; and finally two places were available at the European and African Continental

Qualifier in Palma. Brazil, as host country, would get an automatic place.

One of the often seen injustices of Olympic sailing is that only one team gets to go per event, and this often means that many of the world's best sailors either miss their best chance, or sometimes never get their chance to compete on the ultimate sporting stage. It has happened many times that World champions, European champions and even World No. 1s, fail to qualify. This can sometimes be a tough pill to swallow, but it also means that the qualification process is sometimes even harder and more competitive than the actual Games.

Some sailors become so burnt out and emotionally wrecked by prolonged trials that they also fail to compete at their usual level at the Olympics. How often have we seen a sailor produce a career best performance in the months before the Olympics after more than a year in qualification, only to sail disappointingly at the Games?

While most of the national selection trials for Rio would not begin until 2015 or 2016, most of the psychological battles would begin in August 2014 in Santander, Spain. It was a combined Olympic classes world championship held every three or four years, the first stage of the long and complex process of country qualification for the Rio Olympics. For the Finn Class, the competition was still for the Finn Gold Cup. At the end of the week the first 12 nations would qualify for one of 23 places allocated to the Finn in Rio.

These were not places for sailors in Rio, but rather for each country. Each country had to be qualified by a sailor, whether or not that sailor was finally selected by the country to represent them at the Olympics. This of course means that the sailor who sailed well enough to qualify their country, could yet be beaten in the national selections by someone who had not even started sailing the class.

Of the 23 sailors who would be competing in Rio, 10 had to undergo protracted selection trials. The rest were either alone from their country in their bid to qualify for the Games, or just had to meet the NOC criteria to be selected.

For Rio, for the first time in a long while, all those who qualified their country won selections, and all were selected by their NOC to attend the Games. In the past, too many sailors had been denied the right to sail at the Games, even though they had qualified their country and won their national selections, because their NOC, or MNA, didn't want to send sailors without medal potential or proven results.

Some of the MNA or NOC criteria to attend the Games have been set so high in the past that they don't seem to take into account the vagaries that sailing can produce. Demanding that a sailor produces, say a top three placing, in a specific regatta, when they had already proved they could achieve this in other regattas could be seen as shortsighted and self defeating. Denying sailors the right to attend the Olympics can stagnate the Olympic knowledge in that country and defeats the ideals of Olympic competition. It creates a vacuum of experience that future generations of sailors will struggle to fill as well as providing disincentives to those attempting the Olympic journey in the first place, especially if the crossbar is set so high as to be virtually unobtainable.

AFTER A STRING of major victories over the previous 18 months, the favourite in Santander, and the British favourite for Rio, was undoubtedly Giles Scott. He had won the European title in May by an unprecedented 50 points, and hadn't been beaten in the Finn since April 2013. Due to other commitments, Scott hadn't sailed a Finn World Championship since Perth in 2011. He won that of course, though the event would always be remembered for other reasons.

His selection trials would end up clear-cut, but he was racing against some of the best sailors in the world within the British Team. Former European and World Champion, Ed Wright, was good enough to win an Olympic medal and desperately wanted to go to Rio. Both Andrew Mills and Mark Andrews had trained extensively with Ben Ainslie. The 2013 winner in Hyères, Mills, had dropped out of the race just before Santander – his last contribution to the team was training with Scott in Santander the weeks before. Mark Andrews had also been around the top 10 in the world for many years, but Santander also proved to be his last major Finn event. And then there was Ben Cornish, adding further strength to the team. Cornish would go on to train with Scott in Rio.

The team had huge strength, huge depth, and even though Scott was head and shoulders above the rest, he owed them a huge debt for pushing him hard in training, so he could achieve such success.

The bronze medalist from London 2012, Jonathan Lobert from France, had placed fourth at the Europeans earlier in 2014 before picking up the silver at the first Rio test event in August. He was facing strong competition from teammate Thomas Le Breton, who performed well at the early season regattas in Palma and Hyères.

Lobert's selection trials against Le Breton were very tight going into London, and it looked like it would be equally tight going into Rio. However by early 2015 Le Breton was, ever so slightly, slipping behind Lobert and despite spending time training in Rio was presented with an opportunity to sail bigger boats and so ended his time in the Finn. This left Lobert almost unchallenged for the place, though the rising young star, Fabian Pic, made his mark at a few events.

The Italian selection trials was perhaps the tightest and most contentious of any nation. The Italian team included three former Olympians, Giorgio Poggi, from 2008, and Filippo Baldassari, from 2012, as well as Michele Paoletti, who had crewed in the Soling class at the Sydney 2000 Olympics. All three had produced form at some point over the previous year, and no one was guessing who would prevail. With various automatic selection points throughout the process as well as a points based system, it was also one of the more complicated selection processes, and it would not be over until the final major event before the Olympics.

Another intense battle over the coming years would be between the Swedish sailors Björn Allansson and Max Salminen. While Allansson, who had also campaigned for London in the Finn, had the upper hand most of 2013 and 2014, Salminen, who won gold in the Star class crewing for Fredrik Lööf at London 2012, had fought back and overcame Allansson at the first Rio test event.

Another team of note over the previous 18 months had been that of New Zealand, with a mix of youth and experience making for interesting racing. Andrew Murdoch had produced some great results in his career, with two fifth places in the Laser at the previous two Olympics, while in contrast Josh Junior was much younger, but also bigger and on a faster learning curve. He picked up ninth place at the 2013 Finn Gold Cup, and also won the Santander test event the same year, though in a much-reduced fleet. Both sailors had been training hard together to make the best of the championship.

From Australia, Jake Lilley had placed an impressive 15th overall at the Europeans in May, and took the Junior European title in the process. However, during 2013, his main rival for the Rio place, Oliver Tweddell, was the more dominant of the two. Lilley had been improving fast, though, and had turned the tables on Tweddell in most events going into the Santander competition. He was under no illusions of his goals, and what it would take to achieve them, however even he couldn't have foreseen how long and tortuous, and eventually how close, his Olympic trials against Tweddell were going to be as both sailors upped their game beyond recognition over the coming 18 months.

The numerically strong Russian team seeking selection included the 2007 European champion and twice Olympian Eduard Skornyakov, though he dropped out shortly after Santander. In addition there were the young hopeful Arkadiy Kistanov, who like Lilley, was still a junior, as well as Egor

Terpigorev. After winning the world junior title in 2011 at the age of 17 Kistanov had matured as a sailor over the next few years and was now pushing the seniors. The Russian selections would ultimately prove fruitless as country qualification eluded them time and time again.

Ivan Kljaković Gašpić, from Croatia, was trying to qualify for his third Olympic regatta. Already by this point in time, European champion twice, he had never really produced his best at an Olympics. A fifth at London 2012 was as close as he got to the podium, but by 2014 he was again fully focussed on reaching the top of his game again. He was facing strong competition from Milan Vujasinovic, who had joined the fleet in 2013 and had already put in some good results and showed his transom to Gašpić several times. Like the Italian selections this often heated and scrappy trials would go right through to June 2016.

Other country selections would be less contentious. Often there would be one dominant sailor, or just one doing a campaign. For Argentina, Facundo Olezza and Santiago Falasca did not enter the race for selection until the South American Continental Qualifier in January 2016.

For Canada, the race seemed to be between the double Olympian (2008 in Laser and 2012 in Finn), Greg Douglas and Martin Robitaille. But Douglas dropped out after the Santander qualifier and then in early 2016, a young Laser sailor, Tom Ramshaw joined the fray. He immediately made an impression and the Canadian trials would rumble on until June 2016.

Perhaps the most interesting selection trials were for the USA. The 2008 silver medalist and 2012 Olympian Zach Railey had retired after London, disappointed with his performance there. His younger understudy Caleb Paine, started to excel, briefly moved up to World No 1 and looked set to have a clear run into Rio, especially after qualifying USA in Santander with a top 10 place. However by late 2015 it was clear Railey was on the comeback trail, a route that took them both to the brink in March 2016 as the USA trials came to an extraordinary conclusion in Barcelona.

But before all that, the fleet headed to Santander, on Spain's northern coastline.

7

Lull Before the Storm
The Road to Rio Begins in Earnest

The first Olympic selection event for Rio, the 2014 ISAF Sailing World Championships in September 2014, in Santander, Spain, was beset by many challenges for the sailors, with as many organisational challenges as there were racing challenges.

The Finn fleet started racing in Santander on Monday 15 September, with an opening series of four races followed by a final series of six races and the medal race for the top 10 on Sunday 21 September.

The week turned out to be not only a test of sailor's skills, but also a test of patience for sailors and race committee alike, waiting for wind and trying to run quality races with the odds stacked against them.

The week was beset by problems before it even began, with the organisers running short of money, woefully inadequate equipment and boats and the lack of trained, albeit enthusiastic, staff. Race officers were running around trying to gather everything they needed the day before racing began, with not even enough flags to go around. On the Finn course, set some way outside the Bay of Santander in relatively deep water, committee boats drifted due to inadequate anchors, races were delayed in strong winds because boats were dragging, while on other days sailors were kept afloat for many hours waiting for wind that didn't come, and was never likely to come. Almost all the media boats, when finally enough were found, either broke down or were unsuitable.

Despite all these frustrations and setbacks, the racing itself was not compromised with the Principal Race Officer Peter Reggio overseeing the racing and making sure the sailors had a fair championship. While the event was labelled by ISAF as the Sailing World Championships, it was also the Finn Gold Cup, the name of the trophy given to the winner of the annual Finn class world championship.

The favourite was of course Giles Scott.

"The last Finn Gold Cup I did was Perth and that was actually quite a while ago. It's a little odd to think I haven't competed in a world championships since 2011 because I've done quite a lot of Finn sailing since then."

Before Santander he said, "We've done just under three weeks in Santander now, with two before Rio [the first test event] and one after. I think it is one of those venues that could throw up anything but more likely than not we should get light to moderate sea breezes, but it depends of course."

Scott was keen to pick up a second world title without the distractions that Perth produced. Did he feel it helped to be the called the favourite?

"I wouldn't say it particularly does. Obviously I can take confidence from my previous results but you need to be able to prove yourself like you do at any regatta, which is exactly what I'll be trying to do. In all honesty, I'm just keen to get out there and start racing."

Ivan Kljaković Gašpić, from Croatia was still looking for his first Finn Gold Cup win.

Speaking before racing commenced, he said, "I would be really happy with a podium finish in Santander. As always, it will be very tough, all the guys have been working very hard so we will have some exciting hard racing."

Unlike some other sailors he had only spent limited time in Santander.

"I've not done too much training there. However in the middle of August I did two nice weeks. So far I saw light to moderate breeze."

The defending world champion was Jorge Zarif from Brazil, the first sailor to hold both the junior and senior world titles in the same year. For him Santander was not about qualification, as Brazil had an automatic place as host, but more about testing himself against the world-class field as he prepared to qualify himself for a place in the Brazilian team.

Vasilij Žbogar, from Slovenia, had won the European Championship in 2013 at Warnemünde in Germany, and placed second behind Scott in 2014 in La Rochelle. He was up against Gasper Vincec for the Slovenian place. Vincec had returned to Finn sailing in 2014 after losing an exhausting 2012 trials to Žbogar. However soon after Santander, Vincec pulled out of the race.

Žbogar was the top sailor at the Dinghy Academy in Valencia and was trying to qualify for his fifth Olympics. He placed sixth in London in the Finn after winning two medals in the Laser in previous Games. Žbogar led a strong, and growing, group of sailors who had based themselves at the Dinghy Academy over the previous two years and the results were starting to show.

Another Dinghy Academy sailor, Zsombor Berecz from Hungary placed seventh in the 2013 Finn Gold Cup and was beginning to make his mark on the circuit. He also would have no selection battles beyond qualifying the country.

Before Santander Jonathan Lobert, the London 2012 bronze medalist, had said, "I spent some time in Santander in June and at the end of August and I felt good there. The racing will be very tight, we will have groups and the race course will be not so long so I think it's going to be very intense."

"I think it a very interesting place with a lot of different waves conditions. It can be big swell sometimes but it also can be very messy when you sail more close to the shore. For the wind it's hard to say because it can be very different day after day."

On the competition he said, "I think Giles and Ed will be for sure two of the strongest sailors there but for the rest it's hard to say. Some were in Rio and some stayed in Europe to keep on training. The last race we did all together was the Europeans in La Rochelle in May, a long time ago. We might see some new faces fighting for the top ten and maybe the podium. But I am very excited and I am looking forward to race."

Following his so-called 'retirement' after winning the silver medal at the London 2012 Olympics, Jonas Høgh-Christensen from Denmark was also back. His long-term plans were still unclear, but he said he was not sailing in Santander just to make up the numbers.

"I was asked a number of times to help the Danish sailing team get the results they needed and especially in the Finn. It fits well into my schedule and it was a chance to get a bit into shape. Also I just love the sport and when you haven't sailed in two years you really miss it."

"Since the London Games I have done two days in May for a weekend regatta in less than 5 knots. Then I have done four days in Santander. That is all the sailing I have done since the Games, in any boat."

Høgh-Christensen famously took a year off after the 2008 Olympics, came back for the 2009 Finn Gold Cup, without training and out of shape, and won. Two years later he was back again. He said it wasn't exactly a comeback but...

"For now there are no plans for an Olympic comeback, but I have said that before. To be fair this is where I stand until I change my mind or in reality it becomes a real opportunity in my life."

Another sailor who could have been elsewhere instead of Santander was Pieter-Jan Postma, from the Netherlands. After failing to secure a place in the Brunel Team in the Volvo Ocean Race, he was back full time in the Finn and hungry for more success following his first ever major win in Hyères earlier in the year. After his disappointment of not being selected for the Volvo, his hunger for Finn sailing returned.

"In the last six weeks the hunger is bigger than before. The training is done. I cannot do any more, so I am curious where I stand. We have done three weeks in total in Santander, with lots of great light wind training, though it can be quite wavy. One day we had 25 plus knots with great sets rolling in. It would be superb if we get that one day."

"After the Olympics this is the most important regatta for us. No excuses. Time to be strong." On the prospects ahead he said, "Could be anything. But as you know the Worlds is always intense, and everybody will be ready."

In pure figures, the fleet in Santander contained five world titles, eight European titles, and more than 20 sailors with Olympic experience in any class. It was a deep field of talent with at least 25 sailors statistically capable of winning races.

It was time for battle to commence.

8

Santander Show
First 12 Places Decided for Rio

The racing in Santander got off to a slow start, with no racing on the opening day, Monday 15 September, because of a lack of wind. On the second day, the two groups only got one race in each, with Oliver Tweddell from Australia and Great Britain's Giles Scott taking one win each.

The fleet had spent more than 13 hours on the water over two days for this first race, waiting for the wind to build and stabilise enough to hold fair racing.

The Yellow fleet was won by Tweddell, who led the entire race. The Blue fleet was stacked with big names but the returning London 2012 silver medalist, Jonas Høgh-Christensen of Denmark, back after a two year lay-off, led round the top mark from London 2012 bronze medalist Jonathan Lobert of France. Scott rounded in tenth and made gains throughout to pass Høgh-Christensen at the last mark to take the race win.

The fleet then waited afloat for another six hours with no further racing as the wind performed circles around the fleet. There was plenty of wind around, at one point 15-20 knots came off the land in a very hot blast, but that only lasted 30 minutes before the fleet were left wallowing on the left over swell. By the time the fleet was sent ashore, the sailors had been on the water for more than eight hours.

Tweddell said, "Luigi (the PRO – Peter Reggio) and his race team were actually doing a really good job. They weren't sending us off for a bad race in dodgy wind. We actually got a second race off but they abandoned it after a couple of minutes as the breezed died and then filled in. So they did a really good job, but the breeze was never stable enough to get a second race in."

ON WEDNESDAY, SCOTT produced the kind of form that most sailors can only dream about. He picked up three more bullets for a perfect score after four races to lead overall from Lobert and Ed Wright of Great Britain. The fleet split remained the same as from the first two days, so the sailors had only been able to race against half the fleet so far, the same half, but at least the opening series was completed, which at one point was looking unlikely.

After two days of fitful, unstable, and too light winds, the third day in Santander was completely different. An overnight storm had left behind some solid 15-25 knots winds that kept some classes ashore. For the Finns however it was just what they had been waiting for and they revelled in the big winds early on for three action packed, exciting races. However, there was a long delay as the race committee couldn't get the committee boat anchor to hold.

There was some criticism of the group allocations for the opening series. Perhaps because of the way the groups were selected, they were very uneven in terms of ability with one group having a far higher number of top ranked sailors compared to the other. Normally this would even out with changing the groups each day after racing, but after the first day was lost and only one race was sailed on the second day, the decision was taken not to adjust the groups for the third day.

This meant that all the opening series races were sailed in the same group, and with very unbalanced groups it had the effect of making qualification for the gold fleet much harder for some sailors than it should have been, with several sailors in the blue group feeling aggrieved at being relegated to the silver fleet, after having a much tougher opening series than many sailors in the yellow group.

Scott was never really threatened in any race though Zsombor Berecz from Hungary did steal a large lead on the opposite side of the course to Scott in Race 3, a lead that soon evaporated as the race progressed. Scott wrapped up three race wins to claim his place at the top of the leaderboard at the end of the opening series.

Lobert recovered from a double capsize in the first race of the day to score 2,4 and trail Scott by six points. Ed Wright was unable to sail the opening race after picking a black flag disqualification in one of Tuesday's abandoned races, but channelled his energy into the remaining two races to pick up two race wins and end the opening series in third overall.

It was a tough day for the fleet, starting out with epic conditions with more than 20 knots of breeze that decreased through the day for a tricky final race with some major wind changes.

Scott summed up his day. "Early on it was pretty epic. But it was disappointing that the organisers can't get a committee boat that can hold station. It was very frustrating to be waiting around for two hours while there was a great wind in place. In the last race it turned a bit odd with the wind swinging through 180. The wind just kept going right all during the race."

SCOTT CONTINUED TO extend his lead on the fleet after the fourth day of racing. After six races he held a 13-point lead from Lobert and Ivan Kljaković Gašpić.

The fourth day was another windy and shifty day on the Finn course area with some big shifts mixing up the fleet. Scott recovered from a mid-fleet first mark rounding in Race 5 to record his fifth race win of the championship. He then looked to have a sixth race win all wrapped up, but Kljaković Gašpić picked the right lane on the final downwind to the finish to take advantage of a late gust in the wind and passed underneath Scott just metres from the finish line to deny the Brit a perfect scoreline.

Scott said, "In the first race I was there or thereabouts half way up the first beat and then just got the wrong side of a big shift at the top and ended up rounding in the pack. On the second beat it just slowly started to clock right and I managed to take everything I could right. I managed to take lifts to the right, which is what ended up making it so good. At the top it went really hard right and the leading group had committed to getting across to the right, so I ducked their transoms, and just before I got to the layline it flicked back to the mean direction."

Björn Allansson from Sweden summed up his day. "We had big shifts all day, but it was really only oscillating. It was just about playing the shifts correctly and today a lot of other guys played them better than me. You needed to be able to go with the pressure and capitalise when you had the opportunity. So I think everyone learned a lot today, though some are probably more happy with their results than others."

He went into the day tied on points with Max Salminen, but the Swedish battle had gone Salminen's way. Allansson was not phased though, "I never actually watch the results through the regatta. I just try to focus on my performance and see the result at the end of the regatta. It's only on the final day that it actually matters."

Josh Junior, from New Zealand, continued his consistent form to end the day in tenth. "I did alright today. We had shifty, pretty windy conditions and I managed an eighth and a tenth, so pretty pleased with that, though it could have been slightly better. I quite liked the conditions and managed to get in phase with the shifts. I got on the wrong side a few times, but I have two counters today. It was pretty good racing out there today, with awesome race management, and makes up for sitting around for two days earlier in the regatta."

SCOTT EASED INTO a 20-point lead in after two more challenging races on the Friday. Kljaković Gašpić moved up to second while Lobert dropped one to third. The gold fleet race wins went to Wright and Alex Muscat, from Spain.

The day began windy again but soon moderated once racing was started to 15-18 knots. Large pressure changes and wind bands funnelling down the course caused more than a few upsets, with patience and calm decision making reaping benefits at the top mark. However, some of the top 10 picked up some high scores.

Despite his worst scoring day so far, Scott still had the best day on the water with a third and a fourth. His nearest rival Kljaković Gašpić placed fifth and sixth, giving the Brit a crucial points cushion going into Saturday's two final gold fleet races. And with lighter winds forecast, it was a long way from being over.

Scott said, "It was a hard day; shifty and random. I got a third and fourth which I am actually pretty happy with because that was really difficult sailing. There were big leftys and big rightys and they were long as well so you could easily get stuck on the wrong side. So I am pretty happy come away unscathed. But Bambi [Kljaković Gašpić] was only a couple behind me in each race so it's not over yet."

Kljaković Gašpić explained his consistency.

"I am just sailing simple and waiting for my chances, and waiting for the right moment to cross the group. I guess I am not under pressure so far as I don't have any major mistakes and this just keeps me relaxed. I don't think about the points, just about sailing good races and sailing relaxed. I am pretty happy how I am performing so far."

He remained realistic about whether Scott could still be caught.

"It's hard to say. He has really good results so far and he is consistent. I'll just do my best to sail as best as I can and as I have been doing this week."

Lobert was one of those picking up a high score on the second race.

"Today was a tricky day, quite windy and super shifty and I managed a sixth, which was pretty good, next to Bambi, so that was also good. Then in the second race I was just not in the right wind, I missed it on the first upwind and then on the second upwind I chose to stay on the left hand side but that was not a good choice and I finished 19th. There is now some points to Bambi, but I am still third, and very close to Ed. Tomorrow will be a tricky day again so maybe some big scores coming in, so it is not over yet."

Høgh-Christensen described the start of Race 7.

"I thought I saw a massive pressure line coming down the left side and I just went for it. It was very hard because you had to look up the race course and prepare for the first shift after the start."

"Things went really well in the first race and I got a second. Then I was almost last in the second. I was leading half way up the first beat on the right side. It normally paid to take the big shifts right and stay to the right of the group if you could. And then the wind changed 35 degrees to the left with pressure and we had none. I just sat there watching the other side of the course fully hiked. Then I took a wrong decision on the downwind and another wrong decision on the second beat and then took a chance on the last run as I had nothing to lose by then. It went sour quite quick, but that's racing."

One of the pre-event favourites who didn't find his form was Pieter-Jan Postma from the Netherlands. At the event drew toward its conclusion he was languishing in 26th place, a long way from the Olympic qualification zone.

He said, "Yes, PJ is struggling. Mainly with strategy and decision making. You have to have a lot of patience on the course and it's so hard to pick the right shifts. But my speed is ok, and my starts are all good."

"I think my preparation was good. I trained really hard for this and the sailing was going really well. So I felt quite ready but the results so far are terrible. I don't think I will secure the Olympic place this week. I pushed hard again today but there was still no great racing yet from me."

Vasilij Žbogar, the 2013 European champion, was in 12th place, and just four points outside the medal race, but within the Olympic place selection zone. He hasn't performed as well as expected, but explains why.

"It's hard for me. I was sick before the worlds and had two months off. I lost a lot of training so I was not very well prepared for this event. I knew here would be extremely hard from the beginning and then the wind kicked it and it got harder, so I really struggled in these conditions. If you don't have really good boat speed it's hard to race against these guys. We have two races left. I am close to securing the spot in Rio, and it's going to be close tomorrow, so I hope for less wind. It might give me a little bit more of an edge."

THE REGATTA CAME full circle on the final Saturday with the last of the fleet racing series abandoned in almost identical conditions that led to the abandonment of Monday's racing, six days earlier.

Since then one man had dominated the fleet and had built a 20-point lead, never scoring worse than fourth in any of the eight races sailed. Scott would take this comfortable margin in Sunday's medal race. All he had to do was finish the race to lift his second Finn world championship.

His immediate reaction, "I'm nearly there. It might just seem like a formality tomorrow, but I've still got to finish, without having an OCS and without gear failure to make absolutely sure, but other than that, I am very happy."

On not racing, "It's good for me because I keep my 20-point lead but it was odd out there. There was a big split in pressure. To the left was really light and to the right was probably raceable. By the time we moved over to the right, it immediately shut down and we came ashore. So maybe it would have been possible but it was marginal at best."

One of the stand-out performances of the week was that of Anders Pedersen of Norway. Three years before in Perth he tried and failed to qualify Norway for London 2012, finishing 55th. Wind the clock forward three years and not only did he win the 2014 Junior World Championship for the Finn Silver Cup earlier in the year, but he was also in the medal race for the Finn Gold Cup, guaranteeing Norway a place in Rio.

"I am super happy with this. My dream goal was to qualify Norway for the Olympics, though I didn't really dare to say it out loud. But it was a good week and it has turned out well for me."

"I've known for the last few months that I have really good speed so I was just trying to use that and follow the good guys and use simple tactics and hang with the group. Getting into the medal race is just a real bonus, but of course I will try to do my best in that as well."

The final Olympic qualification space was won for Finland by Tapio Nirkko, of Finland. He said, "It's been quite a tough and challenging week. A lot of waiting, first with problems not having enough wind, but then we had a really nice breeze for three days. There were a lot of ups and downs for everyone in a very challenging and tricky wind, with massive shifts and pressure areas moving across. I could have done better but the minimum goal was to qualify the country so I am happy with that."

On Sunday 21 September, the medal race was played out in the Bay of Santander with a grandstand full of spectators watching in the glorious Spanish sunshine. As was typical of the week, the racing was complex and hazardous for the unwary, with several upsets caused by the capricious wind.

The day started windless and all racing was postponed, though a light sea breeze was expected later in the day. A light, fickle breeze duly arrived and the Finn medal race was characterised by big shifts and pressure changes across the course that ultimately decided the bronze medal.

Junior led out of the right side of the start from Scott and rounded the top mark first. Scott took the lead on the first downwind, but on the second upwind the left side proved heavily favoured. Kljaković Gašpić found the best route to take the lead and he never looked like relinquishing it. To win the race was all that could be expected of him. The rest would just take care of itself.

Lobert just had to beat Wright to maintain third place and take the bronze, and had the better of him down to the gate. However Wright wisely chose the opposite gate mark to the French sailor and sailed straight into a pressure zone and quickly moved from ninth to third, leaving Lobert isolated and helpless in much less wind. From there Wright held on up the third beat while Lobert was unable to recover. Lobert finished a distant ninth in the race and ended up fourth overall, again. Despite winning medals at Olympic and pre-Olympic events, he was still looking for his first major championship medal, and it was beginning to bug him.

Junior sailed a great race to finish second and moved up to fifth overall, passing his teammate Andrew Murdoch, who had been ahead going into the medal race.

Giles Scott's winning ways continued as he took his second Finn Gold Cup with consummate ease, leaving the rest of the fleet far behind in his wake. His only job was to finish the race cleanly to wrap up his second world title in the Finn. Fourth place gave him a winning margin of 14 points.

Having won the first five races in what turned out to be a nine race series, one less than scheduled, he consolidated his seemingly insurmountable lead by never placing worse than fourth in the remaining four races. A fourth in the medal race assured him the gold when all he actually needed to do was cross the finish line.

After this near flawless performance, no one doubted that Scott was on a mission to win gold in Rio in 2016. He made the task of winning against some of the best sailors in the world look too easy. He only had to make recoveries from a poor first mark rounding in a couple of races and generally was at the front early on in most races. His impressive speed, his almost flawless tactics and his relaxed attitude, verging on nonchalance, on the water proved a devastating combination. He never once looked like he was under pressure and that is always a good place to be at the half way stage of the four-year cycle.

For Scott, the win was all the more poignant because of the way he won his first Finn Gold Cup, three years previously at the 2011 ISAF Sailing World Championships in Perth, Australia. The 2011 Finn Gold Cup looked like it was heading for a very different outcome until Ben Ainslie's now infamous incident with a media boat denied him the chance to fight for his sixth world title, and opened the door for Scott to win in Ainslie's absence.

He said, "It's a been a great season for me and I can't really think of a better way to round it off than with the world title. It's been a great event and I am really pleased with the way I have sailed, and there's always a lot to learn from it, but I'm over the moon about it."

Did he expect to be so dominant throughout the event?

"I never really let myself think like that. But the event has gone really well. I have sailed well from day one and managed to keep it going through the regatta."

"It's a big milestone. I try to stay realistic, but my big goal is in two years time. But this is a very big step towards that so I am really looking forward to the next two years."

Reflecting on the Finn Gold Cup in Perth at the last ISAF Sailing World Championships, "The Perth win was an odd one with the other issues going on, so it's great to come out here and feel I have fully won this event outright. It's nice to be able to say I am now a double world and European champion."

On the race, "I just went out and sailed my own race and kind of forgot what was going on with the other guys. You can try and get out of their way but I was racing as much as they were. I wanted to go out on a high and I managed to almost do that."

THE SILVER MEDAL for Kljaković Gašpić was his best ever world championship result. It concluded a great season for the double Olympian, who was arguably one of the best, and most successful, sailors in the fleet never to win an Olympic medal. The medal was a great boost at the half way stage of his campaign.

The Croatian had lost some direction for a while but now seemed to be back, stronger than ever, with new backing and a new resolve to leave no stone unturned. He was the first sailor in Santander to take a win off Scott and his confidence grew race by race and when the pressure was on for him in the medal race he came through.

While many others succumbed to the pressure of the moment Gašpić sailed an outstanding medal race to not only take the race win, but to confirm the silver medal he'd had one hand on for most of the week. He was the only sailor other than Scott to record only single digit finishes.

He said, "The week has been great for me, a really excellent performance. Today I knew I had to be relaxed and keep calm and I did exactly that and it put me right into the lead. Then I had really clear lanes through the race and really good moments. I sailed pretty consistently today, as I did all week, and it turned out to be a winning combination for me."

"It's an important event for me because after a couple of years of some general setbacks, I really made a great performance here, with all my team behind me. This really makes me happy and all of this proves that we are working in the right way and the progress is just going forwards and I hope in Rio it is going to be even better."

On his consistent performance he said, "All my life I was always struggling in the breeze but this week was three days of pretty strong, shifty and breezy conditions which proved I can perform in any kind of wind. That's what I have been focussing on the last couple of years, trying to get myself in shape to sail in all conditions. So I am pretty happy I have succeeded in this and it makes me quite me quite confident and sure about the future."

For Ed Wright the bronze was further confirmation that he was one of the best Finn sailors in the world. But as the years before, he was always sailing in the shadow of the strong British team. Twice already he had his Olympic hopes dashed at the hands of Ben Ainslie, and was again facing an uphill struggle again for 2016, this time against Scott. While he had some catching up to do, the battle was still a long way from being over, but ultimately his ambition would go unrealised.

The 2010 world champion picked up his fifth consecutive world championship medal in Santander.

Talking about the medal race, he said, "On the second beat I got a gust on the left hand side and moved up to third and held that all the way. It was a nail-biting race and I really enjoyed sailing in it. It means a lot to me to get a medal at the worlds and I needed this medal, so I'm really happy with that."

On his tactics, "There were people nipping at our heels, and there was a chance of getting the silver, so to be honest I just wanted to go out and win the race. That was my tactic, and if I had the chance to push Jonathan back I would have done."

"It's been a hard week after I had an OCS early on and I've been struggling a bit with that. But it was all to play for today and it was a real fun race. I now just need to wind it up a bit more and try to catch Giles. I am putting together some big winter plans, with training in Rio and then Miami, so it should be fun."

THE 2014 ISAF Sailing World Championship was an interesting week in many ways with a number of favourites failing to secure their Olympic spot this time around. There were some shock omissions from the list of first qualifiers, as several notable sailors struggled with the Santander conditions. However, three nations had already qualified for Rio, Hungary, Norway and Slovenia that were not present in 2012 at all.

As an event Santander 2014, supposedly a pinnacle event in the Olympiad, was not without its problems. However, the welcome from the city was genuinely fantastic.

The sailors who didn't qualify now had to wait 14 months until the 2015 Finn Gold Cup in Takapuna, New Zealand the following November which would be the next qualification regatta.

9

Santander to Gaeta
The Long and Winding Road to Rio

Between the end of the 2014 ISAF Sailing World Championships in Santander and the 2016 Finn Gold Cup in Gaeta, just over 18 months later, the rest of the line up for Rio 2016 would be decided through a series of qualification events and heated national selection trials, that did not come to a conclusion until the week after the medal race in Gaeta. It would be a long and hard road with several sailors dropping out along the way, some high-profile comebacks, as well as a continual stream of regatta wins from Giles Scott.

The first event after Santander was the inaugural ISAF Sailing World Cup Final in Abu Dhabi. Promoted as an elite level event that was envisaged as new world-class event to showcase sailing, many of the top sailors largely ignored it as interfered with their own schedules and plans, despite the offer of subsidised logistics and prize money. It was an event that would always struggle to gain support from the fleet.

The seven race series was led from start to finish by Vasilij Žbogar. After winning the first two races, he maintained his lead and then just stayed close to Ivan Kljaković Gašpić in the medal race to take gold. Gašpić took silver, with Caleb Paine taking bronze.

Three sailors in Abu Dhabi then continued onto Australia for winter training leading up to the Sailing World Cup Melbourne, where Ed Wright took a relatively easy win from Oliver Tweddell and Jake Lilley. The 2013 winner, Björn Allansson, had to settle for fourth.

After Santander Tweddell completely reviewed his programme. Though he won a race and had some other great races, he finished in 23rd, while Lilley had placed 13th and qualified Australia for Rio.

One of the main things to come out of Tweddell's analysis was to create a productive training group. After Santander he started training with Wright and Allansson, first in Abu Dhabi, then in his hometown of Melbourne for five weeks leading up to the World Cup, and then in Miami prior to that World Cup.

In Melbourne Tweddell had taken the advantage over Lilley for the third time - they finished second and third for the third year running. But Lilley was about to emerge as the stronger and would be almost unbeaten by Tweddell up until the selections, despite both of them raising their game beyond recognition. Their selection process would go right down to the wire.

BY THE START of the pre-Olympic year it would be unusual to expect a lot of changes. However 2015 was quite different to normal. First there were a few changes to team line ups with several sailors stepping out of the race for Rio. Then the London 2012 silver medalist, Jonas Høgh-Christensen, announced his return to the campaign trail, which while issued in a surprise announcement was also not unexpected after his good showing in Santander. And then towards the end of the year the 2008 silver medalist, Zach Railey, from the USA, also quietly launched a comeback. It was never going to be a boring year.

The second unusual matter was that all major boat builders released new hull moulds, and Finn sales took a major upturn. Many were being trialled before Palma with most of the top sailors trying to find an edge on their competition. World champion Giles Scott picked up one of the first new boats from Petticrows but decided against using it in Palma, though he did use it later to win in Weymouth. Devoti Sailing had launched the new Fantastica Finn in September 2014, and in the end this proved the most popular.

In March Greg Douglas announced he was stepping down from Olympic campaign, while in the Spring, Thomas Le Breton also announced his retirement, leaving the way clear for Lobert to compete in Rio for France.

Scott's first event after Santander was the World Cup in Miami the following January. He won five races and finishing a close second in the medal race to wrap up his eighth consecutive major win and defended the title he won the previous year. Ivan Kljaković Gašpić took the silver after a very consistent week, while Lilley was starting to emerge as a force to be reckoned with. A solid medal race win gave him the bronze.

With the World Cup evolving into a more elite series capped at 40 entries, for the first time since the series started, the Trofeo Princesa Sofia was dropped from the series, but Palma remained a popular start of the season training venue and in 2015 the regatta attracted a large entry. Scott secured yet another victory after winning the medal race to take the regatta by 25 points. The other medals went to Kljaković Gašpić and Tapio Nirkko, Gašpić's better medal race result giving him the silver.

Without a doubt the week in Palma threw the most changeable, shifty and often bizarre conditions at the sailors, that produced a very high scoring event all round. That Scott managed to win despite these conditions and despite having to change boats mid-week after a collision rendered his own boat too damaged to continue, said a lot for the world champion. Josh Junior showed plenty of potential and held a podium position right up until the penultimate day, when it slipped away.

Then it was straight onto Hyères where Scott secured his second Sailing World Cup event of the year after winning the medal race to take the top spot by 24 points. Žbogar took the silver while Wright took bronze

Hyères was the first event with the new format of 40 boats, with 30 taken from the world rankings and 10 from the next best in Palma.

In May the Finn fleet returned to Split, in Croatia, the fourth time in recent history for a major championship. After surviving a controversial protest against him for allegedly hitting the pin-end starting vessel, Kljaković Gašpić took his third European title after a close battle with Junior. Žbogar turned around a slow start when he was ill, to finish strongly and take the bronze. Again, a lot of the top sailors skipped the event, preferring to train elsewhere.

Delta Lloyd Regatta and Kiel Week followed, both former World Cup venues that had been dropped. After many years of trying Pieter-Jan Postma finally won in Medemblik, while Deniss Karpak won again in Kiel.

The final major event of the early season was the World Cup event in Weymouth, which attracted just 24 entries. Scott had a fight on his hands against the two Kiwis, Murdoch and Junior, and it was still wide-open going into the medal race after a shortened series. Scott stayed close to Junior throughout the race and they finished at the back. Murdoch escaped, but couldn't get far enough ahead of Scott, who took the event by four points from Junior and Murdoch. It was Scott's narrowest victory for a while.

After the summer break and many national regattas, it was back to Rio for the Aquece Rio 2015 Test Event, which Scott won at the last minute after trailing Postma all week long. Nirkko continued his good season with the bronze.

The fleet was starting to close the gap on Scott. He had continued his run of victories but some of them were perhaps too close for comfort. Scott's response at the end of the year, at the 2015 Finn Gold Cup, in Takapuna, was loud and clear.

THE SAILING WORLD Cup Qingdao was next, the Asian qualifier for Rio 2016. The 10-boat Finn fleet featured nine Chinese boats with a single Iranian, sailor, Ahmad Ahmadi, up against them in the race for qualification. The Chinese controlled the fleet from the first day with 2012 Olympian Lei Gong and Luwen Shen fighting it out for overall honours. The Chinese had done enough by the end of the fourth day to secure the Rio place for China, while Gong showed his experience in the medal race to overcome a DNE (non-excludable disqualification) and a five-point deficit to take the title by just one point and be selected for Rio.

PREDICTABLY, THE ISAF Sailing World Cup Final in Abu Dhabi in October suffered because of its proximity to the Finn Gold Cup in November. Nevertheless six sailors made it to race a tight series off Lulu Island. European champion Kljaković Gašpić took gold after making the best of the six race opening series, with Wright holding second place most of the week. However a great medal race win from Pablo Guitian Sarria handed him the bronze with Alican Kaynar taking home the silver.

Then the fleet converged on New Zealand for the Finn Gold Cup and the second class qualifier for Rio.

The first Finn Gold Cup in New Zealand for 35 years was as sensational as the last time it was sailed there 35 years ago, but for very different reasons. In 1980 there was a huge battle between Cam Lewis and John Bertrand to decide the world title. In 2015, Giles Scott did not just dominate the event, but won his third world title by a huge 45-point margin and with two races and one day to spare. It was the biggest victory in Finn Gold Cup history since Paul Elvstrøm's win in 1959 and just when everyone thought the level couldn't improve, he stepped it up a gear to demoralise his opposition completely.

Jonathan Lobert finally broke out of his medal wilderness to take a confident silver, while Žbogar survived the free pumping medal race in less than 10 knots, to secure bronze, his first Finn Gold Cup medal, and it meant a lot to him.

Just 12 months after being introduced, nine out of 10 boats in the medal race were Devoti Fantastica hulls. Scott had also decided to use one, after using his older Classic Devoti hull at the test event. In fact many sailors had used old equipment in Rio, while the new equipment was travelling to Takapuna.

In terms of Olympic qualification, Pieter-Jan Postma finally secured a place for The Netherlands, the 2012 European Champion, Ioannis Mitakis, took the next for Greece, Deniss Karpak qualified Estonia and Alejandro Foglia qualified Uruguay.

With the World Championship in November, the season never really stopped. For some it was back to Rio for another training event. Only one sailor travelled to the Sailing World Cup Melbourne, for a small fleet of two or three boats, but Oliver Tweddell finally won the title.

The Olympic year began with Brazilian favourite Jorge Zarif winning the World Cup in Miami, which was also the American Continental Quali-fiers for Rio. Facundo Olezza qualified Argentina for the Olympics while Tom Ramshaw qualified Canada. Olezza knew within a week that he had done enough to be selected to represent his country while Ramshaw had to wait until after the Finn Gold Cup in Gaeta five months later. From there onwards, attendances at events decreased as sailors tailored their pro-grammes around suitable dates for training camps in Rio, and many sailors ended up only doing a handful of events in 2016 before the Games.

The 2016 European Championship was held in Barcelona, Spain in May. Pieter-Jan Postma's biggest adversary had always been himself, but in Barcelona, he overcame that as well as 89 other competitors to take his first major Finn championship title after 10 years in the class. Zsombor Berecz also recorded a career best with the silver medal and became the best placed Hungarian of all time. Bronze medalist Milan Vujasinovic sailed the regatta of his life, won two races and narrowly missed the overall win.

The event was also being used by many countries as an Olympic selec-tion indicator, with the most high profile being the US trials, the second in two events after Cup Miami. With the huge numbers, the stage was set for a thrilling week of racing that also brought the worst weather and wind con-ditions to Barcelona for six months. The usual reliable breeze was all used up in practice and the sailors had to cope with wind from all directions during the week. It was very testing on the competitors as well as on the race committee with delays and postponements most days. While notable for Postma's hugely popular win, the event hit the headlines for the match race between Caleb Paine and Zach Railey on the penultimate day.

The Finns also made the headlines for a different reason in Palma a few weeks later at the Trofeo Princesa Sofia, the final Rio qualification regatta, where one place was available each for Europe and Africa.

Josh Junior sealed his first ever European regatta win with a day to spare to take the gold by 27 points, and became the only sailor to beat Scott since April 2013, and the only sailor heading to Rio who had beaten Scott in the quadrennium. Scott ended up with the silver after a Race 10 retirement due to rudder failure when he was in a commanding position and Tapio Nirkko took the bronze, his second major medal inside nine months.

However that is only half the story that unfolded in Palma that year. It was also the final continental qualifier for Rio with one European and one African place up for grabs. The expected strong showing from Africa didn't happen with just two boats. Four time Olympian in the Laser, Allan Julie from Seychelles never lost a point to Karim Esseghir, from Tunisia, and didn't have to sail the final race.

The battle for the final European place was intense and hard fought throughout the week, with 32 sailors from eight nations in the race to come out on top. In the end it boiled down to Russia, Turkey and Czech Republic, with Spain, Portugal, and Poland close behind. Five or six nations were always locked together at the end of each day, with even the smallest mistake severely punished.

Alican Kaynar, the 2012 Turkish Olympian rose to the top of the group trying to qualify on the penultimate day and fended off strong challenges from Egor Terpigorev, from Russia, and world junior champion Ondrej Teply, from Czech Republic, to be able to qualify Turkey. It went right down to the wire. He took a 10-point advantage over Terpigorev into the final race and held it together to finish on top and head to his second Olympics.

As most sailors commented, Palma was probably the most competitive regatta of the year with virtually all the big names sailing, and of course the first defeat for world champion Giles Scott in three years.

Numbers were down for the Sailing World Cup Hyères, with just 33 boats taking part. The week belonged to the Australians as Lilley and Tweddell got to the sharp end of their Olympics trials and both raised their game enormously. It was a battle made for clichés and though Lilley led for much of the week, they both had their ups and downs, and he went into the medal race after claiming three race wins. But it was still so close.

The medal race would decide the week, and maybe also the Olympic selection. In winning the event, Lilley thought he had done enough to win his Rio ticket, but with Tweddell in second, the decision still loomed over them as they went into the Finn Gold Cup in Gaeta, Italy in May, a few weeks later.

The 2016 Finn Gold Cup in Gaeta, Italy was a week to remember. The awesome scenery and hospitality, and the great racing conditions produced a fantastic and fun event, in which Scott won his fourth Finn Gold Cup, his second inside six months. Coming out of his first defeat in three years, at Palma, he only made one mistake all week when the patchy winds on the first day left him with a dangerously high score. But after that he was never worse than seventh to again wrap up the title with a day to spare.

Jonas Høgh-Christensen took the silver after his most promising week since returning to the class in 2014. Only twice outside the top eight, he was only one race away from giving Scott a run for his money on the last day. Everyone fell foul of the light and tricky winds on the first four days of racing. The bronze went to Pieter-Jan Postma, some way back from the top two, but it was enough to take his second major championship medal of the year.

Of course the event was also the 60th Finn Gold Cup, a fact of history not lost on most of the fleet. The championship would also mark the end of the Australian, Croatian, Canadian and Italian Olympic trials, so there was a lot going on.

A fourth overall for Lilley put his selection beyond doubt. Likewise an eighth did the same for Tom Ramshaw for Canada. The extended trials for Italy had gone on for a long time mainly because no one met the basic criteria. In Gaeta, Giorgio Poggi, produced his best ever performance with a fifth overall, and was duly selected.

The Croatian trials had come down to Kljaković Gašpić and Vujasinovic after various changes to the published selection events. Neither sailed very well in Gaeta, but by the last race Kljaković Gašpić had already done enough and didn't sail. Vujasinovic had shown so much promise early in the trials, but at the end, perhaps the pressure or the tension of the occasion got to him, and he didn't sail anywhere near as well as he had in the previous year.

A few weeks later, the cycle of preparation ended where it had begun four years previously, in Weymouth & Portland. Scott won his 16th regatta, out of the 18 competed in since 2012. Lobert took silver, while Max Salminen took bronze.

Next stop was Rio.

10

Development

Finn Class Funds Sailors All the Way to Rio

Development support of sailors had been an important part of the work of the Finn Class over the decade before the Rio Games, and one of the principle activities in the 2012-2016 quadrennium was supporting the sailors that trained at the Dinghy Academy, set up by the 2000 Finn silver medalist, Luca Devoti, in Valencia.

From 2013-2016, the Dinghy Academy was a the principle development tool of the FIDeS programme (Finn International DEvelopment Support). FIDeS was established in 2006 to provide appropriate funding to sailors from countries that were developing Finn sailing.

To date the FIDeS programme had assisted with many projects including: providing funding for sailors to attend the 2008 Finn Gold Cup in Melbourne, a qualifying regatta for the 2008 Olympic Regatta in Qingdao; funding of sailors to reach the Olympics in 2008, resulting in new Finn nations competing in Qingdao, such as Cyprus, Venezuela and India; assisted with transport of moulds to Brazil and South Africa so that local builders could build reasonably priced boats to help with the local and regional development of the class; and supporting a number of sailors both through funding as well as logistical and technical support.

In 2013 the Dinghy Academy and the International Finn Class embarked on a joint venture to fund the coaching and training of sailors from developing Finn nations. The objective was nothing less than qualification for the 2016 Rio Olympics.

The agreement between the two organisations provided free use of equipment and facilities for five days to eligible sailors. It was a great opportunity for sailors from nations without a history of Finn sailing to find out what Finn sailing is all about, with coaching and advice from the best in the world, all freely given.

Over the next three years small groups of sailors received funding from the Finn Class as part of their Dinghy Academy training. Two of them, Alejandro Foglia, from Uruguay and Facundo Olezza, from Argentina, succeeded in qualifying for the Rio 2016 Olympic Games.

In addition, seven other sailors, who had trained for long and short periods at the Dinghy Academy, made it to Rio: Vasilij Žbogar, Josh Junior, Zsombor Berecz, Alican Kaynar, Giorgio Poggi, Tom Ramshaw and Allan Julie.

LUCA DEVOTI NEEDS no introduction. Larger than life both in character and ambition, his vision of a Finn training base came to life as the Dinghy Academy in Valencia. His passion for this was obvious and he found great satisfaction in passing on his hard won knowledge and seeing the next generation of Finn stars evolve.

Valencia had proved a popular training venue for Finn sailors for many years. This really began in the lead up to the 2007 America's Cup, held in Valencia, where sailors from various teams continued to sail Finns in their spare time. It is a great location for the Academy, which is located in the extensive grounds of the Real Club Náutico de Valencia, because of its excellent conditions afloat and great facilities ashore. Valencia was widely regarded as one of the best places in the world to train with almost guaranteed good wind and weather.

His vision for the academy was to assemble a world-class array of talent and coaches to train together during the Olympic cycle. Charter boats were made available and the team of dedicated sailors was led by four-time Olympian Vasilij Žbogar. Into this cauldron of expertise and athleticism the class hoped to introduce emerging talent and give them to tools to complete at the highest level.

In 2014 the Dinghy Academy became an ISAF Approved Training Centre following a full audit of its operations and facilities. Luca Devoti explained, "So far this has not really had much impact on our operations, though with time I hope that such a prestigious acknowledgment will help us grow and promote the sport even more."

When the first sailors arrived he wrote, "They are training hard, spending long hours on the water and getting better at their game. They love Finn sailing, they are racing against the pros and at times their bows are at the front of the fleet. What a fantastic boat the Finn is. Very young athletes, pros and a huge community of masters all share the same passion, the same drive and the same quality. Every boat has a soul and the Finn is special."

The initiative to help with funding some sailors at the Dinghy Academy was a natural progression of the work being done and a no-brainer to try and help these athletes and bring new countries to the Olympics Games in the Finn.

Sailors from nations that are developing Finn sailing mostly experience a lack of technical knowledge, such as tuning and boat handling skills. The Dinghy Academy and its coaches provided this know-how in addition to providing a training camp opportunity and regatta logistics, as well as of course the camaraderie among sailors. There is also an economy of scale factor in the project, which is vital for sailors with low funding. The Finn Class was actively encouraging further globalisation of Finn sailing and this project was a perfect fit.

This scheme was also a natural fit for the FIDeS programme. FIDeS was created in 2006 by Finn class development officer, and 2004 Finn Olympian, Michele Marchesini, as a way to channel funds and expertise within the class towards sailors from nations that were trying to develop Finn sailing. FIDeS aims to help sailors and National Finn Authorities in countries where the Finn and the sport of sailing are not well established, by offering training, information, coaching, logistics and equipment loan, leasing and discounts.

The programme in Valencia began in 2013 with support for Agustin Zabalua from Argentina and Foglia. These two sailors were part of a training group of a dozen or more top athletes benefiting from Valencia's near perfect conditions. In addition, teams from Austria and Russia began training alongside the full time sailors in preparation for the season ahead. More and more sailors gradually began including Valencia and the Dinghy Academy in their training plans for the year, including Masters looking for a winter training base.

For Foglia the Dinghy Academy proved to an essential part of his training. "The Dinghy Academy has been providing me all the equipment to be able to sail in the Finn, because I don't have my own boat yet. My first contact with the boat was in November last year (2012) in Valencia, and since then I have been there three more times sailing with other Finn sailors all over the world. Luca as the head coach of the Academy is helping me a lot to get to know the boat and its basic controls, the boat handling and manoeuvres. Thanks to the Finn Class funding I can access all the facilities there, including accommodation during my stay and access to the gym."

He described a typical training period in which recovery is as much a part of the programme as on the water work and physical training. "We have a routine of three weeks training and one week off, which is basically recovery training. During the three weeks the loads are gradually increased. We train on Monday, Tuesday and Wednesday and then recover on Thursday. Then on Friday and Saturday we train harder and then have Sunday off to recover. We do that with increasing loads over the three weeks and then take a week off. If there is a regatta coming then we take a week off before the regatta."

"We do endurance training from October to January. Then we just maintain that and increase intensity with weights in the gym, and sailing of course. The amount we do of each activity depends on the wind. If we look at the forecast and have a hard week coming then the most important thing is to sail, so we train in the gym but not as hard as if the wind is light, because you want to be fresh when you go sailing to do the best you can."

The 'head sailor' in Valencia was the 2013 European champion, and double Olympic Laser medalist, Vasilij Žbogar. It was largely his need for a training base and training partners that encouraged Devoti to establish the Dinghy Academy.

"For me Valencia is a great training place where I can focus just on the sailing. For a guy like me that is from a small country with just a few Finn sailors, the academy it is a great place to train with other sailors. Valencia is a nice town, and the Real Club Nautico and all the facilities, good weather and wind all year around will ensure a long and successful future for the Dinghy Academy."

Devoti added, "Sailors who come here just get better day by day. The tough training and competition makes them grow at all levels from masters to top champions. The camaraderie between the sailors and the fact that we share all the information makes us grow day by day."

"Since we started we have had more than 50 sailors coming here. All kinds of sailors learn from the champions here and they share their passion. For this, Valencia is magic...I hope the Dinghy Academy will become the reference for dinghy sailing in a modern doping free, friendly and competent environment."

Devoti is keen that the Academy is there for everyone and encourages Masters to train there as much as he does young sailors. The Swiss and Russian Masters frequent the centre on a regular basis.

However he recognises that the future of the class lies with its youth and attracting new blood into the fleet. Together with the Finn Class he actively sought sailors to join the programme, for example Laser sailors who have grown too big, and emerging talents from developing nations. In the two years leading up to 2016, the Academy helped sailors from many nations developing sailing from Africa, the Caribbean and South America, and this is already continuing towards Tokyo 2020.

Santiago Falasca, from Argentina, joined the Dinghy Academy in 2014 and was allocated FIDeS funding. Falasca moved into the Finn from the Laser Radial, where he has represented his country at the Youth Worlds.

Soon after he joined he said, "I have improved a lot and sometimes I am already catching the guys who have done many Olympic campaigns. I think it is probably the best place to learn everything. We are always sailing with the top guys of the Finn class. We have a gym here, we have a top coach coming all the time to give us advice. We have every aspect of the training covered. Coaching on the water, coaching in the gym and physiotherapy. Everything is covered. Of course having a coach that has a silver medal in the Finn is also very positive. He knows a lot about how to sail the Finn and about the materials we need to improve our sailing."

Facundo Olezza joined the Dinghy Academy in 2015 and together with Falasca and Foglia, benefitted from the Finn Class funding to see through the full Olympic campaign, with Foglia and Olezza qualifying for the Rio 2016 Olympics.

Funding has also helped Gareth Blanckenberg, South Africa – he did two Olympics in the Laser and switched to the Finn in 2012 and Karim Esseghir, Tunisia – embarking on his first Finn campaign, but who failed to achieve his goal of qualifying for Rio at the 2016 African continental qualifier in Palma.

FIDES HAS DONE much more than just fund sailors. It has also facilitated new boat building ventures around the world.

In 2008 the FIDeS programme carried out its most ambitious project to date with the shipping of some spare moulds from the Hungarian boatbuilder, Pata, to Rio de Janeiro, Brazil.

This initiative helped Brazil rejuvenate its Finn fleet with locally built new equipment. In 2013, the class attracted 26 boats to its championship, which was the highest for several decades.

Initially the boats were built by Holos under the direction of long time Finn sailor Jorge Rodriguez. In 2013 he took over the moulds and produced them from his own workshop. Since 2008, 11 new boats have come from these moulds. The class expanded considerably as the Rio 2016 Olympics approached.

In 2010, FIDeS also supplied hull and mast moulds to South Africa for the same reasons – so that locally built equipment was more easily obtained without the high costs associated with importing from Europe.

Pata Finns Africa supplied a complete package, including hull, carbon mast, boom, rudder, launching trolley and covers. The company also upgrades older boats, thereby improving their performance and bringing them close to the new specifications.

Pata Finns Africa was set up in 2010, and by 2015, 16 new boats had been built. Of the 16, nine were based on the Highveld (in the Pretoria-Johannesburg area), and the rest were based in the Cape Town area.

11

The First Test

2015 Aquece Rio Test Event

There were two trains of thought about training in Rio. One the one hand, some sailors felt it was essential to invest huge amounts of their time and resources to be in Rio as much as possible to become at home with its many idiosyncrasies, its tricky winds, unpredictable weather patterns, peculiar currents and tides, as well as its atypical living environment.

Others felt that it was better to train at home with a few trips to Rio to acclimatise to the conditions and then to go early for the Games. In the end, the results seemed to show that those who had made the effort to learn the conditions over several years generally faired better in 2016. Perversely, there were also those who spent minimal training time in Rio, performing well in racing, as well as those who spent the most time there training, performing poorly in racing. There was often little direct correlation, though it had clearly been beneficial to some sailors.

However, for the first real assessment of the investment in training in Rio, the time seemed to pay off with most of the top 10, and specifically the medalists, having trained extensively in Rio before the event.

The pre-Olympics, or the Aquece Rio 2015 Test Event was held almost exactly one year before the Olympic Games were due to begin. It was supposed to mirror as closely as possible the conditions expected in August 2016.

The aim of the test event was to test the race management processes rather than anything else, which was just as well because the sailing base was still being built, and the Marina da Glória was littered with temporary tents and fenced off areas that were being bulldozed and rebuilt.

On the water things were also not going smoothly, with a large number of the race support craft impounded on the first day by Rio water police for not having the correct documents. Officials were seen on jet skis coming directly through the middle of a racing fleet and demanding paperwork from boat drivers. If everything was not in order, the boat was escorted back to harbour.

From the sailor's side, many were using old equipment, shipped to Rio for training while their best gear remained in Europe or was sent to New Zealand for the Gold Cup. Among those was Giles Scott, sailing his old boat while the new one was shipped to Takapuna.

Of the 20 sailors who turned up for the test event in 2015, which was limited to one sailor per nation, 17 would be back a year later.

FOR SOME OF the fleet the test event was also their first opportunity to become familiar with the various course areas around Guanabara Bay and out on the ocean. The contrast between the different areas was immense, with inland, flat water sailing in a strong current on the Ponte course by the Rio-Niterói bridge; the ever tricky, shifty conditions on the Pão de Acucar, or Sugarloaf, course area between the towering Sugarloaf Mountain and the Santos Dumont Airport, Rio's very busy domestic airport; and the three open ocean courses, that could offer huge rolling waves, but also a great view over Niterói on one side and Copacabana on the other. To succeed in Rio, you had to be comfortable with a huge range of conditions and racing areas. This is what drove the sailors to spend so much time training in Rio. It wasn't like any venue they had ever been to before. Every course area was vastly different, with different challenges.

Though racing for some classes started the day before, the Finn class opened its regatta on Sunday 16 August with two complex races close to the Rio-Niterói Bridge, the longest pre-stressed concrete bridge in the southern hemisphere, and the furthest course area away from the open sea. The bridge cuts Guanabara Bay in two and handles more than 140,000 vehicles each day. The constant, albeit dull, thrum of combustion engines from above pervades the calmness of the water below, but the sailors were so focussed on the job at hand that it largely went unnoticed.

First blood went to Norwegian Anders Pedersen. The right side of the course, close to Rio and the airport, proved favourable most of the day. Pedersen led at the top mark in the opening race from the right side from Jonathan Lobert with Pieter-Jan Postma close behind. Lobert took the lead on the run and continued to lead round the second top mark, but let both Pedersen and Postma slip though on the final downwind in more pressure.

The second race followed a similar pattern, but with a dying breeze that eventually shifted further right at the end of the race. This time Postma controlled the right and led all the way round from Jonas Høgh-Christensen and Max Salminen.

With a second and first place for his day, Postma had made the best start and went on to wear the yellow bib, for first place, the entire regatta. Max Salminen ended the opening day in second with Tapio Nirkko in third.

Postma said, "Today we had 8-12 knots and it was quite tough because we had the pumping flag, so it was a lot of hard work. For me, in the first race I had a very good start and a great strategy. I started at the boat end and then tacked off all the way to the right and there was a bit more pressure there. I was fourth at the top mark and then I caught up to second. The last race was much the same. I had another very good start, and a very good strategy and am super happy that I won the race."

"Today we had to look for the pressure both upwind and downwind. The winning was in the start and protecting the pressure on the right. You needed to have good starts to play your game and keep out of the boat."

"I think the challenge here is that every day we have a different course. We have just done three weeks of training here, and have done quite a lot of sailing. It feels like there is still quite a lot unknown, but the big things are settling in."

Pedersen said, "It's difficult to get to where you want. There are a lot of good guys here, all with good speed so it's difficult to position yourself exactly where you want to be to get into the pressure."

"I have only trained here for three days, so I am learning a lot, but we hope to spend more time here in the run up to the Olympics."

Second overall, Salminen said, "We had a light sea breeze, with a lot of current coming in so we had long upwinds and short downwinds. I think that the time we have spent here is paying off and I know I am fast in these conditions. I think you have to spend a lot of time here to be able to deal with all the different courses, both outside and inside."

"For me, it was a really good day. I executed my plan pretty spot on. Mostly the right paid, but I think everyone figured that out. So it was really a fight for the lanes today. First of all get a good start and then be fast enough in your lane."

Jonathan Lobert, in sixth overall said, "In the first race I had a good start and managed to be on the right hand side, which was good with the current and the wind. I was second to the top mark and managed to pass the Norwegian on the downwind. Then I was leading at the next top mark but on the final downwind I went a little to far to the left and one or two boats passed me. In the second race I messed up the start and it was hard to come back."

"The start is so important to be able to accelerate and get into a good position to go to the right. It was a little strange because soon after the start there was a left shift and all the boats were coming from the left. I don't know exactly what happened, but then I spent too much time underneath the fleet and I couldn't cross."

AFTER RIO HAD been awarded the Olympic Games in 2008, much had been written about the unsuitability of the sailing conditions during August, with a history of light winds, late winds and non-existent winds, combined with an early sunset providing a nightmare for schedulers. However, the first days at the test event went surprisingly smoothly, with enough wind, on time, to get the schedule completed before sunset. Then it started to go awry.

The second day, Monday in Rio didn't quite go as planned. The fleet was on the water around 11.30 to get out to the Copacabana course outside the harbour for a 13.00 start. However the wind hadn't shown up at the agreed time and the fleet wallowed on the swell for several hours until being sent all the way back inside Guanabara Bay to the Ponte course again. By the time the race started, only one race was possible before sunset.

Nirkko made the best of it, rounding the first mark behind the American, Caleb Paine, with Postma not far behind. There was a bit of confusion though as many of the leaders mistakenly thought that Oscar flag had been flying at the start, signalling free pumping and starting giving it everything downwind. Unfortunately, Oscar was not flying and the jury swooped in to penalise three boats including race leader Paine, Giles Scott and the home country's Jorge Zarif. With Paine doing penalty turns and Scott forced to retire as it was his second penalty, Nirkko had some clear air and sailed clear of the fleet. Postma moved up to second with Josh Junior briefly in third, until Lobert came through on the second upwind.

Nirkko said, "They made a good call to come into the bay with a good breeze on Ponte course, so we had a solid race. I managed to get a clear lane right from the start and had good speed, with pretty safe tactics, and stayed with the other guys and rounded second. There was some confusion about the free pumping and two guys around me got a flag and I got a little bit away from the fleet then and it was a pretty easy job to maintain the lead. It was similar to yesterday, but just later in the day, so the current and wind were a bit different."

Junior finished fourth in the race and was up to sixth overall. He said, "The forecast was that there was going to be some wind but once we got out to Copacabana there was nothing and we ended sitting out there for three hours before they sent us in. When we finally got racing it was a pretty nice breeze, and we had a great race. Yesterday was a hard right hand course, while today was still a right hand course but there were a few more shifts in it so you could go right but could also come back from the left, and so as long as you were on the right hand side there were a few shifts to be had."

So far Postma and Nirkko had not really put a foot wrong, while several of the favourites were making hard work of it. In his own words, Scott had a "very average" first day with a 6, 7, so adding a DNF (Did Not Finish) was not what he needed.

With the sun setting over the picturesque hinterland, there was no time for any more racing. Postma maintained the overall lead, while Nirkko had moved up to second with Lobert up to third.

ON THE THIRD day, the fleet was prepared to sail three races to catch up with the schedule but the wind still didn't play along. Perhaps the predictions of no wind in Rio were correct after all. On Tuesday, it seemed that someone had forgotten to order the wind. The third day was beset by light winds and by the time the fleet had been released to race in the late afternoon, what breeze there was had already started to shift and drop. The event was supposed to be at its half way stage by now, but after three days the Finn class still had only three races on the board.

It was a day of musical chairs. Initially scheduled to sail on the Sugarloaf course area, the decision was taken late on Monday to send the fleet out again to Copacabana for a three race day. However the day started with the fleet being held onshore while the race committee headed out to the course area to wait in vain for four hours. Then an amendment was posted moving the fleet back to the Sugarloaf area for racing once the 49er FX fleet had finished its racing. However almost as soon as the racing area became clear the breeze started to clock right and drop significantly with a calm patch working its way off the corner of the bay. It was clear nothing much was going to happen and pretty soon all sailing was abandoned for the day and the race was on to get back to the slipway to beat the crush.

On the Sugarloaf course area with an onshore breeze the starting boats were just a few hundred metres off the end of the runway at the domestic airport. Throughout each day the air at the Marina da Glória and the Sugarloaf race area was filled with the deafening roar of jet engines as the airport kept to its busy schedule. It became obvious that something would have to be done for the Olympics as not only was the flight path straight over the race area, commentators would be unable to do their job and there could be no aerial filming of the action on the water with the constant passage of air traffic. During the Games, the airport would close during the hours racing was scheduled.

NOW SERIOUSLY BEHIND schedule, the Finns had to use their reserve day on the Wednesday to try and catch up. Three races were scheduled on Niterói course, outside the bay on the opposite side to Copacabana. However, while the other fleets inside the bay got away on tine, the Finns were again postponed onshore waiting for the breeze to arrive outside. The fleet was finally released just after 14.00 and just about completed two races before nightfall, finishing the final race at nightfall as the sun set behind Corcovado and Sugarloaf, making for a spectacularly golden ending to another long day in Rio, as the boats picked up their tow ropes for the long tow home.

The Hungarian, Zsombor Berecz, was first round the top mark in the fourth race from Frederico Melo and Scott. Junior moved into the lead downwind from Scott and Melo, but Scott then made the best of the second upwind to lead down to the finish from Junior and Lobert, who had recovered well from rounding the top mark in ninth.

Then, the Russian, Egor Terpigorev got off to a flying start in the fifth race and was never headed, leading the fleet at every mark, though the chasing pack closed up on the final downwind. Croatian, Ivan Kljaković Gašpić was in second placed round the first lap but Lobert and Scott passed him. The wind had started to drop with the sun and with Oscar flag for free pumping being dropped at the final windward mark, the run to the finish was a tense affair in the sizeable swell, with several boats getting a yellow flag for being a little too over enthusiastic.

Terpigorev said, "I enjoyed the race because everyone in the race is a pretty serious guy. In the last race I was just a bit lucky. I started at the pin and after 200 metres I tacked to cross the fleet and was fast enough to do this, and after that it was easy, because when you are first it's easy to stay there."

"It's a really interesting area for racing, a lot of current, and I think that we should come here a lot of times to learn the water because now we know nothing."

Scott had the best day to move up to fourth, but was still only six points off the lead.

"I felt that I had quite a good understanding of what was going on out there and when we got out Matt [Howard, his coach] and I came up with a bit of a plan and fortunately it was the right plan and I was able to execute it. For the first race it was to try and play the right hand side, but a lot of the good guys ended up thinking the left would be good. PJ fell short on that unfortunately. Then in the second one there were some left flicks in it, but still favouring the right hand side and I managed to get a clear lane out there and rounded in the top three or four and that was kind of it really."

"They took the pumping flag down for the last run and with having two yellows already it's the last thing I wanted to see. So I went down the last run very cautiously. I had a bit of scare when Ivan got flagged next to me at the bottom of the final run. It's something I am going to have to deal with for the rest of the week, but actually there are quite a few people picking up flags out there so I don't think I will be on my own in that."

"It's been a slow start to the regatta, particularly for me as I didn't sail that well on the races down at the bridge course, so that was pretty frustrating, but it's good to get a good day done today and be in the mix for the rest of the week."

After five races Postma still led, but with the narrowest of leads, on equal points with Lobert, while Tapio Nirkko dropped one place to third.

THE FOLLOWING DAY, three more races were sailed out on the ocean, this time on the Pai course area, the furthest racing area outside the bay, and this brought the fleet back on schedule. While the wind never quite reached the speeds expected, it peaked out at around 14 knots with some large underlying swell keeping it interesting. The wind produced some large shifts as well, bringing some new faces to the front.

The first race belonged to Postma, leading most of the way to pick up his second race win of the week. Høgh-Christensen began a great day with a second while Junior recovered well from a 13th at the first mark to cross in third.

The second race, the seventh of the series, was won and lost on a big shift on the second upwind. Høgh-Christensen was the early leader, building a significant lead by the end of the first run. However the left unexpectedly paid on the second upwind with Scott leading a bunch of boats left while the Dane stayed with the main group on the right. The left worked and Scott moved into the lead from 11th while, Paine moved up to second. Postma kept his podium hopes alive after recovering from 18th at the first mark to cross in fourth.

The eighth race was equally as shifty, but Kljaković Gašpić, put his second yellow flag, and his subsequent retirement in the previous race, behind him and dominated the right side of the course to lead round the top and extend throughout to win from Zarif and Nirkko.

After having his lead narrowed to almost nothing the previous day, Postma had again extended it to sit five points clear with just two races in the opening series left to sail. In such a small fleet five points was enough to make the crucial difference. Nirkko was sailing very well and not doing much wrong so far. He was the only sailor to maintain top 10 every race. Scott, who could never be discounted, was still six points back from the lead and was not sailing quite as well as he had hoped to, or that everyone expected, but there were still plenty of points to be won and lost before the end of the regatta, so he had not given up hope.

Kljaković Gašpić was the European champion, but was realistic about his chances. "I still have issues with my speed and in the first race it was really frustrating seeing the guys just passing around me again, but I managed to play again a little later on to save some places, but it's really frustrating to sail without any speed. In the second race I got a second yellow flag on the first downwind, which was a bit of surprise. Then the third race was quite a clear lane for me. I started on the right and went all the way right, quite patiently waiting for a righty which came and in and paid off."

"This event is not important for me regarding results but you know any time you are racing you want to win, so we want to do our best. I know that I came here without proper training and I had just one day's sailing before the racing so I was not ready for the event, and the equipment was not tested, so I am not really happy with the boat and therefore my results are quite bad. I think this is one of the first times in my life when I may not make the medal race."

Høgh-Christensen said, "It was a difficult day with big waves, and a lot of struggling to do, and marginal pumping conditions. Some downwinds were free pumping and some were not. There were some big shifts in the second race, a big one to the right in the first that I got right and I was leading big time and then a big left shift and I went down to third, and then I lost a couple of boats on the downwind, but all in all a half decent day for me."

He said he was happy with his progress since returning to the class, "I still have a lot of work to do, but today was a good day. I finished second, fifth and tenth and I actually thought I sailed a couple of good beats and got a little unlucky but all in all I was quite happy with everything."

Postma said, "First race for me was good and I won. In the second race it started to get more and more shifty and a big right shift came and Jonas was leading by a mile, and on the second beat a big left shift came and Giles and myself came back to the top. In the last race there was again a big shift on the right and the second beat was mixed for me and I finished eighth."

After failing to qualify his country at the first qualification event in Santander in 2014, Postma knew he still had to get that job done in Takapuna, three months after the test event. Also, he still had to meet national criteria, which meant finishing top three at a major event.

"I am leading by five points, but tomorrow will be tricky sailing inside the harbour, and will be very interesting. I have been leading since the first day and it's been a little bit tense. It's the Olympic trials for me and so far so good. I cannot complain and tomorrow and the day after for the medal race will be an epic battle."

With Postma still holding the lead, Nirkko was back up to second. However Scott had now moved up to third, but remained six points off the lead.

POLLUTION AND DEBRIS in the water had occupied much of the sailing headlines for the months prior to the test event, with fears that come the Olympic Games, medal chances could be destroyed by boats hitting submerged items, or sailors becoming ill. Apart from the obvious signs and smells in the Marina da Glória, where an open sewer ran also directly out where the coach boats were kept, there were not many signs of problems out in the bay – at least not as many as many expected.

Rainfall always changes the situation in Rio, and on the Thursday night the skies opened for nearly an hour, filling gullies, streaming down the hillsides of the favelas, washing all manner of rubbish, plastics and debris into Guanabara Bay. The following day, the Ponte (Bridge) course was deemed unsailable, because of the high concentration of debris in the water.

The Finns were racing on the Escola Naval course, located in the middle of the bay, just off the Brazilian Naval School on Villegagnon Island, beside the Santos Dumont Airport. There was certainly a lot more debris in the water than previously seen, heading down the harbour and out to sea, but it was not enough to affect the racing.

A lot was standing on the final day of the opening series. The top of the fleet was very tight and the cut for the medal race was even tighter. After a short postponement on shore to wait for the wind to fill in the ninth race got underway first time.

The 8-10 knots breeze was heading straight down the bay from the opening between Sugarloaf and Niterói. With the fleet splitting into two, heading towards the windward nark in the middle of the channel, Jake Lilley led round the top from Paine and Terpigorev. It all changed downwind though with Postma moving through from sixth to first at the gate, from Lilley and Josh Junior.

As the wind continued to increase, the second upwind was lengthened The right side proved more popular on the second beat with Postma maintaining his lead round the top and down to the finish, and with Scott and Nirkko several places back, he extended his overall lead. Junior crossed the finish in second and Lilley in third.

The second race also got away cleanly after one general recall in near perfect conditions. With the tide under them the fleet was again evenly split heading out to the mouth of the bay. The wind was now at 12-14 knots and Oscar was raised at the top mark. Scott led all the way round, initially followed by Zarif and Høgh-Christensen. However through the gate Berecz was up to second and Ioannis Mitakis, from Greece, was third. Postma had recovered from a bad start to move up to fourth.

It was all on for the final upwind with Scott maintaining his lead to win his third race of the week, while Mitakis moved up to second and Lobert crossed third. Perhaps the pressure had got to Postma, as he slipped to tenth. His overall lead had been dramatically cut to just one point going into the medal race after leading the regatta since the first day.

For many sailors it was a week that began slowly and gathered momentum towards the end. Both local favourite Zarif and rising junior, Lilley struggled at the start of the week and were well outside the top ten. However both had a great second half.

Zarif said, "At the beginning of the week it was a little bit tough for me. I am not used to sailing on some areas, like outside, that we don't normally sail on. It was tough, so to finish in the medal race is good. It's not great to be ninth, but after the way I sailed this week it's not so bad."

"I am very used to sailing inside the bay, especially on the Naval School course, and I think I know a little bit better what is going on, so a fifth and seventh is a really decent day."

Lilley, who had still to be selected, was optimistic about his prospects. "I had a really tough start to the week, and I wasn't having a lot of speed but yesterday and today I managed to have some better racing and get the speed a bit better and nail some tactics and go fast downwind. So pretty happy with how I improved this week to go into the medal race in seventh. We had some really tight racing and really good battles this week. This should make for a good Olympics next year for sure."

"The courses all present their own challenges. Offshore we have a bit more swell, which is more enjoyable but inshore you have other challenges with the shifts and the current. They are all different and everyone seems to do well on some courses in particular."

On the following year, "There is still a gap to bridge, but we are not coming to the Olympics for a track suit. We are here to win and we have 12 months to go and the trajectory is good so we are going to keep working hard."

Scott described his day, "The first race was pretty tricky. I found myself on the back foot getting the first beat completely wrong, but then the fleet compressed downwind because it was wind against tide, but that saved me on the last downwind when I went from about 12th to fifth by playing the left hand side. It was a bit of a rescue."

"In the second race I won the starboard end. The breeze shifted right and I decided to continue and for a moment it looked pretty bad. But it came back and I managed to cross the guys on the right and round in first and held on from there, so a good day."

"Rio is a very difficult place to race and it does seem that you are going to have some challenging races no matter who you are. My week was made pretty difficult with getting two yellow flags on the second day. Everyone has been a little up and down, so it's going to make for some tricky racing for sure."

WHILE POSTMA HAD led the regatta from start to finish, he was always under pressure, but on the final day he ran out of luck, and it all went against him. There was just one point in it and Scott was on a charge, leaving it to the last race, the 10 boat medal race, to pass Postma. Sailed under the Sugarloaf, it was a tense and dramatic medal race, and perhaps a foretaste of what was to follow in 12 months time. Rio dealt up probably the best conditions on the course area all week with a relatively steady 8-12 knots straight over the top of Sugarloaf, under a beautiful blue sky.

Early on it was clear the left was the way to go on the first upwind. Junior won the pin and found a lane of pressure to advance forward on the fleet. He never looked back. Postma was just above him but was soon forced to tack off and ducked most of the fleet while heading to the right. Scott persevered to the left but couldn't match Junior who led at the top from Pedersen. Scott rounded third with Postma in ninth. It looked like it was over...but it wasn't.

Junior extended down the run but a yellow flag for him allowed Scott to close up. The fleet again favoured the left on the second upwind back towards Sugarloaf, with Nirkko going further left than most and hooking a left shift into the mark in third behind Junior and Høgh-Christensen.

Postma had also made gains to round right on Scott's transom and they headed downwind a few boatlengths apart. Junior went on to win while Nirkko moved up to second. Scott pulled away from Postma on the final downwind to make sure of the win while the Dutchman stayed close enough to Lobert to secure the bronze.

Postma was understandably downcast after leading all week and losing the gold medal at the final hurdle.

"It was an exciting week. It was good racing and a good fight, also the medal race. I started left from Giles but then I lost some speed and I couldn't hold a lane and that was a bit of a problem. I had to tack away so it wasn't a good first upwind. I had a nice downwind. On the second beat we came close together, only a few metres apart but on the downwind we were only two boat lengths apart and Giles had a bit more speed so he won."

"I think I'm on a good road, but today was a little bit tough for me."

But there were also positives for Postma. "I qualified [for the Olympic team] as I finished in the top three here. I wanted a top three and I did it. So that's in the pocket. We'll do some more training, and qualify the country in Takapuna but let's not forget we sailed a good regatta here with all the Finn sailors and I'm thankful to be here, thankful for the coaching, my family and our sponsors."

Nirkko described his week as, "Maybe the best regatta of my life so far."

"I was just very consistent, even on different race areas and conditions, so I am really happy, especially with all races in the top 10 and the medal race today was a great race."

"In hindsight the name of the game was to be on the left on the upwinds. On the first beat I was trying to play more in the middle but that didn't really pay off and I was at the back of the fleet, but still not too far in distance. On the second beat I had to get rid of Jonathan who was covering me trying to maintain his position. Then he let me go more in the left and same thing happened as on the first upwind with the pressure and the shift coming from the left. I made a huge gain and had a good last run to pass Jonas, so had a good race."

Scott once again stood at the top of the podium, with a two year unbeaten run now under his belt. He had made hard work of the test event – maybe he needed that more than another easy win – but pulled it together when it counted.

"I felt relatively good at the start. PJ followed me around a bit to try and unsettle me but I kind of managed to stick to my game plan and I wanted a good start with a bit of space in the middle of the line which is what I managed to get. Then I went with Josh to the left and we came in looking quite good at the top and then down the first run the wind dropped off a bit. PJ was a long way behind, but he pulled up down the left hand side and then took the left turn at the bottom. He gained and got right back on my transom and then at the same time, the Finnish was going left and gaining a lot. It was a very difficult race to manage so I was fortunate to just about hang on to it."

"I think those conditions are pretty standard for what I'd expect to see on the Sugarloaf course. When the sea breeze comes from that direction the wind is just rolling off the top of Sugarloaf and it does make for some very tricky racing."

For some his win seemed inevitable. "I wish I could be so confident. After the first three races I was in a pretty dark place. I didn't feel I sailed that well. It really wasn't the best of starts to the regatta for me. It's quite nice in hindsight to have gone through that and still be able to pull my finger out for the rest of the week and claw back to PJ who had been on top all week."

"Every medal race is so different. It's amazing how you do 10 races and ultimately the regatta comes down to tiny little decisions here and there in a medal race, but whether it's easier to defend or attack, I don't think it's either. Medal racing is very, very tricky and it needs a specific skills set."

Once again the leading sailor throughout a regatta had been beaten by the medal race. Pieter-Jan Postma had led the Aquece Rio 2015 Test Event all week but couldn't match world champion Giles Scott in the final decisive showdown under Sugarloaf. While Scott took the gold, Nirkko concluded an outstanding series with a second place to take the silver. Postma went home with the bronze.

You can never read too much into a test event results, but 12 months later only one constant remained: Giles Scott.

12

South American Pride

Three South American Finns
at First South American Games

The Rio 2016 Olympic Games was the first time the event had been held in South America, so there was great interest in getting more nations from the region to qualify and compete in Rio. The Finn fleet had three sailors taking part in the Games: Jorge Zarif, from Brazil, Alejandro Foglia from Uruguay, and Facundo Olezza, from Argentina.

While Zarif was a former Finn world champion, Foglia was taking part in his fourth Olympics, and first in the Finn, while Olezza, the youngest Finn sailor in Rio, was taking part in his first.

JORGE ZARIF WAS the son of the late Jorge Zarif Zeto, who completed at the 1984 and 1988 Olympics in the Finn. The young Jorge Zarif started Finn sailing at an earlier age than most, competing against the Brazilian fleet since 2008 from the age of 15. He started sailing internationally the following year and won the Finn Silver Cup, the Junior Finn World Championship on Lake Balaton, Hungary against an impressively strong fleet.

2013 was an exceptional year for Zarif. He was a year out of the London Games having been the youngest Finn sailor there and finished a lowly 20th place. No one really expected much of him. It was his first Olympics and in his own words he was there for the experience as much as anything, though his goal was to make the medal race and to prepare himself for what he knew would be a home Olympics four years later.

By 2013 he was firmly established on the circuit but had not yet broken through the senior ranks. Coached by the 2004 Finn silver medalist, Rafa Trujillo, he won his second Silver Cup on Lake Garda in the summer and then travelled to Tallinn, Estonia for the 2013 Finn Gold Cup. The light winds and conditions favoured him and while others around him slipped up and made mistakes, he stayed consistent, and ended up winning the title with a race to spare. He looked as confused as anyway, as to how he had done this, but it set in motion his rise to the top.

Within two years he was winning World Cup events and was a regular front-runner at international events. Just before the Olympics he won his first World Cup event in Miami, and then his seventh Brazilian National title, two less than his father's record nine titles. He went into the Rio Games with a real chance at a medal.

ALEJANDRO FOGLIA HAD been to three Olympics in the Laser class, culminating in an eighth place in London. He moved into the Finn in 2013 and based himself out of the Dinghy Academy in Valencia.

"At the 2012 London Olympic Games I was sailing in the Laser and after 14 years in the Laser I wanted to make a change because I was also quite a big guy and I was always on a diet because I had to be 84-85 kg, so it was hard for me. In London I finished eighth. I was quite happy with that and I had achieved my goals, so it was a good moment to quit the Laser and look for another goal. The Finn was my best option."

"I came to Valencia in the beginning with Luca Devoti in October 2012 and it was a great experience because I had never sailed the Finn in my life. I remember it was a windy day and it was quite hard to control the boat in strong wind and big waves because I was still 85 kg, but it was good fun."

"I thought to myself this is a boat I like, a boat I like a lot. I decided to try to make a campaign for the next Olympics, for the next Olympic cycle to Rio 2016, and my best option was to come to Valencia and the Dinghy Academy because they had all the equipment. Luca was the coach and he has such a lot experience with the materials and the construction of the boats, so he helped me a lot."

Foglia's qualification for Rio at the 2015 Finn Gold Cup in Takapuna, New Zealand, made him one of his country's most outstanding athletes.

After missing qualification in Santander, he had two more chances to qualify for Rio, either in Takapuna, by placing in the top four nations not previously qualified, or by placing as the top South American nation not already qualified at the Sailing World Cup Miami in January 2016, the continental qualifier for North and South America.

But he wrapped it up in Takapuna, taking the last of the four available places after a nervous wait on the final day, when the racing was abandoned because of lack of decent breeze.

"I am only the second athlete in the history of Uruguay to qualify for four Olympic Games, so this was something big, because Uruguay is a very small country of three million people, where the only big sport is football and the media talks only about football. Is also difficult to find funding to make a decent campaign. Very few private enterprises want to invest in individual sports."

"We don't have many Finns in Uruguay. The last Olympics where there was a Finn sailor from Uruguay was 1968 or something like that. For Uruguay it would be good, but also for the sport."

"The day I qualified for Rio 2016 there was some noise in Uruguay about me, and I made some interviews when I was there. The Federation doesn't have the budget to support the sailors, but they help us to present our projects to the Government to get some funding from them."

It was also a huge relief for Foglia. "I really wanted to do the job in Takapuna and relax my head for the next year. Although before going to Takapuna I had to organise another boat to be shipped to the Sailing World Cup in Miami in case I didn't qualify in New Zealand."

"It was also very important for Uruguay because I was also only the fifth athlete to qualify in all sports, so it means a lot for me for all my family, my friends, my coaches and the people who support me in this career."

Dogged by injury over the previous two years, 2015 was also a difficult year for Foglia because of injury and he had to retire from two major regattas, but he managed to come back strong and prove that he could compete with the fleet.

With Foglia qualifying for Rio in Takapuna, it opened the doors to a third South American nation qualifying at the continental qualifier in Miami, just two months later. Foglia had sent a boat to Miami but elected not to travel. Instead the favourite to win the place was Facundo Olezza, from Argentina, who like Foglia was part of the close-knit team training at the Dinghy Academy.

IN MIAMI FACUNDO Olezza was up against two other sailors from Argentina as well as one from Chile, but was expected to finish top and be nominated for the Olympics.

He did, but it didn't all go to plan.

Behind the young Argentinean's elation and excitement was a story about perseverance against the odds and overcoming an injury that nearly stopped him realising his Olympic dream. Not only did the Olezza produce a career best tenth place, out of 46 boats, in Miami, he did so with a broken wrist and a mast that had recently been repaired after breaking in two.

"In December [2015] I fell off a horse and broke the scaphoid bone in my wrist. I had surgery on December 7 and the doctors told me that I had to be in plaster for at least two months, but I took the risk and only two weeks after the surgery I came to Valencia and started sailing again. It has been really painful and challenging as this bone takes from three to six months to fix. Now it's still broken but I managed to sail with a wrist protector and also I changed a few things in free pumping and tacking techniques in order to sail well."

His coach, Luca Devoti said, "I am very proud of what he accomplished. He managed to recover from a really nasty injury in record time and got better and better. He is a hard worker and a pleasure to work with."

"I know how much this means for him and am moved by the effort he has put in. When he broke his wrist we decided to go for surgery, and to speed up recovery the doctors told him not to even dream of training before January 1. When he arrived here on December 25 we were out sailing the same day. He learned to tack pulling the sheet with his feet, to jibe with the sheet cleated, and to pump with the opposite hand. Each day was sailing, ice, radiotherapy, more ice, gym, more ice, and again sailing and ice and more cardio. We worked every day, we sailed the last day of the year, and we sailed from New Year until January 13. I was really worried as he was in a lot of pain."

But the use of ice and a few days off worked a miracle. "We were back training using elastics to simulate the pumping and squashing a tennis ball all day long to get the forearm strong again." On January 13 he took the plane to Miami, his wrist still sore.

"Facu has the ability to win a medal. He is a very good sailor. At Miami I told him to ignore email, social media, to rest and relax and block out distractions. So he did that. Every night he would just email me and say how his day went and I would reply with encouragement and advice to prepare him for the next day."

After a tricky start in the tough conditions in Miami, Olezza rallied and left his opposition behind to claim his first ever medal race line-up.

He was quietly expecting to be selected immediately, but was still waiting nervously. "The Argentinean federation told us that if one of us got the place and was above the other guys by a significant difference, they could decide in Miami who was selected for Rio. If not, then the trials would continue at the Europeans and in Palma. So I knew it could be an option that they would decide."

The news came soon after the end of Miami that he had been selected for Rio.

On hearing the news of his selection he said, "I have no words to describe how happy I am. It's an indescribable feeling. It only seems like yesterday that I was 10 years old sailing Optis and saw the great sailors like Santiago Lange or Julio Alsogaray and Juan de la Fuente, representing Argentina in the Olympics and they looked like heroes to me. It's hard to believe that now it's my turn to represent Argentina in the greatest sailing competition."

"It has been my dream to become like Santiago Lange and these guys, and of course it is my everyday fuel for the gold medal that everybody wants. I feel like nobody in this world could possibly desire this medal with so much strength as I do."

Olezza continued, "Our main concern now is to recover from my wrist injury, and then to catch up with the top guys to reach the Games in the best possible shape. I trust in Luca and in my team, and of course in myself."

Olezza was one of the growing number of sailors that had all benefited from Luca Devoti's training at the Dinghy Academy, and had qualified for Rio. Like Foglia, he was also a recipient of the Finn class's development funding programme.

He had made the tough decision to leave his family and his home and travel to Valencia in early 2015 to train at the Dinghy Academy under the watchful eye of Devoti.

"That played a very important role. Luca is responsible for all my improvements. He has a lot of experience and is the best in what he does, apart from being an excellent person. The guys here in the Dinghy Academy are also like coaches to me as I learnt a lot from them, Vasco [Vasilij Žbogar], Zombi [Zsombor Berecz] and Chino [Alejandro Foglia] are already qualified and let's hope that the rest can get their place in their continental place and national trials." At this stage, three more sailors from the Dinghy Academy were still hoping to win a place in Rio.

"When I made the choice of coming here I said to myself. 'One day you will be 60 years old and you will look back and say, what have you done with your life?' I am 20 now and I can do this. I am here [in Valencia] and training and improving really fast. I don't want to be 60 or 70 having given up this opportunity. I don't mind if I don't make it to the Olympics or don't get a medal. I personally think I will because I have it in my mind all the time, but I won't regret it because I don't think that is it time I have lost. I have met incredible people, that always give their best to help me."

"This boat is wonderful. Every day that I sail, I don't regret any decision I made to come here, leaving my home, my family and my friends. It's just amazing to have this wonderful shot of making my dream come true, which is winning an Olympic medal."

"I have watched the Olympic video when Ben [Ainslie] wins the medal 1,000 times. That feeling that he knows he has done it, when he finishes, and I think in that moment, all the training all the hard work, all the suffering and all the pain, just disappears. We'll all do that for the gold, but that feeling is something I want to feel someday."

"I can't rest you know and I got a back injury recently. Luca always punishes me because of this but when I rest I feel that I am letting my family down somehow. I don't want them to think that I am on holiday. I want no rest. I just want to give my best and train. I need to grow up in some ways, but I think it's better to be like this than to not train because I am lazy. But of course I need to grow up mentally."

"The training centre is amazing. The people here, all of us training for the same or similar it just makes for a good environment."

I always wanted to go to an Olympics and hopefully win a medal. That's all what I dream about. Every day when I go to sleep I always think about the medal. I don't think of anything else."

13

Oceanic Battles
The Struggle Down Under

Two of the closest selection trials for Rio came from Oceania. The Australian and New Zealand selections were both staged between two evenly matched, and yet quite contrasting sailors. In New Zealand, the experienced Andrew Murdoch was up against the relative youngster, Josh Junior, while in Australia, the slightly older and more reserved Oliver Tweddell was pitted against the gregarious and talented giant, Jake Lilley.

Murdoch and Junior first appeared on the Finn circuit in 2013. Murdoch, then 31, had already competed in two Olympic Games in the Laser class and had placed a creditable fifth in 2008 and in 2012. He switched to the Finn at the same time as the hugely talented Junior also began his Olympic Finn journey.

The contrast between the two was immediately obvious. Murdoch was a conservative sailor, rarely taking risks, thoughtful, measured and perhaps the more consistent of the two in the early stages. Junior was the younger, at 23, less set in his ways, with a higher risk factor. However at their first event together, the Trofeo Princesa Sofia in 2013, Murdoch was seventh to Junior's eighth. Straight after that Junior picked up the bronze at the Sailing World Cup Hyères, while later in the year Murdoch took bronze at the European Championship in Warnemünde, Germany.

However at the Finn Gold Cup in Tallinn, Estonia, Junior was ninth while Murdoch was down in 29th. These tit-for-tat results continued right through to the end of their selection trials in 2016, but it was clear that Junior had the greater potential and was learning at a faster rate than Murdoch, though both were sailing brilliantly most of the time. The two Kiwis were coached by the 1988 Finn bronze medalist, John Cutler.

Speaking in 2013, Cutler said, "It's good to be back in the Finn fleet. It's great to see what's happened in the past 25 years, and it's all looking pretty positive for the class actually. Josh and Doc are both new to the class, and we just take it as a methodical process, so we rig it up, make a few changes one at a time and see what seems to work best. We're not trying to be super clever, we're just running a methodical programme stepping through the controls and the tuning and seeing what works."

"I always had a good time in the class and always look back with good memories of my time sailing the Finn and the Olympic campaign, so I thought well, if I can fit this is with my other sailing and things I am doing, it would be a good thing to do, especially having two sailors who are good and motivated. It's good to be involved again."

"I think [they have] a lot of potential. They are both new to the class and this is their first season and they've done pretty well already, so the good thing is they both have a good skill set and they had good results in the Laser class, so they know how to start and sail, so it's just about getting a better understanding of the equipment and how to sail a Finn really quickly."

"Just looking at the results, Josh is a little bit younger and probably doing a little bit better, but it's still early days at the moment, and I think the important thing is that as a group we keep learning about what makes the boat go fast."

New Zealand has an illustrious history in the Finn class at the Olympic Games. As well as Cutler, Russell Coutts won gold in 1984, and Craig Monk won bronze in 1992.

Cutler coached the pair right through the four-year cycle, passing on a lot of knowledge and experience. Junior said, "I have learnt a lot from him. He has a very broad skill set and a lot to offer and teach. I am very fortunate to have him as my coach." Cutler also coached Monk to bronze in 1992, along with competing in multiple America's Cup campaigns.

Junior came out just ahead of Murdoch at the 2014 ISAF Sailing World Championships, passing him in the final race. They finished fifth and sixth, just four points apart. It was going to be very hard to separate them.

JUNIOR WAS GIVEN his first boat, an Optimist, when he was eight years old, and immediately became hooked on sailing. He learnt to sail at Worser

Bay Boating Club in Wellington, famous for its strong winds and testing conditions.

Coming from a sailing family, it is a lifestyle for Junior as much as a career. "When I'm not focusing on my Olympic campaign you are likely to find me cruising on my small classic yacht in Wellington."

The story goes that his parents named him Joseph John Joshua Junior, ignoring both their own surnames and making one up. Josh Junior first made the sport pages of his local newspapers at the age of 13, and while at Wellington High School won the silver medal at an under-18 regatta. He dreamed of winning a gold medal at the Olympics ever since.

Junior narrowly missed selection for the 2012 Olympics in the Laser class, against Murdoch, but he would turn the tables on his teammate going into Rio 2016. After losing the 2012 trials, Junior decided to move into the Finn, stopped dieting to keep down to Laser weight and bulked up from 82 to 100 kg, as well as adding much more muscle to his tall frame.

Junior won selection over Murdoch to sail at the 2015 Rio test event and finished well to place an encouraging fifth. However once into the selection trials for 2016 he slipped up. At the 2015 Finn Gold Cup in Takapuna, the old enemies of risk taking and a general lack of consistency reared up and mid-week he was really struggling to string a series together. Meanwhile Murdoch was putting together a string of top ten results and, while both sailors said the event was not part of the selection trials, they both knew the selectors were watching and it was still important to do well.

Junior eventually had a few good races and finished 14th, while Murdoch sailed one of the best regattas of his Finn career to place fourth, and just missed out on a medal.

It looked like the selection trials would end up very close, however as the 2016 season began, Junior came into his own and picked up fourth place at the European Championship in Barcelona, Spain, to Murdoch's 19th, and then won the Trofeo Princesa Sofia in Palma, where Murdoch didn't compete, to become the only Finn sailor heading to Rio to have beaten the gold medal favourite Giles Scott. Another fourth place in Hyères wrapped up his trials and selection to Rio seemed assured.

After his results early in 2016, he was the obvious choice, and was finally named as part of the New Zealand Olympic team on May 10 He breathed a huge sigh of relief.

Junior credited his then training partner, Pieter-Jan Postma as helping fast track his learning and preparation. Postma had spent a lot of time in New Zealand before the Finn Gold Cup, as he still needed to qualify his country, and had gelled with Junior and they began training together.

"PJ has been a really great training partner. He has a lot of experience in the Finn class, with this being his third Olympics in the Finn class. He has a lot of strengths and is obviously one of the great Finn sailors, which I am lucky to have learnt from. He has spent several Kiwi summers down in New Zealand training with me which has helped me improve a lot, especially my upwind speed, due to different technique and equipment."

Like a lot of sailors Junior had spent considerable time in Rio to learn the conditions. The Games would be his sixth trip to Rio.

"Rio isn't like anywhere else to sail. There is a lot going on with the topography, the current, the waves and the wind. All the courses offer something different so it challenges all sailing skills, which will make for a really exciting regatta."

"I spent a lot of time in Rio getting used to the conditions and there was always a good fleet to check my speed against and for great racing to practice on all the courses we will be sailing in the Games. I also used this time to tickle up my boat and get the 'tightey whitey' (my boat name) ready to race."

He said he liked the Rio environment. "The climate is always warm, which is nice, and the landscape is pretty spectacular too."

He tried to cover as many of the race areas as possible, even though he would probably not get to race on all of them during the Games. During the test event in 2015, fleets were moved around the course areas when conditions either outside the harbour or inside the harbour precluded racing taking place, so it was important to learn as much as possible about all courses, in case there was a last minute unexpected course area change.

"There are seven different courses, four being inside the harbour and three out of the bay in the big swells. We are scheduled to sail on four of these different courses but you never know what can happen so it's safe to have an idea of what goes on in all the courses."

Junior went into Rio as of the favourites, but he knew as well as anyone that Rio could be unpredictable and extremely challenging. Without a doubt, it would be the toughest challenge of his career.

JAKE LILLEY HAD fast-tracked his way through the Finn fleet, after first stepping into the boat in late-2012, with a huge ambition driving him forwards.

For Lilley the flicker of the Olympic flame grew into a raging fire as he knew at an early age it was all he wanted to do. His Olympic dream didn't start with sailing; he wanted to be a triathelete. However he grew fast, too fast, and was soon too big to follow his chosen sport, but was fortunately invited sailing by a friend. He liked it immediately, and enormously.

Having gone through the Laser Radial and Laser Standard route, he had quickly grown out of these boats and realised his long-held ambition to join the Finn class. At two metres tall and weighing in at 96 kg Lilley was only 19 years old, but he was soon turning heads after his first few regattas, which included a bronze at Sail Melbourne and a gold at the Sydney International Regatta.

"I always wanted to race Finns since I first stepped on to a sailing boat. In addition, the Olympic Games has always been a massive part of my life. To be sailing the true Olympic boat is a great privilege and there is nothing else I would rather do."

Lilley originally hailed from Brisbane. "I started school sailing in early 2008 and quickly moved on, getting into the Laser Radial. I sailed the radial for two years and finished third in the ISAF Youth World Trials and immediately moved to the Laser Standard for 18 months."

He realised his potential following his 12th place at the 2012 Kieler Woche, a pivotal regatta for him in many ways. "This was the last regatta of my 2012 European season and I really proved to myself that I could mix it up with the top sailors in the world."

"After the 2012 European season, I came to the realisation that I was far too big for the Laser Class. I talked to my mentor, London 2012 Olympian, Brendan Casey, about his thoughts on moving to the Finn, as he himself had been too big in the Laser for too long, and it became clear that the Finn was going to be the class for me."

So after some fast-track training it was off to Melbourne. "I had only been training for eight weeks before my first regatta, the ISAF Sailing World Cup Melbourne. I really had no expectations and was still on a very steep learning curve as to how to exactly sail the boat. I knew the boat was going to be technically challenging and physically demanding to race and that is exactly what it was. In terms of my own performance I far exceeded my expectations for a first regatta."

"I next travelled to Sydney where I consolidated with some hard training and good racing at both the Sydney International Regatta and the New South Wales Finn State Championships. I had an unbelievable start to the NSW States with a 1, 1, 2 in some fickle breeze as we raced up and down Sydney Harbour. I was very star-struck racing against my child-hood idol and three-time Olympian, Anthony Nossiter, but I didn't let this hold me back."

He initially had John Bertrand, the American 1984 silver medalist, as his coach. "Yachting Australia had executed a vision and they targeted John to develop a National Finn programme in my home town of Brisbane."

At the time he described his introduction to the Finn class as a massive learning experience. "For sure there are important things I must work on, but for now I am working on improving my entire game, not just some particulars. The learning curve in the class is so steep and with the knowledge that both Brendan and John keep giving to me, I don't know if I will ever stop learning at this rate."

"I have some very high goals and aspirations, but I think the most important thing is having a good plan and focusing on the correct processes, one day at a time. In saying this, each regatta I will compete in is just as important as any other and I want to give the very best performance in each of these events. The long-term goal of course is Olympic gold."

IN LILLEY'S FIRST season in Europe, he collected silver medals at the Junior World Championship at Malcesine, Lake Garda, and the Junior Europeans at Warnemünde. The following year he won the Junior European title in La Rochelle against 25 other Juniors, but skipped the Junior Worlds, preferring to focus on preparations for the ISAF World Sailing Championships in Santander. He was already thinking further ahead, sailing and talking like a senior.

Speaking in 2014 after winning the Junior Europeans, he said, "It was pretty frustrating that we finished second three times last year; that hurt. We worked really hard over the summer, we went to Miami and put heaps of work in so to win the junior open title is really good."

"Our main focus [in 2014] is on the worlds and the Olympics. I'm really happy that all the juniors were here and we're racing with the big boys, so that's the big one for this year. Then it's all on towards the Games."

Since then his progress was only in one direction. He had followed the 2012 Games on TV and decided that's what he wanted to be doing four years later. He bought a Finn, and starting training hard.

However it wasn't all plain sailing for Lilley. His campaign came slightly off track at the end of 2015, when the selection trials began against Tweddell. Coming off the back of an eighth place finish at the test event in Rio, he was expected to do great things at the 2015 Finn Gold Cup in Takapuna, New Zealand. But it wasn't to be and Lilley struggled to beat Tweddell, ending up just eight points and three places ahead after a difficult week.

The main casualty of that was his coach John Bertrand, who left the team under a cloud. They had worked well together since Lilley first started in the Finn in 2012, and nine months out from the Games is not the best time to be changing coaches. Bertrand had used his extensive knowledge and coaching ability to transform Lilley from his first steps in the class to being a potential medalist, so it was a surprising development.

Lilley said, "It's never easy changing a support network so close to the Games. But I'm young and we are trying to run an accelerated programme."

While Euan McNicol took over coaching duties for the Australian team, Lilley spent the early part of 2016 training with Caleb Paine in Miami, with Paine himself about to start his own fiery selection trials.

This training enabled Lilley to take another giant step forward, placing fourth in Miami, where he was unlucky not to win a medal. His long drawn out selection trials against Tweddell were heading for a very tight conclusion.

TWEDDELL HAD BEEN in the Finn since 2010, when he took the bronze at the Junior World Championship for the Silver Cup in San Francisco. As he developed he became very good in lights airs, often winning major races but never quite breaking through during a whole regatta. He had famously won the opening race of the 2013 Finn Gold Cup in Tallinn, Estonia. The boat he arrived with had measurement problems and was barred from racing. He chartered an old Ukrainian hull, and spent all the next day sorting it out, screwing on fittings and preparing it for racing.

No one would have blamed him for being too exhausted and drained to race properly, but he came out of the start confidently in the first race, got the first few shifts right and sailed away from the fleet, to win by a significant margin. It was clear evidence that he had the talent to challenge the fleet.

Then along came Jake Lilley and, with the retirement of the 2012 Olympian Brendan Casey, there was a two horse race heading into Rio. Tweddell was slightly older, but Lilley was a ferocious talent who was not afraid of hard work.

Bertrand maybe also recognised this and Lilley perhaps got the lion's share of the coaching. Tweddell had to resort to finding other training partners to maintain his learning curve.

Tweddell briefly rose to World No 1 in February 2014 after his 11th place at the 2013 Finn Gold Cup, and second places at both the Sailing World Cups in Melbourne and Miami, squarely beating Lilley each time. In Miami in 2014 he was robbed of the win by Giles Scott, by a clever match-racing tactic that piled points onto Tweddell that he could not afford. He picked up 12 points more than Scott in the double points medal race and lost the gold medal by just three.

TWEDDELL APPROACHED THE latter stages of the quad in high spirits, matching Lilley in the early races of the 2014 Worlds in Santander, and even winning the opening race again. But he struggled in the stronger winds mid-week, while Lilley gradually edged ahead. In the end a 23rd overall, compared to Lilley's 13th was good but not good enough, though Lilley had qualified Australia for the Olympics.

After Santander Tweddell took a step back and did a complete review of his programme to assess every aspect of it including planning, training and equipment. He found this extremely helpful and highlighted some key areas where he was on track, and other areas where he needed to improve. After the review he put in place quite an in-depth plan moving forward for how he was going to achieve his new goals, while maintaining other key areas.

One of the main benefits of this process was to create a productive training group that enabled those in the group to bounce ideas around and work together so that everyone could achieve their desired goal. After Santander he started training with Ed Wright, of Great Britain, and Björn Allansson, of Sweden. They started off in Dubai for the 2014 World Cup Final, and then gathered in Tweddell's hometown of Melbourne for five weeks of training, which also incorporated the Sailing World Cup Melbourne.

"Training with Ed and Bjorn was great. They were both extremely enthusiastic about training in a group and working together. The pair of them brought a certain level of professionalism to the group, as well as their openness to share and discuss information and concepts. This has really helped to make a few breakthroughs in certain areas. I think as a group we really compliment each other quite well, Björn loves getting lots of hours in on the water, while Ed loves getting lots of hours in at the gym, so we end up pushing each other pretty hard both on and off the water."

"We each have our strengths and weaknesses on the water too, so no matter what condition we sail in or point of sail we sail on, one of us will be pretty quick, so that gives the others a benchmark, and an opportunity to improve their weaknesses and compare any changes in speed against that marker. We are all striving for the same goal, and are working extremely hard for that goal."

He was also working with several coaches during this period including Adrian Finglas, Craig Cobbin and Johnny Rodgers, who are all great Australian coaches and really enthusiastic about working with Finns

Recognising his weaknesses after the Santander event his main focus was on improving his strength and fitness, as that was identified as a big area to make some gains that would directly relate to his ability to sail faster for longer. He spent a lot of time on the rowing machine and lifting a lot of heavy stuff to keep him on track for his strength and fitness goals that he felt necessary to be competitive in the Finn. By early 2015 he felt the progress was encouraging. He also gained weight while dropping skin folds, as well as setting numerous personal bests in testing. The rowing sessions involved a work-rest ratio of 1:2 for long durations, and were "brutal". Likewise the strength programmes were extremely tough and draining. He was preparing his body for the battle to come, and though it would take longer than he expected, all this hard work would pay dividends before the selections were over.

"Now Australia is qualified for the Games, the main focus is to perform at the selection events to achieve the result required to be nominated by the Sailing Federation for the Games. Australia was the best sailing nation at the last Olympics and that comes about from setting high standards they expect their Olympic athletes to achieve, that is what I am aiming for. That is the only thing you can focus on and work hard to prepare for, you can't control anything other than the work and intensity you put into every session."

The selection events were intended to be over a number of the major regattas throughout 2015, but in the end continued through to June 2016.

A key turning point for Tweddell was the European Championship in Split, Croatia. Both needed to perform to impress the selectors, and while Lilley sailed well, with a string of top ten places, including a race win, Tweddell had his worst regatta for a long time, back in 31st after a week of missed opportunities. He was sailing well but not capitalising on his chances.

It went from bad to worse for Tweddell a few weeks later in Weymouth, finishing almost last in the 24-boat fleet, while Lilley was up in sixth. On the back of his results Lilley was selected for the test event in Rio in August 2015. Tweddell went home scratching his head, with a lot of soul searching to do if we wanted to stay in the race.

He had some time to work on his response, and come the Takapuna Gold Cup in November 2015, he was starting to reel in Lilley, who for a change, was on the backfoot. The result of this conflict was that both sailors started upping their game, concluding with one of the tightest and most competitive selection trials of the quad. Going into the 2016 season, both sailors were on fire with ambition. It was going to go right down to the wire.

AFTER LILLEY'S STRONG performance in Miami in January 2016, where he finished fourth, the next time the two would meet was at the European Championship in Barcelona, Spain. Here, Tweddell had the upper hand, beating Lilley by 14 places. Lilley though had to contend with a major collision with a catamaran that meant he had to find a new boat for the next regatta, the Trofeo Princesa Sofia in Mallorca. Lilley hit the ground running with fourth place there, but Tweddell was not far behind in 11th in the 74-boat fleet.

As part of the selection process, if one of the sailors had achieved a 'baseline' place, then it was an automatic selection. The question no one had answered was what would happen it they both achieved that.

At the Sailing World Cup in Hyères the battle would reach its peak. The two sailors had not only risen to the top of their game, but they had reached the top of the sport. In challenging each other they had both excelled far beyond where they had started from and in all likelihood, where they intended to go. All week long, the battle went one way, and then the other. There was nothing to separate them. Lilley won three races, but Tweddell was amazingly consistent.

Any number of clichés was not enough to describe the battle going on. Olympic trials always bring out the best in sailors, even more so when it gets to the sharp end of the selections. But no one could have predicted that Lilley and Tweddell would have upped their game so much that they top out a fleet of the calibre that was present in Hyères, including Olympic medalists and former world champions

After four days of brutal competition, they were on equal points, and an almost equal discard. The final day of the opening series was telling with Lilley gaining a points break into the all important medal race.

Rarely has there been so much drama in one 30-minute race with the overall medals changing several times, two huge comebacks out of the start by medal contenders and another comeback by the gold medalist at the final moments. The race was sailed in conditions from 1-12 knots, with heavy rain, and with a wind that died and shifted 90 degrees to further challenge the already challenged sailors. It was TV gold, but a sailing nightmare.

The only constant in the race was Caleb Paine, from the USA, who calmly led the fleet all the way. Behind him there was real drama. Tweddell took turns on the start line and started way back but, fortunately, he hitched out right and hooked into a big shift to make a huge recovery to round the top mark in the top five. Meanwhile Lilley was stranded on the left with no way back.

With Tweddell slowly moved his way up to third, and with Lilley still in last place, Tweddell had one hand on the gold medal. But then there was a new change. The rain was tipping down, the wind was almost gone and then started shifting to the right. Lilley made one place on the downwind. A long way in front of him Paine, Jonathan Lobert and Tweddell inched across the finish line. By then the wind had shifted 90 degrees, which changed the final offwind leg to an upwind leg and this allowed Lilley to get to the right side of two boats and, even though he took a penalty on the finish line, managed to make up the two places needed to cross in seventh to secure his first World Cup win. Tweddell took the silver medal.

Lilley described the stress of the day.

"What an incredibly intense race. There was a lot of pressure riding on it. It is really important in terms of our trials."

"I had an OK start, and then got on the wrong side of the shift and it was looking really bad, but I kept chipping away. On the last downwind it got really light and I got pretty lucky, but just kept fighting and then got two turns on the last work to the finish but just managed to hang on."

"I couldn't afford to think about the situation. I just knew what was happening in the race, and I just had to keep fighting and take the right shifts and get in to the pressure. I didn't always get it right but if you keep trying sometimes it comes good for you."

As far as the Australian selections were concerned, "Our trials have consisted over a lot of regattas over 18 months which started in Miami [2015]. It's all-inclusive and you have to get a baseline performance to auto qualify. That [baseline] is a top two at a European World Cup or top six at the Worlds. We've both done that now by being 1-2 here so it's going to go to the board of selectors who will decide who the best medal chance is in Rio."

Rumours were rife after Hyères that Lilley had been selected and that Tweddell was appealing based on achieving baseline qualification. No one but the inner circle really knew what was happening but a few weeks later at the 2016 Finn Gold Cup in Gaeta, Italy, Lilley put it beyond doubt with a fourth place finish, a career best for him, while Tweddell, who also sailed exceptionally well placed 11th, again. Lilley was announced for Rio soon after, with no complaints from Tweddell.

There is a video from Gaeta of Tweddell performing a gybe in 25 knots and a big sea that for a lot of people summed up the progress he had made in two years. On a day when he had pulled out a 2,6,2, the second best performance on the day behind Giles Scott, in conditions that 18 months previously in Santander he had properly struggled, that gybe was as beautiful as anything anyone had seen in Finn sailing for a long while. You can find it on YouTube, an example of man and boat, of mind and sail, and of reflex and wind, all in perfect harmony, all combining to excel at something that is as ludicrously simple as it is tantalisingly intricate, but most of all, a manoeuvre that is the embodiment of a great sailor and a well trained athlete at the very top of his game. He may not have made the Rio selection, but Tweddell had a lot to be proud about.

AN INTENSELY PHYSICAL sailor Lilley stood head and shoulders over most of the fleet and by the start of 2016 was already beginning to show some of his huge potential on the racecourse, with several top results over the previous year.

Lilley was one of the tallest and heaviest Finn sailors in Rio, but also, at just 23 years old, one of the youngest. Going into the Games he was up to World No. 5 and he had a reasonable shot at a medal.

"Four years ago, I was a little bit of an unguided missile. Just heaps of energy and ambition but not all directed in the right direction. Now I am rather focussed and use the energy in the right areas. As a sailor I think I've learnt the boat well and what is required. It's hard for me, as a lot of the competitors had already been to an Olympics before I could sail. It's a big experience gap to bridge, so I'm just trying to learn as much as I can, bridge the experience gap and race smarter. It's a process."

"I certainly started right at the bottom in 2013. It was a steep learning curve and I was lucky to have Brendan Casey and my coaches help to accelerate that process. I was thankful to do the qualification in Santander 2014 and just focus on preparing for the Games ever since. I know I will be one of the youngest competing at the games, but it doesn't stop me aiming for the top step."

He put his success down to his support network. "I'm lucky to have a lot of people that care, and a lot of people that know this game very intricately, around me. I'm in a very blessed position and at the end of the day I just make sure I do everything in my power, every day to be the best I can be. It's a lucky position to be constantly guided and pushed in the right directions by the world's best sailing team."

"I think I develop and learn at an incredible pace. We are always pushing the upper limits. As such we need to evaluate constantly where we are at in each respect, and work on areas that require more attention."

Surprisingly, he admitted to not feeling any pressure on his young shoulders. "I think I'm really well prepared. I'm fitter and stronger than ever. I have no pressure on me, I'm young and, most importantly, we have been sailing super fast." The key is to "just never lose focus of the goal and always make the right choices every day. That's all you can ever hope for."

He had spent a lot of time in Rio getting used to the conditions. "This year I knew I needed to emphasise my racing practice and equipment testing in Rio as priority and we felt we had a good grasp of the venue. As the

Games drew closer, we decided to spend more time in Brazil, and only once we were happy with what we achieved, touch base with the fleet in Europe."

"Training encompasses all aspects from preparing mentally and physically, to putting in the hours on the water, clicking with the venue, continuing to evaluate our speed and equipment and making sure every box is ticked come Games time. We are just refining every aspect and making sure we bring the absolutely optimal package to the Games."

"We decided to spend our final preparations both at home in Australia and in Rio. Home provides everything we need and where we can get the most benefit out of our prep and Rio is very specific for clicking into the nuances of the venue."

"Rio demands a very holistic sailor. The best sailor will win; there is no doubt. It demands everything from tight flat water shifty racing, to drag racing in the current and chop and of course some real swell, offshore sailing conditions. There's no hiding in Rio, if you're weak in a particular area., it will be exposed."

The best part about Rio? "The atmosphere. It's a really vibrant venue and different from the standard European circuit. Everyone is excited – so are we. Oh and the sailing is pretty good there too actually."

He said he is a "super obsessive individual. I find something and I become really addicted and hyper-focussed. The last four years it has been Finn sailing. But I also go through stages of smaller obsessions. Right now, I'm really keen on squash. I have also always been into cycling. I still love it. It's a brutal sport. I love the physical component and the mental aspect too, especially when you're on your physical boundaries. That's where you see what somebody is made of."

"I think it helps with the sailing."

14

Danish Gold

Fourth Time Around for 2012 Silver Medalist

After winning the silver medal at the London 2012 Olympics Jonas Høgh-Christensen said, "I don't have any sights for Rio. It looks like my time is up."

He made headlines in 2012 as the 'Great Dane' trying to overcome Ben Ainslie on the waters off Weymouth & Portland. The 'battle of the bay', and the story that followed, captivated the sporting world, but afterwards Høgh-Christensen announced that he didn't think he would be back for another campaign.

However, two years later he returned, if briefly, for the 2014 ISAF Sailing World Championships, the first country qualification event for Rio. Though he didn't achieve his goal of making the medal race, he placed 11th to comfortably qualify Denmark for a place on the starting line in Rio.

Many people thought that would be where it would end. Later, he admitted he had used the Santander event to see if he missed sailing enough to come back. "I have learned never to say never about sailing."

And then he slipped off the scene again…until the following March, when he unveiled his return to full time Olympic campaigning with a well planned and well funded campaign for Rio. The decision had been made in January 2015 that, subject to finding funding and the right support group, he would return for a fourth campaign. About three quarters of his funding came from the federation, with the rest having to be found by him.

Considering Denmark's successful history in Finn sailing, it was remarkable that Høgh-Christensen had dominated for as long as he had. While he felt there were a number of sailors coming through for Tokyo in 2020, there was no one to really challenge him for Rio. However did see himself as a mentor to the younger group.

"I will try and pass on all my knowledge and hopefully the young guys can build on that and become the stars of 2020. " He later revealed that the training groups he prepared, to pass on his knowledge to the next generation, took too much out of him.

HØGH-CHRISTENSEN WOULD BE 35 years old by Games time in 2016 so the physical side was one of his biggest obstacles, though he claimed to be fitter than he was at the same stage prior to the 2012 Games. In March 2015, he said, "I am much fitter, but then the whole fleet has gotten much fitter, so I needed to start on a higher level. Also with being four years older, it takes a bit more time to loose fat and gain muscle. It will be a constant fight, pushing myself without breaking. The last 12-15 years in the boat, with some massive breaks, puts its toll on the body"

"I am four years older and my body is a bit more crooked, but I am that more experienced as well. It's my last chance, trying to hit the grave with as little regrets in life as possible, and because I just love sailing."

"Obviously it has constantly been in the back of my head. You think you will not, but I love to sail, and I love the sport. I actually missed sailing the Finn, and it is now or never."

He also still felt that he had unfinished business, saying that even though the silver medal he won in London felt very good, it still haunted him that he didn't win gold.

"Many people think I have an axe to grind, that I need to come back and try and win the Olympics and there is no doubt that is the goal but it is actually the love of the sport that brought me back. I really do enjoy sailing. I think the Finn is one of the most competitive classes for guys my size. And I think it is a lot of fun."

Rio would be his fourth Olympic Games. It would be a long hard road to Rio.

JONAS HØGH-CHRISTENSEN SAILED his first Olympics in Athens in 2004. He had just turned 23 and was the youngest guy in the Finn class and actually did quite well in a couple of races, but he also capsized in a race and had to withdraw. Looking back at it, he said one of the main factors was that he wasn't in good enough shape but he had gone into the Games with no expectations and finished ninth, and was "pretty happy with that".

Going into his second Olympics in Qingdao, he was by now one of the favourites, having the won Finn Gold Cup in 2006, and finishing third at the 2008 Finn Gold Cup in Melbourne at the start of the year. In the light winds and strong currents in Qingdao, he had a really bad start to the event and ended up for him, a very disappointing sixth. He famously trashed his hotel room after a particularly frustrating day on the water when he realised his medal chances were gone.

He ended up taking two or three years off, though returned briefly in 2009 when he won the Finn Gold Cup in Vallensbæk, Denmark, and then a year later returned full time to run for London. "I think most people thought Ben was a shoe-in or whatever you say. I think we managed to put together a campaign on a tenth of the budget and half the time and managed to give Ben probably the biggest run for his money ever."

But it was a hard event for the Dane. Leading from day one, after what he described as his best day of sailing ever on the opening day, he went into the medal race effectively on even points with Ainslie, and watched the gold medal slip away

"It took me probably close to two years to actually even be able to watch the medal race. It was one of those races where we had probably done 300 races on that race course and I would say 80 per cent of the time you had to go left and I thought I played it pretty well. I forced Ben out to the right and went out to the left myself. And then you know, it was one of those races where it went right. I actually look at it and I see a couple of the races turning the event where I didn't do that well and had I not made a couple of mistakes there I probably would have been further ahead and I could have sailed the medal race completely differently. So you know, I put myself in a situation where chance or risk was a big part of the outcome."

"I have huge respect for Ben as a sailor. He is a fiercely competitive guy. He is by far the most talented guy I have ever sailed against. He comes off a little hard to a lot of people because wants to win that bad. I am sure a lot of people have said that about me. I think that is the name of the game when you get up to the top guys and you do this for a while. You push really hard to win and so I think we both did."

The silver medal was a mixture or pride and disappointment. "It meant a lot. Of course I was disappointed for the first couple of days but looking back at it, I am very proud and very happy. I probably sailed one of my best regattas ever. It's funny; it's one of those things. I heard about it before the Olympics that the medal doesn't actually mean that much. It is more the achievement and it is very true. I don't even think I know where my medal is but you look back, it is a very fond memory. And I would like to repeat it. And I think that is why I came back."

After London was over, he returned to his career, stepped away from sailing, again, and no one really expected to see him back in a Finn again. Then in 2014, the Danish federation needed to get a couple of Olympic qualifications and they asked Høgh-Christensen whether he could help them out in Santander to try and qualify Denmark for the Finn class in Rio.

"I decided to do that and come down to do the event. I didn't do a lot of training for it but I did the event. And I realised I really missed sailing. I probably knew before I went but I really did miss sailing a lot. So then we started looking at whether it was a possibility and we managed to get it all sorted by the spring of 2015 and I did my first event in Palma and then pretty much from there, the training intensified. I quit my job and went full time sailing."

One of his conditions to come back for Rio was resuming his work with his coach from London, Kristian Kjaergaard. "We had a great working relationship up to the 2012 Olympics, and it is quite natural to recreate the cooperation and good chemistry, and it will be one of the pre-requisites to succeed at the Olympics. Part of the resources that Team Denmark and Danish Sailing Association makes available are that I can work with Kristian almost full time until 2016."

SO, HE TURNED up in Palma in 2015, with a new campaign and new ambition and a lot of drive to make it to the top of the podium in 2016. He placed 14th out of the 73 boat fleet. It was a good start but a long way from where he wanted to be. He purposely sailed at very few regattas during 2015, focussing on training in Denmark and Florida.

While he was considering whether to try for Rio, his wife was offered a job in New York, where they moved in July 2015. So Høgh-Christensen had quit his job with Live Nation and moved with her to start his fourth Olympic campaign. He resided in New York until after the Olympics. While with Live Nation, he helped to start the now world famous Copenhell festival, before beginning his campaign for the London Olympics.

Later in 2015 he did some extensive training with Zach Railey, Ed Wright and others in Florida, in preparation for the Rio test event in August and the 2015 Finn Gold Cup in Takapuna, New Zealand, in November.

These three had trained together extensively in previous cycles, so all knew each other very well, with former Olympian Chris Cook from Canada providing some coaching assistance. It was at this time that Railey had also decided to make a comeback for Rio. Høgh-Christensen and Railey had trained together leading up to the 2008 Olympics, where Railey had won silver. A year later Høgh-Christensen had famously denied Railey a win at the 2009 Finn Gold Cup. The Dane won the medal race in Køge Bay off Vallensbæk, to take his second world title, while Railey had to settle for the silver. Høgh-Christensen had shown the world he still had what it takes, even after a year out of the class, and with very little training.

His programme through to the end of 2015 and early 2016 was based around training and improving speed, and he soon announced a partnership with the Danish technology company Weibel, a leading specialist in Doppler radar systems, which helped him analyse his boatspeed with far greater accuracy than ever before.

Although a seventh place at the 2015 test event in Rio showed he was heading in the right direction, the Takapuna Finn Gold Cup in November, didn't quite go to plan. He suffered from the first of numerous gear problems that would dog him all the way to Rio. In Takapuna he finished 18th, and went back to Miami unhappy with his progress.

He almost won the next event, the Sailing World Cup in Miami, winning three races, but ultimately consistency let him down in some unusually chaotic weather systems that disrupted the schedule. An 11th at the Europeans in Barcelona and a 16th in Palma was followed by a sixth at the Hyères World Cup and he ended his European season on a high with a silver medal at the 2016 Finn Gold Cup in Gaeta, Italy. Finally he felt he was getting somewhere.

Back in 2012 Høgh-Christensen had famously said, "Next time around there will be no old school sailors with a bit too much fat. They will be fit, tall and young. With that said, it looks like my time is up." He stood by that statement, "The sailors have become much fitter, much stronger, taller, younger and more technically adept. It has not become easier. If you see the picture of the top 10 at the 2016 World Championship, I am the smallest guy there."

Earlier in the year he had spoken of how he saw his chances in Rio. "Right now I see myself as a little bit of an outsider. I have seen it at all of them. At this point six months out, there will be 10 or 12 guys who are actually in a position where they can improve to a point where they can win a medal and even win the Games. Of course Giles is a huge favourite. But what you usually see once you get a little closer is that the fleet will go from 10 or 12 to five or six guys. And I hope and think I can be within one of those five or six guys. I truly believe it. One of the things is my experience and I think we have a very good programme set up. I think what I need to take care about is myself and my body and I don't want to get injured. That's my primary goal at the moment. I think if I can do that I have a very good chance."

He was one the few sailors who hadn't already thought Giles Scott was heading for certain gold "I do think Giles is beatable in Rio. When I decided to come back I looked at the fleet and there is no doubt that Giles is very strong and will be the one to beat in Rio, but if I didn't think I could beat him I would not have come back."

"Giles is a very good sailor. He is a little different to Ben; his strength was his tactical and strategic abilities. Not saying that Giles is bad at this but I think Giles' big force is his size and his physical strength. He is a very technical sailor, he sails the boat really well. He doesn't take too many chances, he just goes fast and tries to stay out of trouble and he has been doing that really well for the last couple of years."

Of course both Scott and Ainslie were also involved in the 2017 America's Cup, with Scott often taking time out of his Olympic campaign to join Ainslie. Referring to this, Høgh-Christensen thinks that Finn sailors are a dominant force in other areas of the sport, due to the skill set needed to become a top calibre Finn sailor. "If you look at the Finn fleet and see how they migrate to other classes – the America's Cup for example and see how many Finn sailors are on the boats, in either a tactical or steering position – it is quite a dominant class."

"I think the depth is big, I think the class is growing. It is growing because it is very physical. And it is a good fun boat where you can be strong and you can be big and you don't have to be on a diet to go sailing. You can actually go to the gym and work your ass off. If you look at the Finn sailors most of them actually look like they are rugby players."

"I think one of the things I learned along the way, was if you build everything up around the Olympics and think that is your only goal for four years, you put too much pressure on yourself. I really enjoy sailing the Europeans, and Palma and the Worlds. They are great events; I really enjoy the sailing. If you can make the Olympics just another event, yes, it might be the most important event of the year but it is just another event, you will enjoy it a lot more. If you enjoy it a lot more, you will be more relaxed and have a good time."

Back in 2012, "That is pretty much what I tried to do. We had a long checklist going into the Games of things we had to achieve and reach and two days before the Olympics, we looked at the list and it was all green ticks on it. And therefore I felt as prepared as I could. There was nothing I could really do to be more prepared so it was just to go out and do whatever we had practised and worked on and that started out really well. And we almost got to the gold."

"I like to challenge myself. I once talked to a guy who was a mountain climber and he climbed Mount Everest twice and he was like, you get down from a mountain and you almost want to say, can I go somewhere that is even higher or more challenging. To me that is the same thing and I think the Olympics is probably the biggest challenge you can have in sailing and therefore I think that is what keeps drawing me back and going for the Games. It's the biggest challenge I can put upon myself. And I really enjoy that challenge and working against those goals and sort of being told you won't be able to do this and then doing it anyway. I like that."

"Going to the Olympics every time is climbing an Everest. I think what we did last time around was as close as it gets. There are times that you are going for a run and it's raining and it's five degrees and it feels like you have to climb Mount Everest. You know this is pretty physically tough to keep doing this every day and so I think for everybody that is doing this full time and really trying to win a gold medal, this is like climbing Mount Everest for them."

After finishing as runner up at the Gold Cup in 2016 he planned three training camps in Rio, two weeks on, one week off. "I tried to spend as much time there as possible as the current, waves and wind are super tricky and really need a lot of work to perfect."

"Sailing in Rio sure does give some new experiences. You have to adapt and reconcile with any challenges coming your way both on and off the racecourse. We had a ton of bad luck with a broken mast, rudder, sails, cameras and other equipment. On the water we sailed in 6-8 meter waves one day, crazy current the next with the wind all over the place, as well as the debris and filth in the water, which gives another dimension to the sailing."

"Also I was trying not to fall apart physically as I am getting old. I try to do minimum 8-10 gym sessions a week and sail 3-4 hours six days a week. I then have some weeks in a low gear with minimum sailing and a recreational training to recover and get ready for the next camp."

Just before the London 2012 he broke his favourite mast in training. Damage to equipment dogged him again in Rio. Firstly, it took a while to find where his container had been stored He finally found it in the outskirts of Rio behind a favela on top of some other containers. It contained his Finn and his coach boat.

He said at the time, "The ability to scramble and adapt is key to Olympic success."

However it was about to get worse when after opening the container he found one of his two masts had been broken in transit. "Not sure how it happened. The luck we have had lately is disproportionate. It should be impossible to be this unlucky. Hopefully there will be some balance and good things are coming my way. The mast is broken, nothing we can do about it other than move on. Luckily we prepared for setbacks like that."

Experience is the key word for Høgh-Christensen regarding sailing in Rio. "If you have superior speed you will do well. But if we all show up and go about the same speed, I think experience will be key. I have been there and know what it takes. I am also probably stronger all round so will be hoping for a bit of everything."

"It is very common in the Finn class that it is very fierce on that water, and people shout and yell at each other and it will almost be like gladiators fighting to the death. But once we get in, we are all friends and people go for a beer and we still have a good time. I think Rio is going to be very different from London. It is probably going to be a little lighter. It is going to be a lot trickier, we are going to see higher scores. But I think we will see some fierce competition."

Jonas Høgh-Christensen sailed his final training camp in Rio in mid-July, focussing on final details and learning to sail with the new equipment, the equipment that he would use for the Games. "It's the small things now. Fine tuning. Checking boxes."

15

Fifth Time Around

Close Friends Compete at Fifth Olympics

Allan Julie, from Seychelles, and Vasilij Žbogar were the most experienced Olympic sailors in the Finn fleet in Rio. Both were competing in their fifth Olympic Games. Both started in the Laser fleet with Julie competing at four Olympics from 1996 to 2008, before deciding to come back for Rio because of the qualification system allocating one place to Africa. Žbogar had taken part in three Olympics in the Laser from 2000 to 2008, winning the bronze in 2004 and the silver in 2008. He sailed in London 2012 in the Finn and placed sixth.

The two friends met when they were training in Lasers in the SailCoach programme run by Trevor Millar, who coached them both for many years.

Julie started to sail Optimists from a young age in Seychelles. Then he went into 420s for about six months and then straight into the Laser standard. He sailed three youth worlds in the Laser standard then after that he started his Olympic career with the Olympics in Atlanta.

"The first Olympics in Atlanta for me was more to gain experience but I did quite a good job there. The federation, and the people behind me, sponsored me to go for the next one. And again I did well in Sydney. And this time I was competing. I was still gaining experience. Then I went on to Athens. Before the Athens Olympics I had very good preparation. In Athens I finished 21st and I would have been very happy to finish top 20.

That was close. In Beijing I struggled with the light wind because I am not very good in light winds. I knew it would be very difficult. But I managed to do some good races. I managed to get two top ten races so in the end it was ok. I really cherished my Olympic experiences – I think about them every day."

"The first one was on invitation because it was the first time the Laser went to the Olympics. But for the other Olympics, I had to qualify. Qualification was done at a world level and it was more difficult but I managed three times to qualify so it is my training, and the sacrifices that I made that got me to the Olympics."

"Nowadays we can qualify on a continental basis and I saw that a good opportunity was there and almost no one was sailing Finn in Africa and I thought with the experience I have in sailing, I could probably qualify for the Rio Games. Also, all my friends who I have been sailing Lasers with, they are now sailing the Finn. So I thought it was a good opportunity for me. To meet up with them again and try to race in the Finn."

"Vasilij and I, we go way back a long time since he was sailing the Laser. I have known him since 1998 and we have been travelling together and we were coached by the same guy [Trevor Millar] for over 10 or 12 years. So he knows how much experience I have in the Laser. He was the one who convinced me to jump into the Finn. And since I started he was very helpful."

ŽBOGAR STARTED SAILING aged seven in the Optimist, sailing out of the same club as he still does today, JK Burja. "The first three of four years were probably, like all the other kids starting with the sport at that age, a bit like a game rather than as a sport. We did it for fun. I tried different sports handball, basketball soccer, tennis, and table tennis. I tried them all and somehow actually my father introduced me to sailing but I continued because it was a nice group of friends and we had good fun together, sticking around the sea, swimming, and it was a lot of fun."

After Optimists he joined the really strong 470 team until he was around 20 years old then he moved to the Laser.

"I think I started in 1995/1996 so I had five years until Sydney. That was a bit unexpected. We had done the qualification in Dubai in 1998, where I met Trevor, so I was a bit surprised to be competing in Sydney Games, but it was an extremely good experience."

"I met Trevor after doing the international qualification for my country, and then until the Games I was working with Trevor, and for me and my country at that time it was a big thing. I learned a lot and after the first day in Sydney I was top three. It was a big surprise for us but of course I couldn't keep the results up, but it was a good experience."

He spent most of the season training at the SailCoach base on Ile des Embiez near Toulon in France. This is where he met Allan Julie.

"We have a really good relationship because we have known each other 20 years already. He was from a small country, I am from a small country and we have grown up together in the laser. We had Trevor Millar as our coach through all these years in the Laser. We were fighting and trying to be the best. We made really good improvements and great results and I'm extremely happy that he came back to the Finn, which I think is an extremely good class for him. It takes me back 20 years when we were sailing together and trying to be the best we could."

"We were like brothers because we spent 15 years every day together training and sharing houses and everything so there are a lot of stories. A lot of determination to prove that we can be good sailors, because as I said we are both from small countries so we need to prove to the others that we can be good. So a lot of memories are linked to the sailing challenges we had on the water. He was extremely good in some conditions; I was good in some conditions. I was good in lighter, he was good in stronger conditions so we linked up and we had definitely a lot of fun in the end."

"I was trying to convince him for many years [to come to the Finn] and I don't know what was his final decision but I was pushing really hard and I always offered him a boat for when he wanted to come and sail in the Finn."

WHEN JULIE DECIDED to campaign the Finn for Rio it was already late in the cycle with just eight months to go before the first race. He had a steep learning curve ahead of him.

He first stepped into a Finn about three weeks before the 2016 European Championships in Barcelona. He worked a bit with coach Paul McKenzie who introduced him to Finn sailing, and also received a lot of help from Žbogar. It was still a baptism of fire, with a few good moments to encourage him.

"The Finn is a bit different from the Laser, trying to figure out the angles because they sail a bit higher angles than the Laser. One good thing about the Finn class is that everybody is very friendly and we get along very well. It is definitely a bit different to the Laser where everyone is keeping to themselves."

"It's getting used to the boat. Knowing the tuning of the boats because it is a bit more technical than Lasers. For me it is a great experience. I am getting a lot of help from many people and I am happy."

"I really like the boat. The Finn feels like a more stable boat and it feels like a real boat. I like it. I think it's probably better for people more like my weight." Weighing 93 kg, Julie was in the lower weight range for Finn sailing.

After the training, it was onto Palma for the Trofeo Princesa Sofia, the final qualification event for Rio and where the single African place would be allocated. Initially it was thought that he would be challenged by four or five sailors from Africa, but in the end only one showed up, Karim Esseghir from Tunisia. Julie never lost a single point against the Tunisian and could pack his boat away before the final race with the job done.

Rio would be their fifth Olympics in total and their fourth Olympics together.

GALLERY

Above: The Olympics began with two tense and tricky races on the Sugarloaf course area. This is the start of Race 1

Below: Busy mark rounding in Race 1 in very light and patchy winds

Above: Giles Scott didn't get off to the start he hoped for, with a 17th in Race 1 (above) but recovered to third in Race 2 after several boats were disqualified

Below: As well as the spectacular backdrops, this sculpture of a high jumper, by French artist JR, was one of many several large installations across Rio

Above: Vasiliy Žbogar managed to get two top ten results on Day 2 to stay in the top three overall

Below: After rounding the windward mark in Race 3, Tom Ramshaw escapes on a huge rolling wave, while Max Salminen briefly loses control

Above: Jake Lilley rounds the top mark in the extreme conditions on Day 2 and heads downwind in huge rolling waves

Below: Shortly after the start of Race 3, heading upwind towards Sugarloaf Mountain through huge waves, relentless rain and bad visibility

Above: The second best performer on Day 2 was Ioannis Mitakis with a third and a second in extreme wind and weather conditions

Below: Vasilij Žbogar in Race 3, with Cristo Redentor, standing high on top of the 700 metre high Corcovado, in the background

Above: Approaching the windward mark in Race 6 in huge waves • Allan Julie (right) leading Giles Scott into the gate in Race 5

Below: Giles Scott struggling to catch up in Race 5 after going the wrong way on the first upwind. Rio's rugged hinterland made a spectacular backdrop

Above: Jonathan Lobert fighting upwind in the huge waves in Race 6

Below: The first mark rounding in Race 5 in huge seas and big winds with Copacabana beach in the background

Above: Zsombor Berecz (left) had the best results on Day 3 • Jorge Zarif (right) leads round the top mark in Race 5

Below: Alejandro Foglia (left) coming into the gate in Race 5 • Tapio Nirkko (right) placed thid in Race 5, his best result of the week

Above: Giles Scott on Day 4 on Ponte course area. A first and a third was enough to take an 18 point margin into the final day of the opening series

Below: Racing on Day 4 inside Guanabara Bay under the shadow of Corcovado

Above: Max Salminen leads a very tightly packed group across the finish line in Race 8, after a very close race

Below: Jake Lilley (left) had a great Day 4 to jump to third overall • A thoughtful Pieter-Jan Postma (right) after a 14th in Race 7. He went on to win Race 8

Above: Caleb Paine trying to survive in Race 9 and stay in contention for a medal

Below: Day 5 was sailed with the windward mark directly upwind of Sugarloaf Mountain, providing some great silhouette photos

Above: The start of Race 10. Caleb Paine (USA) had a great start at the pin, while Giles Scott (GBR) had a more conservative mid-line start

Below: Facundo Olezza (left) on Day 5, doing just enough to make the medal race • Giles Scott (right) celebrates after winning gold with a day to spare

Above: Caleb Paine looking around as he approached the first mark in the lead in the crucial medal race

Below: The fleet heads downwind from the first mark during the medal race

Above: Caleb Paine (left) celebrates as he wins the medal race to take the bronze medal • Giles Scott (right) crossed in second

Below: Vasilij Žbogar celebrates after crossing the finish line of the medal race in sixth to secure the silver medal

Above: Vasiliy Žbogar, Giles Scott and Caleb Paine walk onto the podium stage with the builk of Sugarloaf Mountain just visitble behind them

Below: The three medalists looking happy after receiving their medals

Above: Giles Scott (left) turns to watch the Union Jack raised • Caleb Paine (right) waves to the crowd as he mounts the podium

Below: Vasilij Žbogar (left) still not not qute beleiving what he had achieved • Giles Scott (right), the undisputed Finn champion in Rio

16

In the Footsteps
Taking Nothing for Granted

As he headed into the Olympic Games as the overwhelming favourite in the Finn class, the fact that Giles Scott had won almost every regatta since his failure to beat Ben Ainslie for the British place at the London 2012 Olympics meant very little. Rio 2016 was just one more regatta he wanted to win; perhaps more than all the rest put together, but he knew it would not be easy. The others knew he was the favourite, but they also knew he could be beaten, and that was the challenge facing them.

Scott was also expected to continue the winning run of Great Britain in the Finn class. Starting with Iain Percy in 2000, and followed by Ben Ainslie in 2004, 2008 and 2012, Great Britain had won four consecutive gold medals in the Finn class. Scott maintained that this fact was not important to him, but that it also brought some confidence. However he surely felt the weight of expectation on his broad shoulders.

"In honesty it doesn't really matter what's gone before. We have to get out onto the race course at the Games and fight for the win; that what it's all about. The pressure is certainly there from various outside sources, but I've put a very high amount of internal pressure on myself throughout my sailing career; it's something that motivates me."

In the final week before racing in Rio commenced, he revealed "I'll just try and race as I normally do, keeping a cool head and deal with what are some very tricky race courses. The fleet is always getting better and I've been trying to do the same. I'm confident with where I'm at, so we'll have to wait and see. But I'm sure Rio will be a very tough fight."

He spent his childhood in Canada – where he was granted citizenship – before returning to the UK aged seven, when his parents began his sailing career with a beginner's session at Grafham Water, one of the UK's largest reservoirs. He soon demonstrated an innate and tenacious ability to win races. In one season he won every Topper race, but could not tell anyone how he did that. To some people, sailing just comes naturally and Giles Scott was clearly a natural.

He was always competitive, but the passion to race didn't begin until he was about 10 years old. He was more interested in just making the boat go as fast as possible. But when he did start racing he was soon Topper national champion, something that was as unexplainable to him as to those around him.

He moved into the Laser class and won gold at the 2005 ISAF Youth Sailing World Championships in Korea, a title that brought him to the attention of sailing chiefs because of his calm manner. Two years later, still at the age of 19, and standing at 6ft 5ins, he stepped into the Finn. The following year he was junior Finn world champion, and was training alongside Ainslie in the run up to the Beijing Olympics in 2008.

He was quoted as saying that he didn't even know sailing was part of the Olympics when he started, but after watching the sailing during the Sydney 2000 Olympics, he was hooked and knew what he wanted to do. It was an incredibly successful Games for the British Team with Iain Percy winning the Finn class Gold medal, watched by the impressionable 13 year old Scott.

By 2011 Scott was already viewed as a potential Olympic gold medalist. He won the World and European Championship, but only after losing the crucial British trials against Ainslie. With Ainslie then winning the 2011 Olympic test event, also in Weymouth, selection to London 2012 was assured, so Scott stepped away from the class for a year to focus on an America's Cup campaign with Luna Rossa. Scott returned full time in 2013 and only lost two Finn regattas between the 2011 British Olympic trials and arriving in Rio. That's a record of some 19 wins in 21 regattas starting with the 2011 European title in Helsinki.

Ainslie did not compete in Helsinki, preferring to focus his efforts on training in Weymouth for the 2012 Games. However both competed at the Finn Gold Cup later that year in Perth. It was the only Finn Gold Cup that Ainslie ever lost. Angry at press boat interference during one of the final races, Ainslie sailed up to the press boat after the race, boarded and remonstrated with the crew before diving back into the water to chase after his Finn. He picked up two disqualifications for his outburst, which put the title beyond reach.

That opened the door to Scott, who capitalised on Ainslie's absence in the medal race to win his first Finn world title. In receiving the Finn Gold Cup, he looked quite bemused at the turn of events that had conspired to make him world champion. It would be another three years before his next Finn Gold Cup, in Santander, and he completely dominated that to win a second world title, and shed the shadows surrounding the first title.

The 2011 trials still niggle in his mind as a lost opportunity. "Absolutely. I've had no choice but to use that as motivation. That period in time has become the reason and foundation for this Olympic cycle, clearly a very disappointing time for me. However I've always maintained that I wouldn't be as good a sailor now had I not been through it. I may have had a shot at a medal, but I don't think I'd be as driven and hard working as I now am. That and clearly I had a great guy to train with and learn from."

The were often fiery moments on the water when Ainslie and Scott clashed, though generally what happened on the water stayed on the water and they remained close on shore.

It was widely recognised that had Scott won the 2011 trials, he would have been very likely to go on to win gold in 2012. Scott still credits that loss and the disappointment with making him the sailor he is today. He learned many crucial lessons about running a campaign and making the best use of time and energy that he simply did not have at the time.

He has been compared a lot with Ainslie, however Scott admits he is very disorganised, and his demeanour suggests he is easy going and he always looks pretty relaxed on the water. He learned a lot from watching the London Games, even though it was tough to sit and do nothing. The disappointment and frustration at letting the trials slip through his fingers remained raw. He wouldn't make the same mistakes again.

On the water, by the time of the Olympics in 2012 he was almost unbeatable. Scott thinks his progress was just six months too late. In the final run up to London 2012 he beat Ainslie at both events they both attended. First the 2012 British Nationals in Falmouth, just prior to the 2012 Finn Gold Cup, also in Falmouth, where Ainslie collected his sixth World title on his home waters. It was where Ainslie had learned to sail. Then Scott squarely beat Ainslie again at the final event before the Olympics, this time at Sail for Gold on Olympic waters in Weymouth.

Scott didn't sail the 2012 Finn Gold Cup and excused himself for America's Cup duties, but returned a month later for Sail for Gold, in Weymouth, where he dominated, beating most of the Olympic hopefuls on Olympic waters, just eight weeks before the Games commenced. The message was clear.

SCOTT'S COACH, MATT Howard, was a crucial part of Scott's success. Howard gave up Finn sailing in 2007 and immediately started to coach Scott. The pair formed a near-invincible team, and Howard felt that by the time of the Games, Giles was a good match for Ainslie, at least in the breeze.

Referring to the 2011 Olympic trials, he said, "Their trajectories were slightly different and Giles was always improving and by the time we got to the Games he was at least a match for Ben, though maybe not across all the wind ranges. When you look back at the Games, and it was quite a windy Games, you could say that Giles would have had a good chance at winning that relatively easy – as easy as it gets I guess, but equally if it had been a light week I think that Giles at that time would have potentially struggled to medal, whereas Ben, if it had been light would have walked it."

"So he was in a pretty dark place in that he knew he was good enough to be at the Olympics and good enough to win a gold medal and if he wasn't sure of that when the trials ended in 2011 he was definitely sure of it by the time we got to the Games. He did a couple of events that year and also we trained as a group with Ben and Sid [David Howlett, Ainslie's coach] in Weymouth and all the way through the build up so Giles knew how well he was going compared to other people. So it was an opportunity missed for him. But Ben was the right person to go. He won the trials and I think as an all round sailor at that time, Ben was better."

However, Howard concedes that Ainslie was not that well at the time and he didn't really want to do Sail for Gold before the Olympics because it was an opportunity that he didn't need.

"It was another opportunity for competitors to learn the venue, the racing environment and just two months before the Games, and it was an event that was far higher pressure than it should have been. There are not many other Olympics in recent history where there was effectively an Olympic turnout at the Olympic venue just two months before the Games started."

Giles won that event fairly easily, with Ainslie famously capsizing in the medal race and nearly dropping off the podium. "It was a big story and was the last story that anyone who had been selected for an Olympic Games wants to have to deal with: someone who they had beaten in the trials had just beaten them before the Olympics. It was a great story for the media but not a particularly good story for your confidence and your mindset."

Following the event there were a lot of questions about Ainslie's fitness and whether it had been the right decision to select him for London, after all the problems he had faced over the previous year, including the outburst in Perth and surgery on his back over the winter.

"But hats off to Ben. I am not sure everyone would have been able to turn round from that event two months before the Games and come back and do what he did, particularly as he had that capsize in the medal race. It wasn't great timing for him, but as we know, the more on the back foot Ben gets the better he gets."

Even at that time Scott was fully set on doing another campaign. "Fundamentally, the amount of money that he would have to go forward into the Rio campaign relied on Ben winning that gold, especially with Perce [Iain Percy] narrowly missing out. Our funding was secured by that gold. If Ben had not won it or not medalled then Giles' campaign would have been significantly hit financially in the following cycle for sure and that's one of the reasons why everyone is very supportive of the people who go to the Olympics. Of course you have the patriotism and the rest of it but medals means money and everyone needs that to do a proper campaign."

For the Rio campaign, funding secured, no stone was left unturned.

IN THE PERIOD between the 2011 European title and the Rio Games, Scott only lost two events, taking silver at both: the Sailing World Cup Hyères in 2013 and the Trofeo Princesa Sofia in Palma in 2016.

Following Sail for Gold in 2012, Scott didn't race the Finn again until the spring of 2013. He had sailed the autumn of 2012 with the Prada America's Cup team and after the winter they had an enforced break while the team moved its equipment from Auckland to San Francisco. That break happened to fall when two of the major early season regattas were taking place: the Trofeo Princesa Sofia in Palma and the Sailing World Cup event in Hyères. Scott decided to sail them and they were the only events he did before his full comeback in October 2013.

Scott won in Palma, and in Hyères took a six-point lead into the double medal race. Both events were trialling some new scoring systems, which were later discarded, involving a two-stage event, with the first stage counting for one race. The win went to Scott's team mate Andrew Mills, who sailed a great series, but Scott did little wrong, only coming adrift in the light wind final races.

After that Scott returned to the America's Cup with Prada Luna Rossa, but remained in touch with Matt Howard every few weeks planning and getting boats and equipment bought so that Scott could "hit the ground running" in October. It was in October that they hatched their plan for Rio.

The Semaine Olympique Française in October 2013, in La Rochelle, France, was Scott's first event in the Rio campaign. The America's Cup was over and it was time to focus on that gold medal in Rio.

Howard remembers, " We did about a month of sailing, three to four days a week, in Weymouth before heading to La Rochelle and that whole planning thing was quite a big process. We debriefed his last cycle, and there were some home truths on both sides, and also interestingly we had a look at everyone else's campaign that we had an insight into and we kind of debriefed those as well, as if they were ours. What they did well and what they did badly."

They not only looked, of course, at Ainslie's campaign, but also at other campaigns within the British team and other Finn sailors. It was all valuable input on how to run a successful campaign.

Howard continued, "And we also looked at how it all turned out. If you look at that last three months before London, we were in Falmouth and Giles wasn't and I was there with the other Brits, and Ben absolutely destroyed that world championship. On big Wednesday when we had three races in 25 knots in one of the worst sea states I have ever seen, he got three bullets. That is an incredible result. And then two months later he's struggling to hold Jonas [Høgh-Christensen] off in less wind, so we were looking at how your strengths can get you through World Championships and stuff, how they convert into the Olympic Games. And also how things can change very quickly."

"The 2012 Finn Gold Cup in Falmouth, with 90 boats, really played to Ben's strengths. He's an incredibly strong starter, incredible good at holding his lane and very fast downwind. And with 90 boats if you can't hold your lane, it's going to be hard, but then you go to the Games and there are 23 boats and there is room all over the place, so if you are really fast, you get a bad start there is room and the speed comes into it."

"And we tried to plan for that a little bit and tried to plan for the Olympic Games rather than for a World Championship."

"We did plenty of sailing between Falmouth and Weymouth. I would say that the training we did leading up to the 2012 Games, as is Ben's normal kind of thing, he trains incredibly hard and if you are not careful he will train seven days a week, and in hindsight we thought we probably did too many days sailing in the run up to London, but that's just an opinion."

After winning in La Rochelle, Scott remained unbeaten until four months before the Rio Games, at the 2016 Trofeo Princesa Sofia, after his rudder pintle broke in the penultimate race when he was in a regatta-winning situation. But in spite of that he went into the medal race determined to still take home a medal, and it worked as he won the silver. However the breakage had another cost.

Howard explained, "The loss had a huge effect on both of us. You can't imagine how many different types of pintle material and diameters, and gudgeons that we then went through on the back of that. And also the problem with something like that breaking is that the corrosion is internal so the only way to stop things like that breaking is to life them, and say, change them every three months. But that pintle was only six weeks old, so it had been used enough that it was beyond the 'never use anything new' but it certainly wasn't enough to be an issue, so when it failed it was like, 'what else is going to break?'"

"If you look at poor Rafa Trujillo, he had a horrid London Games because of gear failure, he had things breaking that just don't normally break that were new but not too new. So that made us look very hard at our equipment, even harder than we had before. Giles is pretty obsessive about his kit preparation and it went to another level frankly. So we did lose a few hours trying to sort all that out, but we had some clever people. We were pretty sure it wasn't going to happen again."

On the actual loss and the only defeat in three years. "We were not fussed about losing. If we had gone and he had underperformed, then we would be looking at everything, but as it was, Josh [Junior] had sailed incredibly well. It was a really good regatta, one of the last where everyone who was at the Olympics was there, and Giles went into the penultimate race in a position to engage in match race with Josh."

"It was fantastic watching it. It was 18-22 knots offshore and there were three general recalls. And for each recall Josh and Giles were engaged from four minutes to go, which was absolutely riveting to watch, and they both did a really good job of it. But it must have been incredible demanding with the circling and gybing and tacking and all that. So Josh sailed really well, but it was it the breakage that lost it for Giles."

MID-CYCLE, SCOTT HAD become about an unbeatable as it was possible to imagine, winning regattas with two races to spare and sometimes by as much as 50 points. His almost casual demeanour sailing the Finn was in stark contrast to the man whose shoes many felt he was stepping into. He had a natural skill in the boat that set him apart from the rest of the fleet and he barely seemed to break a sweat in the heat of competition. He rarely looked rattled or under pressure.

His continuous success was a wake up call to the fleet, many of whom had considerably upped their game over the two years before Rio to try and match Scott's supremacy. Scott continued to win every regatta, but just occasionally the winning margins became less. Several times he had to fight himself back into a regatta.

Nevertheless, in the cycle from London 2012 to Rio 2016 he won three more world titles from 2014 to 2016, the European title in 2014 and perhaps more significantly, both Olympic test events in Rio. At the 2015 test event he struggled all week only to get break in the medal race and snatch the gold at the last possible moment.

With more preparation in Rio than most of the fleet, his focus in the final weeks before the Games started were on getting to grips with "small things", the courses and final details on the boat set up.

He knew very well – all the sailors in the fleet knew – that the racing would be tough, that the sailors would have to cope with a wide variety of sea states with big tides, and a very shifty wind, which was generally expected to be between 7-14 knots. However no one could have imagined the diversity of conditions during the Games.

Training on the different course areas and with other teams was a vital part of Scott's preparation. "We made sure that we were in a venue with other teams present, often the French, Finnish and Swedes. We'd then often do half sessions on our own and come together for some racing. I think it worked pretty well. This is something we constantly tried to put in place."

"We ran a rolling development plan in regards to kit and sailing skill, so all the camps were of equal importance. As long as the structure of the camps enabled you peak when you want to they have worked in my opinion."

He was by now also sailing as part of Ainslie's America's Cup team as well as campaigning the Finn and his salary for that was ploughed back into his Finn campaign.

While he was happy with his development programme over the cycle, there was always more than could be done.

"There are always a few things that I'd have changed, avenues I investigated that didn't end up producing anything of use. But that's all part of it. If I hadn't investigated something, I'd have this sinking feeling that I didn't look at everything I should have."

Since the 2012 Olympics, the techniques in the Finn class had moved on considerably, with increased physicality. "I think the major change is that sailors are really beginning to make the most out of the free pumping rule, which you can see by the shape and athletic nature of the majority of the top guys. The Finn hasn't lost its history in techniques and strategic sailing, but it just seems to be growing in the athletic direction at the moment."

At 29 years of age, Scott was perhaps the most athletic of all the Finn sailors in Rio. His record of wins was proof enough.

Scott had won almost everything in sight since 2011 – in fact he had won 19 out of the 21 regattas he had sailed. He was clearly a cut above the rest and his smooth, almost casual style spoke volumes of an innate skill in the boat that to some minds transcended his previous training partner and mentor, Ben Ainslie. He was bigger, stronger and fitter.

He made it look too easy.

17

The American Question
No Paine, No Gain

One of the most absorbing and hard fought national trials before Rio was the USA selections. Though many more sailors took part, it was only ever going to come down to two sailors, the 2008 silver medalist and 2012 Olympian, Zach Railey, and his former younger understudy, Caleb Paine.

The US selection trials were held over two regattas, the Sailing World Cup Miami in January 2016 and the 2016 European Championship in Barcelona in March. The disparity of these events was obvious to everyone, so it was always going to end up with a showdown in Barcelona, but it exploded in a way that no one really expected and made global sailing headlines after Railey employed some very aggressive tactics in the penultimate race to try and seal his third consecutive Olympic ticket.

With two Olympic Games under his belt, Railey had experience on his side. He followed the largely unexpected silver medal in Qingdao in 2008 with a disappointing 12th at the London 2012 Games. He expected more in London after an intense, and largely successful, campaign following 2008 and went home perhaps slightly discouraged and contemplating his future in sailing.

After London he felt his life needed a change in direction. He was 28 years old and was left thinking what he was going to do after his Olympic career was over. The family business had been managed by his aging father, and his sister Brooke, while he and his other sister, Paige, had sailed almost all their lives. He felt it was time to put something back, so for the next three years he focused on his business life and almost forgot all about the Finn. He put on weight, and lost most of his fitness.

Then in the autumn of 2015 he decided to give it one more chance. He put together a very late campaign for Rio and knew it was going to be tough. He returned to the class after a three-year break, training in Clearwater, Florida with his old sparing partners Jonas Høgh-Christensen and Ed Wright. He returned to the race course at the 2015 Finn Gold Cup in Takapuna, New Zealand, but didn't give anything away about his true intentions, even if deep down inside the Olympic flame was burning bright. He was there to have fun, compete and 'see what happens'. He didn't make headlines, but it was clear that Railey was back and wanted more.

In making his comeback he had also lost 26 kg of corporate hospitality bodyweight in the process. He had been sailing for a only a few months by this point and was happy with the good training group that they had put together, which also included the young Norwegian star Anders Pedersen and the Danish junior, Andre Højen-Christiansen, who had been invited by Høgh-Christensen to join the group, as a possible future Olympian for Denmark.

Høgh-Christensen had already made a comeback for London 2012, where he ended up winning the silver medal, and was six months into his comeback for Rio 2016, so he knew what Railey would be up against. In Takapuna, Railey finished 30th out of 75 sailors. It was not a completely unrespectable result after three years out of the class, but crucially for him, Paine had been several notches better, placing 12th. There was still a lot of work to do. The fast track training continued, but it was not long until the first selection event in Miami.

IN THE COCKPIT of the Finn belonging to Paine there was a decal that read 'No Paine, no gain'. This very much summed up his attitude towards making sure he was absolutely the best prepared he could possibly be come the start of the Olympic Games in Rio.

He explained, "I think that no matter what, in the toughest times when you are out there training, it is being able to keep pushing no matter what. I think I've always been hard working but you are going to do everything you can to win that one spot and be the better sailor or athlete in the end."

Paine started off sailing the Finn when he was 19 years old. "I was introduced to the Finn by a guy named Scott Mason from Long Beach, California. I sailed the boat once, totally loved it and realised it would give me the ability to go to the Olympics and possibly win a medal."

The Finn also offered the chance of international competition for him. He had sailed the Laser before, mainly youth events, and did quite well on the youth circuit with a few regatta wins, but hadn't competed internationally so far. The first time he had ever been out of the country was for a Finn event, Kieler Woche, in 2009 after which he sailed the 2009 Finn Gold Cup in Denmark.

As soon as he had graduated high school he was given the opportunity to sail with Railey and train with him and acted as his training partner leading up to the 2012 Games. He also sailed alongside Luke Lawrence as Juniors through 2010, including the 2010 Finn Silver Cup in San Francisco, which Lawrence won.

After Lawrence, and then Railey stopped Finn sailing, Paine assumed his place as the top Finn sailor in the US. He won World Cup regattas in Miami and Medemblik and briefly rose to World No. 1 in late 2013. Since then he had been a regular at the front end of the fleet, including a seventh place at the 2014 ISAF Sailing World Championship in Santander, Spain, where he qualified the USA for its Finn place in Rio. He was clearly making great progress and the results were starting to come. In 2014 it looked like he had a clear path to the Olympics, with none of the other American sailors able to touch him.

Lawrence made a short-lived reappearance early in 2014, squarely beating Paine at the World Cup event in Miami that year and also winning the medal race. He started the European season full of campaign grit, but eventually he decided to focus on his other sailing commitments rather than mounting a campaign for Rio, and pulled out of the race.

From then on, Paine's campaign went very smoothly until the autumn of 2015, when Railey suddenly appeared back in the boat, threatening to wreck Paine's dreams of Olympic qualification.

THOUGH HE HAD crossed paths, and swords, with Railey in Lasers prior to his Finn sailing career, Paine had not even started Finn sailing when Railey had won his silver medal in 2008, and now he found himself battled against his former training partner in a bitter and often overheated selection series.

Born in San Diego and raised there, his parents didn't come from a wealthy background, his mother being a nurse and his father a teacher. Paine fell in love with sailing at a young age and always had a dream of going to the Olympics and winning a medal. Supported by his parents he travelled the USA, sailing in youth Laser regattas with moderate success, until that day, aged just 19, he came across the Finn. He had been pursuing his Olympic dream ever since.

Railey's background was very different, coming from relatively wealthy east coast family, but the two worked well together up until 2012. Railey's return in 2015 clearly had Paine slightly rattled about realising his Olympic ambition, but for him at least it was not unexpected. He had convinced himself that Railey would return at some point: this was the perfect incentive to make him work all the harder.

"I just told myself that he was going to come back to sail, even if he was or he wasn't. I think that helped drive me and work harder and obviously once he did come back it sparked a fire in me. It would have been easy to just sit back and do the best I could, but when you have someone to push you, it drives you to get more out of yourself."

Paine has been regularly labelled as 'hard working', going the extra mile, doing the extra session and leaving no stone unturned. He said this is because he doesn't feel he is a naturally talented sailor so it takes time for him to get the right technique.

"Over time I learn lessons and work with the coach and we seem to get the job done. And what it does as well is to really make the lessons that I learn concrete so that I don't forget and get them wrong, so it makes a big difference in the end game. You are not always going to win every drill or be the fastest downwind, but you keep working on it."

THE SHOWDOWN BETWEEN the pair began in Miami in January 2016. Paine was the most consistent in the early races, even leading the regatta overall after the second day. He had been training with Australian Jake Lilley in preparation for Miami and both were sailing fast. However Railey was beginning to show his old form, winning two races, albeit mixed up with some high scores.

Mid week, Railey moved ahead of Paine by a single point when the discard came into play, but then struggled on the penultimate day to trail Paine by five points going into the deciding medal race. The medal race proved to be a foretaste of what would happen in Barcelona two months later.

Paine, who was by now struggling with illness that he said affected his performance, held the early advantage in the medal race, rounding the top mark in seventh to Railey's eighth. They were locked together downwind, but Railey took the opposite gate behind the eventual race winner, Russian Arkadiy Kistanov, and found better wind on the left to come back ahead of

Paine. But Paine was still right behind at the top. Railey needed to put two boats between himself and Paine, and coming into the bottom mark there was barely a boatlength between them.

At the gate they were still locked together. Railey attacked, letting four boats through and then forced an error on Paine, who was given a jury penalty. By the time Paine had completed his turns, he was in last place, and then to add insult to injury, due to a finish line error, he scored a Did Not Finish. With Railey crossing the line in sixth, he had done enough to leapfrog Paine in the overall rankings to place fifth to Paine's sixth, and take the early lead in the US Olympic selection trials.

Railey explained his strategy, "On the last run I tired to slow the race down as much as I could to put boats between us and let other boats pass Caleb so I could reduce the overall spread between us. I have a lot of respect for Caleb and he has worked hard, but we are two competitors fighting for one spot. It's tough that only one of us gets to go, but it's going to be a hard fought battle. I'm going to do all I can to win that spot."

Finishing just one place apart in Miami meant that whoever beat whom at the second selection event at the European Championship in Barcelona, would win the selection trials and go to Rio, as the Europeans had priority over any tie breaks. It would be a vastly different event with a fleet of double the size and with virtually all the sailors who would end up in Rio taking part for one of the most competitive events of the Olympic year.

IF RAILEY REPEATED his Miami success in March in Barcelona he would carry on until the Olympic Games in August. If he failed it would very likely be his last Finn regatta. Not knowing which way the week would go he bought a one-way ticket to Europe. If he didn't qualify for Rio it would be the end of his Olympic sailing career and he would be back in his office the following Monday. If he managed to qualify for Rio he would board the ferry to Palma for the next regatta. It was make or break time.

"When I was 28 years old I had to figure out what I was going to do for the rest of my life so I took a few years off to figure that out, and now I love the business world. I love the competitive side of the business world. I am a very competitive person. I don't like to lose. It doesn't matter what it is. We can play a board game, I don't want to lose the board game. I hate losing. And I hate not reaching my goals."

"So when I got into the business world, I found there's goals there too, there's things you can obtain, and obviously there's money to be made. There's employees and business growth, there's competition against other people who are selling the same products as you. And you are trying to beat that competition, so it's just like sailing or athletics, but you are not out on race course racing in your boat. And of course I miss that side of it and I really missed sailing."

"That was the draw to come back. I missed being in the boat and I enjoyed being out on the water. There was the right group of guys that were coming back sailing and that was very important to me."

"My history with Jonas is very well known. We have known each other since Optimists and we've been friends since we were 11 years old. We have gone to two Olympics together and have each been very successful in individual Olympics, so when I got that phone call that he was going to give it another go, then there was a bit of peer pressure to get out of the office a bit more. And it's been really good and a lot of fun."

"I love the Finn. It's a technical boat, highly physical; it's a really fun boat to sail. It also fits my body really well. I'm a big guy, I'm 6'4" and my weight can range up and down depending on how much I am training, but I am usually 100 kg, and that's what the boat was made for."

"It's been a very successful Olympic boat and it has a lot of great history; a lot of amazing sailors have come through it, and have been very successful in the Finn, and in other endeavours after that. I've enjoyed sailing it and I'm always going to want to sail it. And you never know where sailing takes you. It's a sport you can do for your entire life, so I'll find some way to stay in the sport somehow."

The competition was the biggest attraction for him. "Sailing in general is a test of our best against someone else's best, and you don't always come out of top in high level anything. If you are trying to do anything that most people won't even make the effort to do because it's hard, you have to accept that sometimes you are going to lose. You take the wins and you take the losses and move on."

"A lot of people don't like to embrace the fact that failure is something that happens, especially when you are trying to achieve really high goals. I think, as I have gotten older, I am been able to embrace that a little bit more and just accept that's it part of the process and just worry about what you can control. And in the end you're going to win or you're going to lose and you'll see what happens at the end of the presentation or the end of the competition."

"I knew it was a late comeback, so there were no disillusions or fantasies on what it was going to be like or how hard it was going to be, but we had a good group of people and worked really hard."

"And all you can do it put your best foot forward and see what happens."

AS THE CHAMPIONSHIP in Barcelona opened, both sailors were upbeat and exuding confidence, perhaps Railey slightly more than Paine, but both knew what was at stake. And it couldn't have been much closer. Tensions were running high, but no one really expected what followed.

Railey came out ahead after the first day, with Paine carrying a big score that would haunt him all week. On the second day they traded high and low scores, though Paine managed to close the points gap, and then on the Wednesday Railey made a mistake, allowing Paine to post a better result in the only race of the day to draw them almost even. Railey faired badly, was about 65th at the first mark with little chance to get back into the race in the light wind. Paine also faired badly early on but was happy with a recovery to 19th considering Railey could only scrape a 38th.

With the wind evaporating in the Mediterranean spring, there were no guarantees as to how many more races could be sailed. Everyone realised that each race could well be the last. Thursday was lost entirely with no racing possible. On Friday the racing started late to wait for the wind to arrive and there was no guarantee there would any wind on Saturday.

In Race 5 they were locked together for the entire race. At the finish, Railey won by just three boats, but with Paine now able to discard his opening race mishap, he moved into a 10-point lead. That turn of events set up a sixth race skirmish that was broadcast around the world.

As the momentous Race 6 started, both of them knew it was probably the last race of the day and it could even have been the last race of the selection trials. There were no guarantees. It was vitally important to end the day ahead in case there was no more racing. If there was no more racing the Olympic trials would be over there and then.

It was a race that few who were there will forget, and turned into an absorbing battle of skill and steel nerves, pushing both the sailors to their limits. To understand why Railey did what he did in that race you have to understand the situation they were in. As Paine said, "You are out there to try and win one spot and you have to do the best you can to do that. Zach is a great competitor and a great Finn sailor and he's going to do whatever he can in order to succeed."

As Race 6 began, Railey got the perfect start at the pin, sailed a blistering first beat and rounded the top mark with a 20-boat lead on Paine. The tables looked stacked in Railey's favour. But it was a long way from being over.

Paine never gave up and chipped away on the second upwind, while Railey made a few mistakes. To compound his frustration he was given a yellow flag for a Rule 42 violation at the top mark and had to complete two penalty turns before carrying on. By then Paine was right on his transom with just one leg to sail. The seemingly insurmountable lead had vanished.

Railey's frustration was almost palpable. Paine was oozing relief. The situation looked calm half way down the leg, which perhaps left Paine a little too relaxed, but that was when Railey took his chance, gybing back across the course and attacking Paine and setting the stage for a mark trap at the final turning mark on the course before the short reach to the finish.

Railey knew if he could draw Paine back through the fleet, and let enough boats pass them, he could end the day ahead. And that is exactly what he did. He expertly blocked Paine from rounding the leeward mark for long enough for about 50 boats to sail through. Railey positioned himself between Paine and the mark and manoeuvred his boat with skill and accuracy to keep Paine from rounding the mark. They moved forwards, backwards, turned circles, but always Railey was blocking Paine's approach to the mark. It was ballet on water, except it was also now getting heated with loud, but polite, calls for mark room and protests.

Paine tried many times to escape and even fouled Railey a few times, before taking penalty turns. When he finally found a way through, ducking Railey's transom and nipping round the mark, the damage had been done. It was just a 200-metre reach to the finish line.

With Railey continuing to shout 'protest' at him the pair crossed the line in the 60s. Paine once again had to count that high score, that 58th, from the opening race. In turn Railey had ended the day with a 10-point lead. It could have been the decisive points margin he needed to secure the Rio berth.

Railey described his thought process. "I was already on the back foot yesterday points wise. And when Caleb came back in the last race from about 20th to tenth, just behind me, I needed to get some points between us because he was going to be quite far in front going into the final race. His worst race was a 58th and mine was a 38th so at that point I had to try and slow the race down and get him as far back in the fleet as possible."

"So I set a mark trap at the bottom to try and let boats goes by us. That's a normal part of racing in match racing and fleet racing. It's happened for the last 20 years."

With Paine desperately hoping for another race, the fleet was sent ashore for the day. They both knew it could be over. The forecasts for the final day were not particularly encouraging.

But first, the two spent most of the evening in the protest room. Both were convinced they were right and it took some diplomacy from the jury to sort out the various situations. Luckily there was some video evidence, which was taken by one of the jury when he saw what was developing. Railey was disqualified from the race, but that actually made no difference to his score as he was discarding that race anyway. He still had a 10-point margin over Paine.

Paine said, "I felt like there has been an infraction during the incident, so obviously I intended calling on that (the rule that Railey ended up being disqualified for) but I continued to just sail the race as best I could and get across the finish line. Then I would look at the process, file a protest and continue to think about the rest of the regatta."

"I did some turns. I fouled a couple of times and did my circles just like you should. Then I ducked inside at the mark: I was clear ahead. I did nothing wrong in that situation. I was clear ahead. We have multiple videos showing that and I was clear ahead."

SPENDING TIME DEALING with a protest is the last thing anyone wants after a sailboat race, least of all when your Olympic future could depend on the outcome, but that is where Paine and Railey found themselves, arguing their cases to the international jury. Even though Railey was disqualified for infringing Rule 18.4, the points penalty he inflicted on Paine remained, and in terms of overall positions there was no change.

Rule 18.4 says once an outside overlap has been obtained the inside boat must gybe round the mark – take their proper course. Neither sailor understood this rule. Railey even went back to the jury with his rulebook as he still thought it was wrong. But neither one of them had interpreted the rule correctly in that situation, but when they got into the jury room and it was explained, Railey accepted the disqualification.

He explained, "It was for when you are inside the zone you have to gybe round the mark once there is an overlap established. The way I had read the rule was that if the boat clear ahead entered the zone beforehand then they were able to hold the boat up to go round the mark. And the interpretation that the jury gave was that if an overlap was established, regardless of if a boat was clear ahead, once that overlap was established, you have to at least gybe to go around the mark. That's what the disqualification was for. It's an interpretation of the rule that obviously I hadn't heard before, or understood, and quite frankly Caleb hadn't either."

Paine has also tried a Rule 2 protest to get the disqualification turned into a more serious Do Not Exclude penalty. "I think a Rule 2 protest was a little bit of a stretch on his part. I wasn't unfairly sailing and that's what he was arguing, that I was unfairly purposely breaking rules to hold him up, which was not what was occurring and I think the jury saw that very clearly. That's why that part of the protest was disallowed."

RAILEY RECEIVED MUCH criticism for his actions, even though it is a common tactic in sailing at this level. He himself was the subject of a similar match racing tactic at the hands of Ben Ainslie, during the abandoned, first attempt at the medal race at the 2008 Olympics.

Paine was generally supportive of Railey and said if the situation had been reversed, he would have had no hesitation in dealing the same on Railey. "Bad blood? Absolutely not. I would absolutely try and do everything that's within the rules. The fundamentals of what Zach did are fine. I totally understand what he did and there are no hard feelings at all."

The incident caused widespread interest and media comment as well as setting up the last race decider. Railey said, "There's an opinion out that there maybe it shouldn't be happening in a fleet race, but at the Olympic level and at this high level of athletics in sailing it's very much an accepted part of the sport. And I'll think you'll find everybody in the boat park agrees with that."

"It's not a bad thing. I think a lot of people look at it and say this is not part of the sport, but the reality is that it is, it's a tactic of the sport, a very well accepted part of the sport. We're not going out and crashing into each other's boats and putting holes in each other's boats, and violating rules over and over to do that. We're sailing within the rules and making the best decision you can to benefit yourself as much as possible to win the race."

"I've never had a problem with it and I don't think anyone should have a problem with it. I don't think anyone here on the Olympic level here will have an issue with it. Maybe there are some people who think that it's not how the racing should be sailed. I don't think you should be match racing on your Tuesday evening beer can races, but when you get to the Olympic level and only one person gets to go to the Games, there's no issue with it."

The end result of the day was that Railey switched from being 10 points behind to 10 points in front of Paine, with one race to go.

That evening, Paine did a lot of soul searching. Faced with the chance that there would either be no racing on the final day, or that he would be unable to overturn Railey's 10 point lead if the final race was actually held, he was staring at the stark possibility that he wouldn't be going to Rio.

You could forgive Paine for feeling angry, frustrated, upset at this point, but he remained calm. "That's one of the things that surprised me about myself. Thinking about that incident and the final race I was a bit nervous before we went sailing but once I got on the water I was automatically going into the right zone. It's not emotional; you just make decisions based on what's in front of you."

"It was kind of a late night anyway because of the protest, but the night before the last race I was thinking about everything that had happened. I can't view this as a career; it's a passion, it's something I love to do. So I was OK with all the experiences I've had, all the hard work, and the lessons I've learned and the places I've travelled to and the people I've met. It was all worth it regardless of whether I was going to the Olympics or not."

"And I came to terms with that and I was OK with that, but that doesn't mean I was giving up or once I am out on the water I am not going to do everything I can to achieve that, but I had come to terms with it."

With a dire forecast, the final race was brought forward in the day to try and use the early morning breeze. As it turned out this was timed to perfection as there was just enough wind to start and it died out just as the fleet crossed the finish line.

Some close quarters pre-start manoeuvres between them were forgotten as the starting gun went and both sailors sailed away in opposite directions. Railey got stuck on the left as the wind started dying and could only finish mid fleet, while Paine sailed well to round the top mark in second and then went to on cross the line in seventh and win the US selection. The expected final battle never really materialised after the start.

Paine, "First thing I did was check the board [on the finish boat] to make sure I was not OCS [a starting penalty]. That would be the worst thing ever, but once I saw it was all clear, it was a rush of emotions, relief being the biggest one. It's something I have dreamed about ever since I was a child and it was quite emotional to finally be able to say that I've done it."

Next thing he did was to sail up to his coach Luther Carpenter and share the celebration and emotion of the moment.

He described it as a challenging race. "It was something I debated about this morning. I thought it would be difficult to push him [Railey] over the line, because he knew he couldn't get a DNF [Did Not Finish]. So my strategy was if the opportunity presented itself to go after him. I had a feeling he was going to come after me. Because of that I was a little hesitant to go and attack right at the back, so as soon as I saw I had a little space, I knew if I got a few shifts, I could put some boats between us."

"We were pretty close in the pre-start. He actually split off, I believe thinking that the left would come in. I was just looking for a bit of space to go sailing and put some boats between us."

Railey hedged his bets on the wrong side of the course and rounded deep, too deep to recover in the light winds. It was game over for the US selection at the first mark.

"I was trying to force Caleb to have a bad start and he had a bad start and tacked and went behind a bunch of boats and I thought I was in a pretty good spot half way up. And then the wind died and the pressure stayed on the right and the boats on the right were able to go straight to the mark."

"The plan was to protect the left side of the race course. We really felt the left was the side that was going to pay on the upwinds. The breeze was dying and in the practice that we did beforehand, and in the time that we spent there, the left side usually paid when the breeze started dying. We came off the line and Caleb had to clear out to the right after a not very good start, and I felt really good with the position I was in."

"Half way up I was looking pretty good and trying to cross back from the left with a group of boats, but then the breeze started slowly dying and the pressure just remained on the right. I tried as much as I could to get over to it but I just couldn't get there."

"The reality was that those boats were in 4-5 knots more breeze and Caleb was one of those boats and I think there were 35-40 boats between us at the first mark. So it was a pretty dire situation from there and I had to start taking really big risks on the downwind and the next upwind, to try and hope for a big shift on the side that I went to. That didn't happen, but that's racing. There's got to be a winner and a loser in this unfortunately."

As they came ashore Railey went straight up to Paine, shook him firmly by the hand and said, "Good work, buddy," and then hung his boots at the top of his mast to signify, that for him, the game was over. This was the end of Railey's brief comeback and his Olympic career. It was so very close, but in Olympic selection trials there is no second place.

Railey paid credit to Paine and predicted a successful Rio Olympics for his former understudy. "A lot of people, I don't think, gave Caleb, his due respect as an athlete and as a sailor. It was incredibly hard to catch back up to where he is. I came very close, I gave it a really good run, I had six months to do it and I think I did everything I could to try to get there."

"People are underestimating where he is at. I said that before I came back. They are underestimating the work that he has put in, and how good he has got. I think he has a good shot at being in the top 8 or 10 boats at the Games, which means he'll have a shot at one of the medals."

And of himself, "I have no regrets. That's why I came here, so I don't have any."

For Paine, it took a while for the realisation that he had qualified for Rio to sink in. He was one of the last few sailors to qualify, even though he had qualified his country some 18 months before in Santander. It had been a long road, but one that would ultimately prepare him for the biggest challenge of his life, winning a medal in Rio.

"Dealing with the sport of sailing, it is what it is. There are so many variables out there, and it's so unpredictable, it could have easily not swung my way and that would have be tough, I don't know how I would have dealt with that, but luckily I didn't have to."

What doesn't kill you makes you stronger, and for Paine surviving that final race, and saving the regatta, would inevitably make him a stronger sailor in the long run. Six years of training, six years of sweat, hard work and effort had boiled down to one 70 minute race to decide whether he was good enough to represent his country at the Olympic Games.

There was no illusion he was taking it easy. He had a goal and that was Olympic gold, but realistically, he would be happy with "anywhere in the top five".

This working ethos would undoubtedly mean that Caleb Paine's performance in Rio would be his best work to date.

18

And Then There Were Two
Palma Showdown for Final Two Rio Places

Almost immediately after the Europeans in Barcelona, the fleet headed to Mallorca for the final continental qualification event at the 47th Trofeo Princesa Sofia Iberostar regatta in L'Arenal, which pulled in 74 entries.

The Trofeo Princesa Sofia in Mallorca is the traditional start of the European sailing season, but in 2016 it took on a whole new significance for the small number of sailors still hoping to qualify for Rio. Under the new continental qualification system, one European place and one African place were up for grabs in Mallorca. Just two places in Rio were left to decide.

For those still chasing the Olympic dream, it was the last chance, and many had been training through the winter since the Finn Gold Cup in New Zealand for one last opportunity. It would complete the country qualifications for Rio, even though many of the national selection trials still had a long way to run.

The stakes couldn't have been higher and with eight countries targeting the single European place it was by no means certain. However, only two sailors were vying for the single African place, so that was much more clear-cut. It turned out to be one of the most competitive regattas of the year with 20 out of the 23 sailors who would go on to sail in Rio competing, including for the first time since the 2015 Finn Gold Cup, Giles Scott, in one of only three regattas he took part in during 2016 before the Olympics.

On paper, the African spot was expected to go the way of four-time Olympian in the Laser, Allan Julie, from Seychelles. Even though he had spent less than four weeks sailing the Finn before arriving in Palma, he was placing well enough in regattas to be reasonably confident about heading to his fifth Olympic Games. The other African sailor in Palma was Karim Esseghir, from Tunisia, who had been in the class for two years. It was widely expected that several sailors from other countries would also attend, but at the last minute the entries dried up or the sailors pulled out.

The European spot was much harder to call.

Based on performance so far in 2016, the main fight was expected to be between Russia, Poland, Spain, Czech Republic and Turkey. At the European Championships, just two weeks previously, the 2015 world junior champion Ondrej Teply, from the Czech Republic, had ended up as the leading sailor out of this group, but Egor Terpigorev, from Russia, and Alejandro Muscat, from Spain, were immediately behind him. Piotr Kula, from Poland, who had competed in the Finn in London 2012, was only five places further back. It was about as tight as it was possible to get.

HOWEVER THE CONDITIONS in Palma would be very different from Barcelona, with generally stronger winds, and bigger waves. The strong Russian team were widely viewed as the favourites. Terpigorev and Arkadiy Kistanov had both put in top results in the previous year including finishing top 10 at the 2015 Europeans, where Kistanov had also picked up the Junior European title. More recently, Kistanov had taken the bronze at the Sailing World Cup Miami in January.

The Russian team numbered eight sailors, including Oleksiy Borysov, who had previously sailed for Ukraine at London 2012, and had been a stand out performer for Russia at many events since switching nationality. However none of the Russians had so far performed well at the qualifying events.

Muscat and Pablo Guitian Sarria were the two Spanish favourites in a strong team. Poland was fielding a relatively young team of six, led by the experienced 2012 Olympian Kula, who hadn't really produced many promising performances during the cycle. He had finished sixth at the 2012 Finn Gold Cup just before the London Games, and had finished well outside the qualification zone in the both qualifiers so far for Rio 2016.

Also in the mix were the 2012 Olympian Alican Kaynar, from Turkey, the strong but young, German pair of Philip Kasüske and Max Kohlhoff,

Frederico Melo, from Portugal, Andrii Gusenko, from Ukraine and Oisin Mcclelland, from Ireland.

Overall the event pulled in 74 entries from 31 countries, and in addition to the continental qualification it was also used as a national selector for many other countries, both those who had already qualified and those who were still hoping to qualify. Just five months before racing started in Rio, selections were still ongoing for New Zealand, Italy, Canada and Australia. To further complicate the situation, there was still an outside chance that some of these countries would not select anyone, and then the place would revert to the next country not yet qualified from the results at the 2015 Finn Gold Cup. If any already qualified country didn't select, then the next country spaces would go to Russia, then Spain, then Czech Republic. But in the end this didn't happen, and every country that qualified sent a representative.

THE WEEK ALSO hit the headlines for another reason. It was the only time in the three years between the Sailing World Cup Hyères in 2013 and the Olympics that Giles Scott was beaten.

It was his first major regatta since becoming the world champion for the third time at the Finn Gold Cup in New Zealand, in November 2015. He had sailed the Coppa de Brazil in Rio straight after the Finn Gold Cup, and won, but otherwise had limited his Finn sailing to training at home or in Rio. He had dominated the Coppa de Brazil against the small fleet of 11 boats, though most of them were sailors already qualified for the Olympics.

"Palma is quite an important step for us as we did a lot of work at the beginning of the year so we wanted to come here and see where we are at with the work, and hope it is moving in the right direction. Ultimately you can convince yourself of something in training, but it doesn't really count until you race with it, so that's the main purpose of the regatta for me."

He opened well on the first day, but an uncharacteristic 45th and 11th on the second day would leave him without any margin for further errors. Over the next three days he was never out of the top four, at least until the final decisive opening series race.

Meanwhile, Josh Junior from New Zealand had been putting together an excellent series, but Scott still had the opportunity to close down the event before the medal race, as he had done so many times in the past. No one really expected any other outcome.

The final day was sailed in miserable conditions. Not only was the wind shifty and patchy, but also the incessant rain and bad visibility made the

Bay of Palma a pretty miserable place for everyone. With the wind first dying and then clocking, the last race took a while to happen, with the fleet sent ashore to wait out the changing wind and the heavy rain. It was a very wet and cold day in Spain, with the sailors finding shelter wherever they could.

When the final race finally got underway, it was sailed in the strongest wind of the week. Scott rounded the top mark in fourth, and had he maintained that position, it would most likely have been enough to win the week before the medal race. However, at the first downwind gate, as he gybed round the starboard gate mark his rudder popped off the boat. After a few moments hanging over the back of his boat trying to put his rudder back on, he realised something was broken and was beyond repair. In a rare moment of anger and frustration, he lobbed the rudder quite fiercely towards his coach Matt Howard, who was positioned in his coach boat just downwind of the gate.

He knew that he had now lost all chances of winning the regatta and continuing his unbeaten winning streak.

"Josh went on the aggressive in the pre-start and we had one recall. I kind of felt I did a good job with him, and in both starts I managed to come off the line ahead and had the option to tack off. In the second start that's what I did and sailed clear, and by the gate Josh was in about tenth and I was in second or third, and as I rounded up my rudder pin snapped. It is a bit annoying but these things happen and it's better it happens now than in a few months time."

The stainless steel pin holding the rudder had come loose from the aluminium surround and the two had parted ways.

"The bit that broke was a three month old fitting and is something that I check regularly and it didn't have any wear and it just decided today it was going to break, so I'll need to work on the boat tonight to be able to sail tomorrow. The event is lost and I suppose that's the way it is, but it's always a frustrating way to lose a regatta. We'll go away and look at it to make sure it doesn't happen again. It's certainly something you'd kick yourself for even more if it happened again."

The regatta win, with a race to spare, was Junior's first ever regatta win in Europe. In spite of winning through Scott's misfortune, it also placed a target on his back as the only sailor going to the Olympics who had beaten Scott in the cycle, as well as reinforcing the increasingly heard message that the invincible Scott was actually beatable. Whether they believed it or not is conjecture, but it was perhaps more important to believe it, whether true or not.

"All I needed to do was to finish the medal race so I am ecstatic to have won the regatta, really happy. I am lucky enough to have John Cutler as my coach and we have been working hard all summer on technique and going faster and consistency, and I think we have achieved that and now we need to keep building until Hyères, and hopefully the Olympic Games."

Cutler, who had won the bronze medal in the Finn at the 1988 Olympics in Seoul, had been Junior's coach since the start of his campaign, and was a key part of his progress.

"We are not missing many people here so it was probably the hardest regatta of the year, and it's just awesome to win it. It's my first ever win in Europe."

Junior's win came at a crucial time for him in his preparations for the Olympics, for which he still had to win selection for the New Zealand team.

"Giles has proven to be fast again, so to come out on top is great. This is probably the most competitive event leading into the Olympics, so this is a great one to win. I am very pleased to have chipped away with a lot of top five places and won the regatta with a day to go."

Junior had just come out of an intensive winter training schedule along with double Olympian and the recently crowned European champion Pieter-Jan Postma.

"PJ and I have spent a lot of time training together over the summer [southern hemisphere summer] and worked on a lot of things and it seems to be paying off, so we'll continue to work together and look at more ways to improve and hopefully do even better come Rio."

Scott rallied in the medal race to take the silver medal ahead of Tapio Nirkko, of Finland, who had sailed an impressive week with a string of top places.

Scott said, "This week has gone really well apart from the day I got a 45th and 11th and ultimately, what really killed me was the breakage. But that being said, if Josh had a breakage, he'd have picked up 14th and not 45th, so in that regard you have to take your hat off to Josh."

"But where I am at the moment, it's going very well. We have been experimenting quite a lot this week and are pretty happy with what we've been doing. Matt and I still think we are in a very strong position."

Fourth place went to a fast improving Jake Lilley, from Australia, who had picked up a couple of race wins during the week. Despite the disruption of changing coaches at the start of the year, and almost destroying his boat at the Europeans following a collision with a catamaran he was upbeat about his progress.

"I've been working really hard. We changed our setup drastically and I also have new boat because the one I had in the Europeans was totalled by a catamaran. So I am really happy with how things are going now."

The Australian trials were heading for a dramatic finale, with Oliver Tweddell, who finished 11th, also producing a noteworthy performance. As often happens when Olympic trials reach the sharp end, many sailors make Herculean efforts and surpass themselves to achieve their dream. The Australian trials were about to take a turn that no one could have predicted.

Lilley said, "It's been a tough few weeks, so coming here I am super motivated. I am training every day after racing, so staying fit and ticking all the boxes, trying to race well. Everything we have been working on with the new coach and equipment is obviously proving itself to be pretty good so I just have to get off the start line and keep racing well."

THE AFRICAN CONTINENTAL selection was largely routine with Allan Julie outgunning Esseghir with nine straight victories to seal his fifth Olympic qualification with a race to spare. After the ninth race he packed up and left when the fleet was sent ashore, with no need to sail the final race. Neither were going to make the medal race.

Alican Kaynar won the European continental selections after an intense week, with plenty of scrappy racing through the fleet and allegations of team racing directed at some sailors. Egor Terpigorev took the early lead for the Russians. Then it was the turn of Pablo Guitián Sarria from Spain, before Terpigorev again lead after the third day.

Kaynar moved into the lead for the first time after the fourth day. However, the points were tight and any of the top five eligible nations could still have won the fight, so it went into the final day, right down to the wire.

In the ninth race, Kaynar was the highest placed at the first mark with both Terpigorev and Teply some way back. Kaynar made the best of the downwind to move into the top 10, but on the second lap the Russian and Czech gained some places to close on the Turk, but it was not enough. Kaynar finished 14th to take a 10 point lead over Terpigorev going into the final decisive race.

Kaynar did just enough in that final race to finish 18th overall, two places and 10.5 points ahead of Teply and three places and 17 points ahead of Terpigorev, to secure the final European spot in Rio. On that last tricky day, it could still have gone either way, but Kaynar was heading to his second Olympics.

"When we started today I had two very close opponents, the Czech and the Russian, and in the first race I tried to concentrate on my race to make a good result to put a few more points between us, and I managed that. I finished in front of them. Then in the second race I just had the Russian close to me and I stayed close to him to guarantee my place. It was a nice but difficult day, and everything went well."

"It was a very tough week. More than 30 people were trying to qualify their country. And also all the time we had windy conditions, from many directions, so it was very challenging. I have improved in the last years and my goal in Rio is to make the medal race. This will be the goal and of course it's still preparation for the next Olympics to go for the medal."

19

The Thirst for Gold

London Medalists Chase a Second Medal

Three of the Finn sailors in Rio had won medals at the previous Olympic Games in London. Jonas Høgh-Christensen had won the Finn class silver in London while Jonathan Lobert had taken the bronze medal. In addition, Max Salminen had switched from the two-man Star boat, which had been dropped from the Olympic slate after London. Salminen had won the gold medal crewing for Fredrik Lööf.

Almost as soon as Salminen joined the Finn class he stepped into Lobert's training group, along with Tapio Nirkko, and early on, Thomas Le Breton. This group all used similar gear with sails from WB in Finland and trained extensively together in Europe and in Rio.

Lobert had won the bronze medal in London after a consistent series that left him just in touch going into the medal race. He had always performed well in Weymouth Bay, medalling at the 2011 test event and the Sail for Gold events, but a win in the Olympic medal race in August 2012, gave him bronze medal by just three points. Over the course of the week he had only broken into the top three on two occasions, and the medal race was his only victory, but that win in Weymouth on that sunny August afternoon in 2012 set the scene for a remarkable Olympic cycle that, though frustrating for him at times, created a better all-round sailor than he ever was in 2012, and he went towards the 2016 Olympics as one of the medal favourites.

When he left Weymouth he was buoyed for the next four years with new energy to repeat, or better, the achievement in London. Over the next quad he was one of the best Finn sailors on the circuit, and epitomised the type of sailor that the new athleticism in the class had introduced through the free pumping rule. However, Lobert had a problem in that time after time he failed to convert his potential into a major medal.

Back in 2012 he was one of the new breed of younger, taller, stronger and fitter sailors with an athletic style around the boat that made Finn sailing almost gymnastic. The free pumping rule had changed not only the way the boat was sailed, but also the physiques of the sailors and now fostered a taller, fitter sailor, rather than just a large sailor. The sailors were still large, but they were also much, much fitter.

"Since 2012, the Finn has again moved forward a lot. Most of the sailors are very fit and very fast downwind. If you make a mistake it's very hard to come back. I think it's tighter racing than ever between the guys."

Though he was rarely out of the top five at any major event since 2012, it took him three more years after 2012 to win another major medal: silver at the 2015 Finn Gold Cup in Takapuna, New Zealand. He had lost count of the number of times he lost a medal as he closed down an otherwise successful series. After he had overcome his medal shortage, his confidence took a major boost and he went into Rio as one of the top favourites.

His selection for Rio came after long time training partner Thomas Le Breton dropped out of the race, after switching to big boats, and was later involved in the French AC challenge with the Groupama team. Though he had lost a crucial training partner – they had trained well together for five years, learning from each other all the time – his departure did allow Lobert to focus on training in Rio rather than worrying about selection, though of course he still had to qualify. He spent a huge amount of time training in Rio, first with Le Breton, and then with the young Fabian Pic, over the three years before the Games, often skipping major regattas in Europe to make it happen.

"I sailed many times in Rio during the campaign and I realised that it's not an easy place to sail especially outside with the big swell. I hope with all the hours we have spent there I will be able to be fast in most of the situations."

Over the final winter, "In Rio, we have been training a lot. And not so much racing. I really like the time we spent in Rio because it's very interesting to be there and to learn the place. I think if we keep on following the plan we have I am totally convinced that is the best way to be successful in the Games."

Lobert's training group was often located in La Rochelle, where he based himself, and was one of the most close knit teams in this Olympic cycle. Fabian Pic joined after 2014 and they tried to join the British group, including Giles Scott, when the schedule fitted together.

Lobert explained his training, "I always try to give my best on the water and I push all the time even when I sail alone in La Rochelle. I think it's the best way to improve. Of course I try to don't break the rules but if it happens I learn from those situations for the regattas. When one guy is faster I try to understand what I can do better to catch him We have in my point of view one of the most complete training groups with very good sailors in the light, medium and strong, upwind and downwind, so every day on the water is a very exciting challenge depending who is on the top of his game."

Lobert was one of the more experienced in the group but said, "From my experience I learn that you can not be perfect, but to win you need to make less mistakes than the others. So I try to learn from my mistakes and keep on improving my skills."

"I think fitness is very important to be successful in Finn sailing so I train six days a week with usually one day in the gym and the next one more on the cardio, with core exercises every day. When I am alone in La Rochelle I try to sail four times a week, and when I meet the boys we sail five days, one day off and five days sailing again."

During this time Lobert was working on a new French mast project, which was ultimately unsuccessful. He was also still chasing his first major regatta win (something that didn't come until 2017), but remained philosophical about the challenge.

"I am not a superstitious man. I don't look back so I am just looking forward to the next championship and I will try to do my best as always. My dad always told me that the most important thing in sailing is to have fun and I still have a lot of fun on the water."

In 2016 he prioritised sailing in Rio against events in Europe. "When we were looking at the schedule and the various races we have during the season, the main goal for us was to spend time in Rio, so we had to chose some and skip some, this year I also won't be at the worlds, we are trying to take the time to recover."

Speaking in March 2016, just before the Trofeo Princesa Sofia, "Every time we go to Rio and come back we are very exhausted. This time was very short. We flew back just five days before coming to Palma, so the energy is not fully high. Next time we are planning a longer recovery."

And there have also been the unusual situations to deal with. "During the camp we had in March I discovered what heavy rain means in Rio. It started to rain around midday and after only four hours of rain most of the streets around the bay were under 70 cm of super dirty water."

His training group included Salminen and Finland's Tapio Nirkko, both veterans from Weymouth in 2012. Nirkko, in his second Olympics, had got as far as the medal race. Together these three sailors produced one of the tightest multi-national training groups ever, but as the Games came ever closer, the needs of the one started to outweigh the needs of the group.

Lobert explained, "I think it was a great chance for us to be able to work together. We learned a lot from each other and we all have improved a lot during the last four years. As the Games approached we were each of us focusing more on ourselves. But Tapio and Max are both very smart, and very good guys, and we keep on working in a good spirit and in the end we know that the best of us will win."

To be successful in the Games, Lobert said he needs to be a very good sailor in most of the conditions and be able to adapt very quickly for the different race areas. "Most important of all you need to have a strong will to keep pushing in the difficult times you will face during the regatta."

"I try to get the most of every situation and every training camp. With François we always try to figure out what we can improve or learn from the training or the regattas." François Le Castrec was himself a successful Finn sailor in the 1980s, and had been Lobert's coach since before the 2012 Games.

"To be in the best shape during the Games I try to listen to myself and use my experience from big championships to be ready at the right time. Of course François keeps pushing me all the time, to get the best from me." But as the Games approached, "I am just focusing on details. Most of the work has been done already during the last few years."

Lobert said he had developed both as a sailor and an athlete over the last four years. "During the last four years I believe I have become a more professional sailor, and I have been trying all the time to get better and stronger. I have been most of the time top five in the regattas and in all the conditions I am able to reach the podium. I am also more calm these days than I was before, so maybe I am starting to be a grown man."

"Becoming a father has for sure, also changed my life for ever. It has been very hard to get in shape in training and regattas during the last 15 months, but I learned a lot about myself: when it's too much, when I need to rest. But most of all I realised I can push myself much more than I thought before."

French success in the Finn class has been limited to gold for Serge Maury in 1972, and then bronze Guillaume Florent in 2008 and Lobert in 2012. It's an interesting fact that after 64 years and 16 Olympic Games, no medalist in the Finn had ever returned and taken a higher medal. Lobert is fairly well placed to take on that challenge, but joked, "I hope I can break the cycle!"

He didn't.

SALMINEN CAME FROM a country with an even less successful Olympic history in the Finn class. Rickard Sarby, the designer of the Finn won the bronze for Sweden at the Finn's first showing at the Olympics in Helsinki in 1952, and his Star helm, Fredrik Lööf had won bronze in Sydney in 2000.

Salminen was attempting to find Olympic glory in Rio, but this time, by himself. He said that to win a Finn medal, he would be in great company. "It's a dream that has been chased for four years now, which is not a lot for some, but I have really given it my all." Salminen was well suited physically to the Finn at nearly two meters tall and weighing 98kg.

Since he made the decision to do it all again, the 27-year old said it had been an upward curve. "When I looked at 2012, I thought how am I going to be able to win another one? So I made a plan for my progression, and of course you have to advance faster in the ranking the first two years, while expecting that the last places are harder to conquer."

"So I said in 2013 I'll be top 20 in the world, and I think I finished seventh at the Europeans, but some were missing. And in 2014 I'll be top 10 in the world, and I was tenth at the Worlds that same year. And I'll be top five in 2015, and so I was in Takapuna at the Finn Gold Cup. And that would lead me to a top three in 2016. It's been a nice progressive curve."

He said the two campaigns are quite different. In 2012, "I came in pretty late to a ready set-up. This time around I had to build it all from scratch. On the other hand I feel that the experiences from the last campaign have made me a lot wiser, and will I go into this Olympics with much more routine."

For the Rio campaign, "I pretty much filled the empty space Daniel Birgmark left in the group." Birgmark sailed the Finn for Sweden in 2008, narrowly missing out on a medal, and in 2012. "I was really fortunate. I would have had a much harder journey on my own. And as soon as I could afford it I hired Dayne Sharp as coach. After a seventh place at the 2013 Europeans I got more funding and could look around for a coach. Tapio [Nirkko] felt we had a lot of the pieces in place such as the material and the sails from WB-Sails, in Finland, so we needed a coach who was specialised in boat on boat tactics. But I have to say I was impressed how quickly Dayne caught up with all the material and technical parts of it."

He said the final preparations were going to plan. "I am very happy where I am today, because it's been a long journey to get to where I am, with changing class."

In Rio the group trained out of the Iate Clube Rio de Janeiro. "It's really convenient. It's a great club where you can find all you need and it's really close to where we usually stay in Rio. We did 14 days in Rio from the end of June until beginning of July, then home for a week then a short visit to Garda, to eat well and spend a lot of time sailing downwind and then pack and go for the big one."

He estimated that he spent around 150 days in Rio. What did he learn in that time? "That's what we are about to find out isn't it. I think it is always hard to put in to words. Maybe what I've learnt in Rio I could have learnt somewhere else as well. But why take the chance. It's a pretty special place where you race closer to high land than most places. There are a lot of local effects to learn."

"I think you have to be an overall sailor. You race both inside the bay close to land on almost flat or choppy water. And the next day you're out on the ocean with huge waves." He said his strengths were, "speed both up and down and then hopefully that my time spent there will help me take good decisions on the race course."

"Mostly it has been smooth sailing, I have to say. But the nature in Rio is something, it is so much more wild in Rio. I have never seen it rain as it rains in Rio and I have never seen as big waves as we've had in Rio."

Salminen got married a few weeks before the Olympics, with his wife, Suzanne, producing their first child in the autumn of 2016. He said apart from sailing he is not that interesting and lives for his muesli and coffee in the morning. Then he "gets outdoors and moves". He loves his toys, mostly bikes. "I have all the equipment for all possible sports and outdoor activities. I think sport was my saviour. I actually don't know how I'd cope living behind a glass window and a desk."

20

Dream Ending
Vasilij Žbogar Going for the Hat Trick

Vasilij Žbogar was preparing himself for what he said was his last Olympic Games. It would be his fifth Olympic Games and though he already had two medals from the Laser, he wanted to add a Finn medal to the collection before hanging up his boots one last time. After winning the Laser bronze and silver medals in 2004 and 2008, he switched to the Finn in 2009 and immediately began carving out a heavyweight career. He placed sixth at the 2012 London Olympics, won the 2013 Finn Europeans and the 2014 World Cup Final in Abu Dhabi. By the time he got to the start line in Rio he would be 40 years old, the oldest sailor in the fleet.

"It is definitely very hard when you are my age. Also to recover from racing takes much longer than before."

He suffered a setback in 2015 after coming off his bike and broke two ribs, causing him to take half the summer season off. His body mended in time to take part in the 2015 test event in Rio, but he was not in shape and out of practice.

"The good thing is that last winter I was working really well and I got really good boat speed in stronger wind, which I needed, so only time will tell how much I lost in those two months when I was not training."

This said the campaign for Rio was quite different to what had gone before. "This time is quite different, especially the last year before the

Games. For the last Games I was fighting with Gasper Vincec for qualification up until almost the last month before the Olympics and I didn't have
so much time to actually train for the Olympics. I spent a lot of effort and
energy just qualifying." This time he qualified early, "So I can just focus on
the Olympics and for sure the programme will be much different from last
time."

The 2015 test event was his first chance to race on the Olympic sailing
areas, and he highlighted the importance of spending time more in Rio.
"The racing area is different from the usual race areas we have in Europe
so for sure, we need to spend some more time there and learn how all the
systems work. At the moment I am not very positive. Many sailors have
been here for years and you can really see the difference between who has
been sailing here before and who has not."

After 34 years competitive sailing, he said he finds the need for improvement the main motivating factor to keep going at this level. "For sure
changing class was a good motivation for me because I spent many years in
the Laser and now if I look at the Finn I am still very motivated because I
can still see room to improve. I don't think too much about the results but
I feel that I can still improve a lot. Of course I think for all of us the biggest
opponent is Giles Scott, who is one step ahead of everyone, but the rest are
quite close so the battle is very open. As Giles is much better, it is pushing
everyone to get better and at the Games I think it's going to be very close.
Now in the Finn class you have many sailors that can be in front and many
sailors will fight for these three places at the Games."

While age was becoming a problem, there were also many other changes
in the campaign that were keeping it moving and helping him to improve.
"As I said, age is playing a big role. I need more rest. I cannot sail as many
regattas, and the problem is very different. Also over the years you change
your coaches." From 2015 his brother Jure became his coach, and stayed
with him right through to the Olympics.

"Technology is changing. The approach to training is different. Physical
training is changing. This is developing over the years all the time, so you
just need to keep following the new trends in training and you are fine.
That's why I am still sailing. You see room to improve and all the time we
are trying something new to see how we can get better. Basically everything cannot stay the same. Every month something changes, depending
on many things."

"I am from a country where there are normally very light winds. From
the Optimist until when I was a 470 sailor we used to sail mostly in light
winds. In winter it was too cold and in summer it was really light winds,

so from the beginning I was good in light wind. In the Laser I was good in light to medium winds. In the Finn in the beginning I was good in light winds. I have never been extremely good in strong winds, and I probably never will be. It's not in my DNA, but I am trying to improve so I can get closer to the best in strong winds and try to make a difference. That was always my strategy in sailing. I like the events when you have a mixture of everything. For me London was really hard and when I look back and see I was very close to a medal in really challenging wind strengths I really did a good job. In Rio, it's a mixture and I think that helps me a little bit."

After so many years does he still enjoy the sport or is it all about the medal? "Of course it's both, but I can spend hours on the water. Many of my coaches will tell you they force me to come in from the sea. I really enjoy sailing and especially competing, but it has to be both. It's a really, really nice sport because it's a mixture of fighting against nature and fighting against opponents, and that has a really special charm."

After the 2012 London Games he played a crucial role in helping Luca Devoti set up the Dinghy Academy in Valencia in his bid to continually improve. "I am from a small country and Luca was working then with the Italian Federation and I said why can we not do something similar but for sailors who cannot afford to have bigger budgets and to have good sailors to sail with. As I did the same before with SailCoach the idea was to do something similar with the Dinghy Academy. To have good sailors who want to improve and don't have many possibilities to do it. We had 5-6 very good sailors willing to go to the Olympics and pushing hard. And for me this is excellent. They are young, they are motivated and they pushed me as well to improve, so the Dinghy Academy for many sailors is the opportunity to follow their dream, to go the Olympic Games and make a good result."

ŽBOGAR IS ONE of the most famous sportsmen in his home country of Slovenia. In a nation where just a few years ago sailing was a little known sport, it hasn't happened by accident and he is quite outspoken on the need for sailors to be more professional and pro-active when it comes to sponsorship and media exposure.

"You have to understand that my budget is quite big and the federation is maybe covering 20 per cent of that. I have to find the rest myself and this is through sponsors. I put a lot of effort into getting sponsors. So the PR thing is really well organised back home and everyone is happy. We fight for every supporter we have back in Slovenia and we give them information about me and keep them up to date. For me, apart from training and sailing, the PR part takes a huge amount of time and a lot of effort."

His advice to the younger sailors is quite simple. "You have to believe in yourself and believe in what you want to achieve and then to make a nice story out of it. Make everything look very professional. You have to look extremely smart and extremely professional. I have had many doors closed and I didn't get anything, but this is part of the experience. But then you refine your story and change it to find solutions and new ideas."

"Of course first it helps if you have made a good result so people start to trust you when you speak to sponsors or any kind of foundation or the people who want to help you, because if you have results, such as an Olympic medal behind you, they trust you when you speak."

"If you make a story, and especially with the biggest companies, they don't look at the return of everything. They want an image. For example a telecom or insurance company is not going to make more money because they sponsor me, but if there is a story behind it they promote this story. And they are happy to be part of this story. You have to have this story."

"So I can have a decent programme over the years I really have to work hard to have sponsors, make events back home make, events for sponsors, because in the end the sponsors help me to do my programme and it becomes a roller coaster when you have to be in the media all the time. Now it's a bit easier, but in the beginning it was really hard. You had to push everything to the media and TV. Now they ask for it, so it's easier. They ask and we send a video and know it's going to be on TV, but when I am home I really work hard to make sailing as popular as possible because many people see sailing as quite an easy sport: they should try the Finn and then they would definitely change their mind."

"I remember my first commercial for Telekom. We gave them the idea for the commercial. It was very popular back then. "When there is no wind I am surfing." So the commercial was about the wind and then no wind and I had this laptop and I was surfing on internet. We gave them this idea and they made a 40 second spot. And we ended up making four spots for them. And they were really successful."

HE EXPLAINED THAT however successful you are, you still have to look for sponsors. They very rarely come knocking on your door. "It always starts from me. It's almost impossible in sailing that someone comes to you and offers support. I have two private supporters who have done that but bigger companies always look at the return, and in sailing at the beginning they don't see the return but then I usually try to get to the top of the company and I try to explain what sailing is. If you have a good story then they usually help."

In Slovenia sailing was almost an unknown sport but now it has become very popular, and a lot of people follow it. "When I go back home everyone knows about my results and what I am doing. For sailing this is really hard because you don't have supporters on the water, so all they see is what they are given. It's hard to get people to follow."

Promoting the sport is a high priority for Žbogar. "I had a lottery and the winner went with out the Finn for a day to try it and it was a really nice thing. We always have to be one step ahead to be popular as a sport. If we look at other sports, they have big influence, such as soccer, so we always need to have new ideas. Luckily I also have some good friends with me, helping me with this."

"Nowadays for the sponsors, the main thing for them is to create a good name for the company. They don't want trouble. For example, if a soccer team is sponsored by a car maker, and then another team who are against them are not going to buy those cars, so that's part of the game."

"Sailing is a very quiet sport on this whole, so if you guarantee a good image then they are going to be proud of this and what you can achieve together they are wiling to help, and for sure in sailing the budgets are smaller."

Speaking about the Finn class initiative, the FINNTEAM crowdfunding programme, he said, "This was my idea. This was my diploma at University. To have a sponsor for three or four guys in a multinational team. It's a good idea, but it needs someone who has time to do it. It will work though. It worked similar with SailCoach and it shouldn't be a big budget for some big companies and it could be a really good return and a good story for everyone who is a bit famous in their country. It works for everyone."

He said he was happy the direction sailing was taking but, "I think the only problem now and especially back home, everything is always a bit different, there are always different rules, discards, medal races, so the formats we set for every regatta should be the same, then it might be a bit easier for people to understand."

Žbogar finished by saying that Rio would be his last Finn event. "After Rio I will stop. Rio is my last race in Finn. Then I maybe will race in the Masters. It's been a already a long and successful career and it's time. I have been sailing 34 years already. It's going to be hard but there should be an end. We'll see what time brings."

21

The Puzzle Completed
Complex Rio Qualification and Selections Complete after Gaeta Finn Gold Cup

One of the final pieces of the puzzle in the make up of the Olympic Finn fleet was the selection of Giorgio Poggi following his fifth place at the 2016 Finn Gold Cup in Gaeta, Italy, leaving the Italian selectors with little choice but to allow the 2008 Olympian a second chance at Olympic glory.

When it really mattered and there were no second chances, Poggi took an emphatic win in the Italian trials, with a career best Finn Gold Cup fifth place in Gaeta, at an event that he played a part in bringing to his home country.

The Italian trials had drifted on for many months, with not one of the four or five sailors really meeting the necessary criteria for selection, and with intense competition, and a little controversy, along the way. So Gaeta was the final chance. Poggi produced his best performance ever to be the only Italian to make the medal race, which he almost won to cement his fifth place overall, and eventually, selection for Rio.

"I knew it would not be easy to reach the result that my federation asked for [top 6] at the Finn Gold Cup to be eligible for the Olympics."

For Poggi, this moment had been a long time coming after missing out in 2012, after similarly tense trials against the same group of sailors. For Rio his focus and preparation was almost flawless. He said he would not have changed anything. And now he had the chance he had been waiting for, for eight years – to better his 11th place at the 2008 Olympics in Beijing. There, he put together a reasonable series but just finished outside the medal race. He had unfinished business.

His coach for the Rio campaign, Emilios Papathanasiou, was also his rival in 2008. "Emilios and I were sailing partners for Beijing 2008 but mostly we are just friends; we call each other brother. In April 2014, I was a bit confused with my target and what to do, so I spoke with Emilios to get some suggestions for my preparation for the trials for Rio. He came to Hyères in 2014 to see me racing and then everything happened."

Poggi also teamed up with Alican Kaynar, for training, who would also be heading into his second Olympics in Rio. "I met Alican in the Dinghy Academy. We had the same view and target so we decided to have a training camp together with Emilios. It is a pleasure to work with him, and I can really say that we are a real team."

Poggi had spent long time at the Dinghy Academy before and then came back there for three months in December 2014. "In the last four years a lot of things have changed. We have new boats, new masts, a lot of new models of sails. I worked a lot in the training to understand which is the best combination of material for my way of sailing."

He has had a lot of help along the way from sponsors and supporters. "To make all these things happen, I need to say thanks to Filippo La Scala, who was not only the sponsor (Garnell Sailing Team) but also a friend that follows all my regattas, and all Alican's regattas, until both of us got selected by our national federations for the Olympics. He also brought a lot of things to the team that we were missing. Emilios, Alican and I are almost only sailors, so Filippo brought a vision from the point of view of a manager and this was a big value added to the team."

"Without the work we did as a team before, it would probably be impossible to have this result and the best part was to share with them all the emotion after the medal race in Gaeta."

Going into Rio "I don't have any expectations, as you know, it is a game, you can win, you can lose. Who knows? I only know that I will be well prepared. I will spend my last days at home and spend most of the time with my wife and my daughter, fix all the things so that when I will leave my home for Rio I'm fully focussed only on me and sailing."

"I HAVE BEEN thinking of this race for four years now. And every day is a next step in the preparation for Rio," declared Anders Pedersen, of Norway, as he made final preparations for what would be his first Olympics. With high expectation and no pressure, he was, "looking forward to seeing and feeling the Olympic energy."

At just 24 years old he was one of the youngest Finn sailors heading to Rio, but had proved himself many times on the water. Junior world champion in 2014, later that same year he qualified Norway for Rio at the first opportunity at the Santander world championships. Since then he had been a regular at the front of the fleet and was showing some real potential.

To become the top sailor he was, he first had to overcome his fear of being alone in a boat. "When I first started sailing in the Optimist I was really, really scared of sailing by myself. From when I was six years old, and for the next year and a half, I was scared every time I went training at my club. But I soon found out that you could actually master basically everything if you practice. So I started practicing."

"I am preparing for the Games as for every other important race. I have been good at picking out my peaks in the season, so I have full belief that I will be at my best in August. I'm going into the Games with no pressure except what I put on myself. I believe I am strong mentally and am good at focusing on the things that matters, and pushing away everything else."

"The last four years have been a bit of everything. I was out most of the 2013 season with illness. In 2014 I did a lot of training in the boat and saw big steps in my sailing. I managed to win the Silver Cup (the Junior World Championship) and did a good World Championship in Santander, and that did well for me regarding funding from my federation. This meant that I could take my campaign to a different level. In 2015 and 2016 I put in a lot of hours in the boat and I think we are on our way to something now."

In 2015 he was contacted by the 2012 silver medalist, Jonas Høgh-Christensen, from Denmark, to see if he wanted to join his group for training in Clearwater, Florida. "I saw this as a very good opportunity to train with a successful and more experienced sailor. I'm trying to learn as much as possible, and I hope I am putting in some good things by pushing hard on training every day. I hope we have success in Rio, and can cash in all of our training. The group has worked well and we have good fun."

"Jonas is the King, and I am the clown," he laughed.

Over the previous four years, "The development has been huge. I am more determined in everything I do. Through help from Olympiatoppen in Norway we have been able to use experts on physical training, and mental preparation. This has taken me to a whole different level from where I was four years ago."

He said his preparations were all going well. "Right now it's going good. We try to use our time wisely on the courses we will race on during the Games. Our time there has showed us that all time spent in Rio, is time spent well. The conditions are challenging wind and current wise. It is great to have some experience from all the different courses."

In the final months before the Games started, he said he spent about 18 days training in Rio and about the same number of days training at home in Norway. In total he had about a month in Rio, considerably less than some teams.

"From there on the focus will be to keep everything up to date, and not lose any feel. Apart from that it's about staying away from any illness and injuries before we start racing."

"The best thing about Rio is the days when you have 20 knots and four meter waves outside. We have been so lucky to train out of Rio Yacht Club in Niterói, a small, but excellent club. Nice people, good food. What more can you wish for?"

"The fleet is full of talented sailors who push hard in every race. This is my first Olympics and my expectations are great. I'm going to give it my all and then we will see. Hopefully I am going to give 'the big boys' a fight."

FOR DENISS KARPAK, from Estonia, his Olympic Finn ambitions were more than a singlehanded drive for the gold. For him it was very much a family affair. While his mother, Marina, was the team manager, his father Igor was the head coach. They travelled with him everywhere, working together as a very tight unit, but also making sure it was always fun along the way.

Eleventh place at the London 2012 Olympics was not the position that he had hoped he would finish. Though he had briefly risen to the World No. 1 a few months beforehand, he only managed three top 10 race finishes in 2012, including one of the biggest race wins of the week. He had much higher hopes for Rio. "All my techniques are sharper."

He qualified Estonia and himself for Rio at the 2015 Finn Gold Cup in Takapuna.

Before London he had sailed the Laser in Beijing, finishing a lowly 24th (though he had won Laser bronze at the 2007 World Championships in Cascais), but even before the end of the regatta, his thoughts were focussed on his next steps in sailing, and the Finn. He was two metres tall and the Laser was not big enough for him any more.

He comes from a very sport orientated family, with both his parents at some time also trying for the Olympics. His father campaigned a Flying

Dutchman for 1984, but missed out because of the USSR boycott, while his mother, a top swimmer, also missed out. Both his parents will be with him in Rio as usual. "With them I feel always like I am at home, because home is the place where my family is."

Apart from one training camp in Rio in March, Karpak was content to train in Europe doing all his normal routines, and not travel extensively to the Olympic waters. "It's risky to stay too long in Rio. And there will be nothing new that I already saw in March. Maybe even less wind."

"We were in Rio a few weeks, and I like it. It has a beautiful landscape from the land and from the ocean. Not so dirty water, with some doors, kitchen machines and plastic bottles, but I like the venue. There was a 'funny' moment, when we came from Niterói to Rio by ferry, and I heard some shooting, thinking it was some fireworks, but the people near told me, that is the mafia speaking."

"The weeks before Rio Games will be the same as the usual weeks of summer. Fun and sailing. It will be a few weeks after my 30th birthday, so I will be almost a new person there. A matured sailor." At the Games, he said, "Mental strength and focus will play a major role."

So, "Between now and the Games I'm doing my regular trainings. Water and fitness. No changes."

His favourite venue has always been Kiel Week. "I like the place and it's very similar to my hometown Tallinn." In 2016 he was trying to win for the fourth time, "…but it was a hard week and I was ended up battling for one of the lower medals, not gold. I was a bit disappointed but I made a lot of mistakes…in spite of three bullets and the medal race win." After that he largely trained in Italy before heading to Rio at the end of July.

Karpak keeps busy outside of sailing. "I'm developing as a person, a multi-tasking person, where not only sailing exists. That's the big difference between Beijing 2008 and Rio 2016, where sailing was all I had and all I could do. Now it's a part of my life, my hobby, my work – I get paid for my sailing – and I'm very happy to be a part of this beautiful sport."

He also writes books. "Not many Finn sailors do that." He was promoting his book 'Breathe underwater'. "I have written since 2011 and when I have some free time, I write small novels. The plan is to finish my first real – 150+ page – book before 2017." He said this book is just a demo, but he has already got a lot of 'awesome feedback'. He writes under the pseudonym of Ivan Brait. "Hopefully you will be able to get my book on iTunes soon."

Karpak is perhaps the most famous sailor in Estonia, winning the Estonian Sailor of the Year award eight times, and this fame has led to some spinoff activities.

Just before the Games he appeared as a model for some big brands.

"It was just a photo shoot for a big Estonian brand Baltman, which makes suits. And my friends from another big international brand, American Crew, (professional line of shower gels, shampoos…etc for barbers and saloons) wanted me to be a face of their new campaign named 'My first suit' in Estonia. That's it. I was previously also in some fashion campaigns and I like it, and hope to continue one day."

But for the moment, "Sport is a game, and I hope Rio will give us this opportunity – to play."

ONE OF THE nations qualified for Rio but which did not select a sailor until late in the cycle was Canada. Tom Ramshaw qualified his country at the North American Continental Qualifier at the Sailing World Cup Miami in January 2016, but the selectors wanted the trials to continue. For a while there was doubt whether they would send anyone, but Ramshaw had shown a lot of promise, so the trials continued.

Martin Robitaille had been in the class for many years, including winning the 2012 Junior World Championship, while 2016 was Ramshaw's first season after just stepping into the boat in August 2015.

Ramshaw explained, "I was taking a break from the Laser and some of the Finn guys suggested I try the Finn at CORK which was the North Americans. So I tried that, had a good time, and ended up winning. So it was like, I have to continue as it was so much fun."

In the Laser class he was consistently in the gold fleet, some top 20 finishes in Miami and a few podiums at CORK, but nothing very spectacular.

He always had problems staying down to weight for the Laser. "I am almost the right size for the Finn, maybe a little short, but putting on the weight was pretty easy. In the Laser I really struggled to stay down. I was on the heavy end of the spectrum and so it was a pleasure to be able to eat properly again. Also I like going to the gym, so it was good to be in the gym again instead of cycling and running all the time."

But then the Rio dream became a real possibility. The Canadian trials were on a selection basis but there were certain criteria that the sailors had to meet. Because Canada had qualified in a lot of classes through the regional qualifiers, the selectors decided were not going to send all of them because in a lot of classes they were not competitive in the international fleets.

So Ramshaw had to prove he was competitive in competitions such as the Europeans and the Gold Cup. Speaking of Robitaille, "We're competitive, but I am not so worried about beating him, but just focussing on getting good results at regattas. If he sails well that's great but I am just trying to beat as many boats as I can."

His first major Finn event was the Sailing World Cup Miami. "I wasn't really putting together full races. I always seemed to be having comebacks and then on the last day it was shifty offshore and that's always appealed to me growing up sailing on lakes. I had a good last day moving up from maybe 20th to 13th, so it was nice way to finish the regatta on a good note. But my goal was really to make the medal race. I wasn't too far off but I wasn't going to make it on the last day even if I made two firsts."

On his long-term goals he said, "When I was in the Laser I was thinking about going until 2016. I was a little burnt out, but as soon as I decided to switch to the Finn there was a decision for a five-year commitment through to 2020. It would be a little ridiculous to just sail for a year and go to the Games, so I'd rather have a better goal of reaching the podium and a successful full campaign for 2020."

He said he loved sailing the Finn more than he could have imagined, especially the physical side. "I love it. It's more physical. The more physical you are the faster you go and that really appeals to me. I wasn't sure whether I was going to like all the tuning and the different types of rig but it's a variation, but now I enjoy tweaking with it and am learning a lot."

"I don't have much time and I don't have a big a budget as some people, so I am trying work with what I have got. I am looking to get a new boat as well. When I am going slowly I try not to think about whether it's something in the rig, I try and make it go fast. But I have been pretty fast and I am have been happy with how it's been going."

Ramshaw impressed everyone with a tenth place at the 2016 European Championship in Barcelona, and then placed eighth in the 2016 Finn Gold Cup, enough to convince the selectors to choose him for Rio.

HEADING INTO HIS third Olympics, Pieter-Jan Postma, from The Netherlands, said he was taking more time over his preparation and was calmer and more prepared than ever before. He wanted a medal, but he knew that it would be a big fight on the water to achieve that dream.

He got very close in London in 2012, but reflecting back four years before when he lost a medal after a mistake on the final mark rounding, he said, "It's a different campaign; all areas needed work. Then I came a little short. This time there is more in the tank, so let's give it all again."

At the 2015 test event in Rio, he wore the yellow bib for the entire regatta, only to lose the gold medal on the medal race. After that he won the European Championship in Barcelona, and took bronze at the Finn Gold Cup in Gaeta during the most successful period of sailing in his 11 years in the Finn. Postma badly wanted to put the spectre of the London Games, where he finished fourth, behind him. Since 2012 he'd had, as usual, some ups and downs, but over the 12 months leading up to Rio, he was most definitely on the up.

"I think every year the level goes up and in Rio it will be the highest level. So in a few areas you want to step up way before the Olympics, for example in materials. Then you have to step up in other areas just before Rio. I think my level went up, up, up. I will be among the medal contenders. I feel good about it. I have got to trust, but you have always got to see where you end up and how it will go.

"This is my third Olympics and I would put myself possibly for the top five. But I want to go for a medal."

He said his previous campaigns have felt rushed. This time he was, "Taking a bit more time, to actually see what is happening. In the last two Games I felt too much in a train – just keeping pushing. This time I am keeping calmer. I am getting more all-round and seeing the process picture more clearly, so I can train more effectively."

"I feel my timing is good; much more comfortable than London."

Since 2015, Postma had been training alongside Josh Junior from New Zealand. "JJ is a great man to have around. We motivate each other off and on the water. It's a really good experience. And we are sharing lots of tricks with each other. To train every day with the best is an honour. He is not that old, he is not that experienced but he is sailing amazingly. He has got a great feel for the boat, sailing downwind very well."

"For Rio, we didn't leave any stone unturned. In every area there are gains, and if the gains are big enough, we focus on it. So for example, the psych area we try and connect, handle the pressure, focus. So the right priority with the right leverage, with the right gain will bring out the best performance. The main thing is that you look at every area and make the best out of it."

Starting and strategy were always Postma's strengths, but he said the key skills for Rio would be to be "fast and smart, cool and ready". He added that winning the European title has added to his confidence, "It's great to celebrate that, to win. I was the best then. It was an amazing experience and it does give you a boost. But every race is a new race. Everybody has got fitter. Sailors have shaped their techniques and topped their level. Everybody is faster."

"I like the conditions in Rio, but at the same time Rio is different every day – so you have to be open."

The Olympics always had a special appeal to Postma. "It is always nice that the pressure is there. It makes it something special. Makes it something enjoyable and sometimes if the pressure is too much, you can feel it like a load, but I feel most of the time that I enjoy it. And the pressure in the Olympics is the biggest in four years. You work towards this goal for such a long time with the team. But I hope there will be pressure and I know there will be pressure. So it will be a great event."

He said that in sailing, as in any sport, everybody was getting stronger and stronger. "What you see in the level of sports in the last 50 years, there is a totally different level. In another 20 or 50 years there will be also a different level. Everybody is growing in every area. And the competitors will be strong also in different areas."

After many years visiting and training in Rio, he felt at home there and enjoyed the culture and the people. "I live with different artists of art and music in a big old school building. I feel at home to see different aspects of life, to be conscious of all choices I make, and what our role and responsibility is as humans in this wonderful world."

By he also had concerns. "It's a different culture, great to see how Brazilians can live day by day and make every day a day to smile. They drive like crazy but don't hit each other; it's like a dance on the road. At the same time, political and economic Brazil has a long way to go. And for example, the sewer cleansing and garbage services are behind the times. So we live and sail with dirty water in a beautiful bay. Start with basics, good schooling and basic services, because this great country with these people deserve the best. But it's great to be here with the people of Brazil, and I am very thankful to be able to take part in the Olympics."

Finally, "I think the Olympics is a special event and I am really looking forward to it. I speak to the other guys; they will be prepared. It will be a big fight, it will be fierce, I hope it will be beautiful and let's all enjoy that."

APART FROM BRAZIL as host nation, which had the right to enter one athlete, 12 nations qualified at the 2014 ISAF Sailing World Championships in Santander: Great Britain, Croatia, France, New Zealand, USA, Norway, Sweden, Denmark, Slovenia, Australia, Hungary and Finland.

Next, China, won the Asian place at the Sailing World Cup Qingdao. At the 2015 Finn Gold Cup in Takapuna, The Netherlands, Greece, Estonia and Uruguay qualified immediately, with Italy added later in the year as no new nations took part in Melbourne, the Oceanic qualifier, so that place was backtracked to the Finn Gold Cup. Canada and Argentina won the North and South American places in Miami, and finally in Palma, Turkey won the final European place, with Seychelles winning the African place. The puzzle was complete.

For a change, all those who qualified met their National criteria and were given their tickets to Rio. Of the 23, just seven would be sailing in their first Olympics, seven would sailing their second, five would be sailing their third, two would be sailing their fourth and two would sailing their fifth: Vasilij Žbogar and Allan Julie. Žbogar was the oldest sailor heading to Rio at 40, though the average age had dropped from 30 in 2012 to 29 in 2016.

And of course there were those who had failed to make it: Poland, Russia, Spain, Czech Republic, Germany and Ireland, all of whom who now had to wait until Tokyo 2020.

Looking at it quantitatively, based on performance, about 10-12 sailors had the capacity to medal in Rio, and around 18-20 had performed well enough to make the medal race on August 16.

THE SCENE WAS set and the players were ready. There was much speculation about what would happen, who the favourites were. Josh Junior was perhaps uppermost in most people's mind as a possible toppler of Scott after his victory over the Brit in Palma. Junior's biggest problem used to be consistency, but having won the New Zealand trials against Murdoch, one of the most conservative sailors in the game, he looked to have that under control.

His training partner Postma had lurked near the top for years, but always failed to convert potential to gold, but over the previous year he had been of the most successful sailors.

Of the 23 sailors in Rio, only 11 sailed the Finn at London 2012, including two of the medalists, Jonas Høgh-Christensen and Jonathan Lobert. Both had performed well in the lead in to the Games, so both were confident, though they had followed very different journeys to get to Rio.

One of Lobert's training partners, Max Salminen, already had Olympic gold at home, in the Star from 2012, but wanted more and wasn't going to be happy going home empty handed.

Of the new young group sailing their first Olympics, Jake Lilley was perhaps one of the brightest stars. He towered over most of the fleet and had been steadily rising through the ranks over the preceding three years and looked likely to pose a threat at the front. Caleb Paine and Anders

Pedersen were equally promising and were both capable of a result.

And then there were the sailors from the Dinghy Academy – Zsombor Berecz, Facundo Olezza, Vasilij Žbogar, Alejandro Foglia. Nine of the 23 sailors in Rio had trained in Valencia at some point.

But whatever had gone before, nothing mattered now. It was time for the Games to begin.

PART 3

FIELD OF PLAY

22

The Final Countdown

Keep Your Mind Open
and Be Ready for Everything

Four years of training and four years of careful preparation and it came down to 23 Finn heroes lining up alongside each other in Guanabara Bay in front of the awesome spectacle that is Rio de Janeiro. The training was complete, the testing was done, everyone was ready and the sailors just wanted the battle to begin.

The racing would open on Tuesday 9 August under the imposing heights of the Sugarloaf Mountain, on what was effectively the spectator course, as well as one of the trickiest courses the sailors had ever experienced. Over the next seven days the fleet would sail ten 50-55 minute races before the all–important medal race back on the Sugarloaf course on Tuesday 16 August where the medals would be decided.

In the final months before the Games started most of the sailors spent a lot of time in Rio and even organised an ad-hoc coaches regatta amongst themselves, with the tongue in cheek name, 'The Zika Trophy'. It was run by Fabian Pic from France, Jonathan Lobert's training partner, through a Facebook page and group to inform the sailors at the various locations around the bay about starts times and results.

Racing was run over four days from 4-7 July, with the handwritten sailing instructions posted on Facebook. While not the full Olympic fleet, 14 Finns took part and without doubt the fastest boat on the water from Zsombor Berecz from Hungary, winning most of the races and the medal race.

IN THE FINAL days before the racing started for real, some of the sailors were interviewed on their final thoughts.

On the last few days before the official programme started with the practice race on Monday 8 August, it was windy in Rio. In the unusually strong winds the London 2012 bronze medalist, Jonathan Lobert, was the only Finn sailor to venture out. "Ah you know, I always like to train in every condition. I thought it was a good chance to practice the manoeuvres. You never know what will happen. It came in very quickly, so we could have one day like that and you need to be ready for everything."

"I think I am ready. I am just going on the water to check that everything is OK with the boat, no stupid mistakes like crossing the ropes."

On the unusual weather. "We've been training here a lot and we realised that the weather can change really quickly. We had some days the weather forecast was saying no wind and suddenly the wind was kicking in and sometimes it's raining when it shouldn't and the opposite is also true. So you need to keep your mind open and be ready for everything. And this why I thought it was a good chance to practice in the strong breeze."

"To be honest I never look at the forecast. I always take what I have. We have this joke with the team weather guy, he's always mad at me because I never read the bulletin."

On sailing the opening races on the Sugarloaf course, "I would say it's the most tricky course, so it will be quite interesting racing."

While Lobert headed into his second Games, Pieter-Jan Postma, was sailing in his third. "I am fully ready. It's obvious to say but we put the emphasis on the Games and it feels like that and it feels ready and it feels totally different from the last Olympics. Then I felt I had a lot of nerves, but now I feel really prepared."

He said he was looking forward to the first races. "It feels nice. There will be some action and I am really looking forward to it. Let's make it a special one, a very special one, and let's enjoy this."

"The people here are great. It's a great place, with great conditions. It's great to be here, it's amazing."

Anders Pedersen, was sailing in his first Olympics. "I am really looking forward to it. It will be really nice to finally get started racing."

"It's going to tricky for sure. Anything can happen there, so I see that as a plus for me and I think it's challenging for everyone. The favourites are not so favoured on the Sugarloaf course when basically everything can happen. We've been a bit behind schedule but now everything seems to be sorting itself out so I think it's all good."

Pedersen had been suffering with the remains of a virus that had affected the end of his training.

"I had a small bump last week. I went to the hospital with some stomach issues, but luckily it got better really quickly so I am back in business and all good."

He wasn't the only one who was suffering. Both Deniss Karpak and Jonas Høgh-Christensen were not at their best and later revealed this was a contributory factor in their poor performances.

There was not much doubt that Rio's waters would provide perhaps the biggest challenge of the sailor's careers. The unseen currents, the changeable winds, and the hidden dangers beneath the surface would all conspire to create a fascinating Games that even the favourite, four times world champion Giles Scott, and favourite for the gold, did not take for granted.

Looking ahead to the Games, Scott was asked about his confidence.

On a scale of one to ten, "I'm an eight or nine. I'm confident, but also aware it's another regatta and on top of that it's the Olympic Games and anything can happen. The conditions are really difficult to predict. The test events we've had here over the last couple of years have actually turned out to be pretty good from a sailor's point of view. Hopefully if we get what are regarded as 'normal conditions' for this time of year we should get good racing."

"We've spent a lot of time here now. Over the past three years we've done at least three trips a year. When we first started coming here we came with a bit of apprehension. There were a lot of rumours flying around about what Rio was like and actually the more we got used to it the more comfortable we felt. It's really vibrant, clearly it's got its darker side but fortunately I haven't seen too much of that. We've enjoyed our time here."

The much-heralded road to Rio was almost at an end. What came next was an engaging and demanding challenge that would showcase one of the most physically toughest events in the Olympics.

Sailors had spent longer training at the venue than at any previous Olympics. Many had started three years earlier to familiarise themselves with the conditions. Many had based themselves there for protracted periods to get to grips with Rio's idiosyncrasies. Most were fully aware it wouldn't take much for everything to go wrong for them.

The intensity of the qualification and physical training periods had evolved into fine details and making sure everything was ready for when the starting gun went on August 9.

However, what all the sailors were saying, whatever their past results would otherwise indicate, was that Rio would be an Olympics where past form meant very little; the Rio Games would be very tough to manage, and very difficult to predict, and to win you would have to be the best all round sailor - and perhaps a little lucky.

23

A Day for the Young and the Old

Day 1 – Tuesday 9 August

There were many predictions about how the start of the 2016 Olympics would go, but no one really expected that the race winners on the first day would be the youngest and the oldest sailors in the competition. Out of the crazy conditions, the youngest, and most inexperienced sailor, Facundo Olezza, from Argentina, won the first race, his first-ever Olympic race, while the oldest and most experienced sailor, Vasilij Žbogar, from Slovenia, won the second race.

After the first two races, held under the shadow of Sugarloaf Mountain, on the so called spectator course, Žbogar led overall from Alican Kaynar, from Turkey, and Olezza. Many of the favourites faired badly on a day that, had it been any other event, would have likely been very different, but because of TV timings and the waiting world, had to proceed on schedule, despite huge pressure variations and huge wind shifts that shuffled the fleet on several occasions.

While the start line was almost within sight of the spectator area on the Flamengo Beach next to the Marina da Glória, the top mark was almost hidden under the towering Sugarloaf. With the sea breeze coming from the ocean, the only way it could reach the course area was by going round or over the top of Sugarloaf. The result is a very confused wind pattern at the top mark, which sometimes extends a significant distance downwind. While the sailors had found patterns in the wind, it didn't always do as expected.

Percentage wise, the left would normally pay, but as it often the case on big occasions, the right side came in more frequently than anticipated. The wind was never more than 7-9 knots all day, meaning that the patchy wind would be sluggish at times with no clear direction.

Tuesday 9 August was a day that many of the favourites would see a different end of the fleet to normal and some would prefer to forget. It was always going to be the hardest day of the week, but no one expected it to be as hard as it was. It turned into one of the shiftiest, random days on the water that most of the Finn fleet have ever been forced to endure. It was a day was full shocks and surprises as the fleet suffered 40-degree shifts and huge pressure changes that mixed the order on almost every leg.

Kaynar, sailing in his second Olympics, was the early leader in the opening race before Deniss Karpak, from Estonia, took the lead on the first downwind after a huge right shift turned the run into a reaching leg. He held it round the following top mark, even if only by a few seconds.

However on the next downwind, Olezza moved into the front and led for the remainder of the race to win the first race of the 2016 Olympics. After dropping down to fifth on the first downwind, Kaynar made some gains on the second and third upwind legs to retake second into the finish. Meanwhile, Žbogar oscillated between sixth and third and finally crossed in third. The leading pack crossed very tightly packed with just four seconds separating the top three, and all boats finishing within two minutes.

One of the biggest gains in the race came from the local hero, Jorge Zarif, who climbed from 19th at the first mark to fourth at the finish, but he was not alone in making big gains, or big losses.

THE SECOND RACE was sailed in slightly more stable winds, at least in terms of pressure but still lacked any particular direction. Žbogar held a nice lead at the top mark after favouring the left, and led through the gate after a tricky light wind run. However on the second upwind, Hungarian, Zsombor Berecz went further right than anyone, picked up one of those 10 per cent shifts and popped out ahead.

Sailing conservatively, Žbogar sensibly covered the majority of the fleet over on the left side of the course, and succeeded in protecting his second place on the water until the finish line, just ahead of Alejandro Foglia, of Uruguay.

However, the Hungarian, along with Jake Lilley from Australia and

Foglia were all pulled out after a starting penalty disqualification – a UFD – to leave Žbogar the race winner from Jonas Høgh-Christensen of Denmark and Giles Scott, from Great Britain.

There was further disappointment for some on the opening day with Josh Junior from New Zealand picking up a disqualification for an incomplete penalty turn while Ioannis Mitakis of Greece and Lei Gong of China were both forced to pull out of the race after collecting a second yellow flag for breaking Rule 42 (kinetics).

Olezza was pragmatic about his race win and a better start to his Olympics than he could ever have hoped for.

"I think it was really important to get the first shift and I got the first right shift and just split with five or six more guys and from there it was a completely different race. It was just staying in the pressure and trying not to lose any places."

"It was super challenging. This course was one of the trickiest in the event so it was important to always be aware of what was happening around me."

"I never thought I would actually win the first race here, but now it's over and it's time to think of tomorrow. I am not trying to be emotional about it, just focussed. For me the races are in the bag and the next are coming, so I am preparing for that."

Žbogar, a double Olympic medalist in the Laser, and now sailing his second Games in the Finn, explained his day.

"The fleet is really strong and everybody is very close so making small mistakes can lose you five to ten places very easily, so to be a little bit in front and be able to cover the others makes the job much easier. We knew the left was much better but with this place you never know actually."

On the second start, "I was just next to these guys that were UFD. It was just a matter of seconds. But when there is a small group that start to push you have to push as well. The course was very tricky to get clear starts. So my goal today was just to be free of the others, because I have good speed and I don't need to push the start as much as the others."

"By the end of the week I think the average points will quite high."

He explained that these were his conditions. "I like these conditions and when you like some conditions everything is much easier. At home in Slovenia we have these kinds of conditions, with no waves."

He thought the key to a successful week was to make the best of your opportunities when presented with the chance and then to minimise any points loss when you are struggling. Being a bit lighter than more of the fleet, and older than all the other contenders, he knew his weak spot was in strong winds and big waves, exactly what was forecast for the following two days.

"It's a better to have a good day than a bad start, but there are two days ahead with strong winds, when I will try to get as less points as possible and be close to the leaders."

One of the day's casualties was four time world champion, Giles Scott, who picked up a 17, 3 to sit in tenth overnight. As favourite for the gold, he was always trying to downplay the pressure that had been heaped on his shoulders. He admitted to being slightly nervous before the first start, but was keen to get it out of the way.

"The Sugarloaf course is notoriously difficult. The wind was that little bit further right than yesterday, which basically means the breeze comes straight down over Sugarloaf, which provides really tricky, unpredictable winds. There is a lot of scope for big gains and there is also a lot of scope for some big loses so managing those is particularly difficult. I'm not massively happy with how today has gone, but there is still a long way to go."

"My game plan for both races was very similar; in the first one it was the execution that went wrong. One minute you think you are going to be in front and the next you're not. It was about as hard as that course gets."

In the second race, "I came off the start a bit better and was able not to be dictated to, which helped me make my own decisions. It is hard in the light winds; not physically hard work but it's mentally draining. I think the vast majority of people today had a good and a bad race."

"It's certainly not the way you want to start an Olympic Games but unfortunately these things happen in regattas, and they have certainly happened to me over the past four years, so it doesn't make things easy but there is still a lot to play for. It doesn't make things easy. I survived today by the skin of my teeth and I just have to look forward to tomorrow."

Brazilian favourite Jorge Zarif faired better and sat in fourth overall after a 4, 6. "I feel like I had two bad starts and had to recover a lot, which was quite bad because the conditions were really tricky. If you ask someone if they are OK with a fourth and sixth, then on a normal day some guys would say, no, but on a day like today it's two good results."

"On the Sugarloaf race area it's the worst course to keep a good average. It's the worst area to predict anything and we can see that in the results."

Sixth overall Høgh-Christensen was more outspoken, "The wind was shifting 30-40 degrees with pressure and there was swell coming across the race course at the bottom half. The wind was going all over the place. But it is what it is. We knew it was going to be tricky on this course and there was a good chance that we would have some randomness in races and we sure did. But we're through this course and onto the next one, until the medal race."

AFTER TWO RACES, Žbogar held a three-point lead over Kaynar and a six-point lead over Olezza. All three sailors had been involved in the training programme at Luca Devoti's Dinghy Academy in Valencia, as well as Zsombor and Foglia.

Speaking after the racing Devoti paid tribute to his sailors. "The guys from the Dinghy Academy did extraordinarily well."

Referring to the UFDs he said, "It's a bit of black and white. They sailed very fast but of course starting over is very costly. It's the most expensive mistake. The conditions should change a lot for tomorrow."

"Vasilij is an unbelievable champion, very experienced and very consistent. Facundo is a champion to come if he manages to control his mind."

With a lot of the favourites sitting deep in the results after the opening day, the Games would come down to clearing the mind each day and starting afresh. It was certainly the tricky start that everyone expected.

24

Big Day on the High Seas
Day 2 – Wednesday 10 August

The contrast between the first and second days could not have been more striking. The calm water, light winds and hot Rio sunshine from Tuesday had been replaced by strong, cold winds, huge seas, incessant rain and bad visibility. On the second day of racing the Finns were outside the bay on the Niterói course area, opposite the Copacabana beach on the north-eastern side of the entrance channel to the bay. It proved to be a gruelling test of stamina and wits.

Giles Scott put his worries from Tuesday behind him to record the performance of the day to move in to overall lead. Vasilij Žbogar achieved his goal of minimising too many points lost and only dropped one place to second overall, while Alican Kaynar also dropped one place to third.

The conditions were full on in every aspect. With a cold front crossing the region, it brought strong, cold winds straight from the Antarctic, with big, breaking waves catching out the unwary. Beyond the windward mark the horizon was just visible with the lights along Copacabana showing up brightly through the murky conditions. Even the starting boards on the committee vessel were brighter than usual as the sunnies came off and photographers ramped up their ISO settings to capture some amazing images. It was definitely not the Rio in the brochure, but the Finn sailors loved it all the same, excelling in the huge waves in big winds, and showing the Finn as it truly is, a great sea boat capable of pushing athletes to the limit while also fostering intense competition.

IN 20 TO 25 knots of wind and huge seas, Ioannis Mitakis was the early leader in the first race of the day after some confusion over the location of the top marks. A number of boats sailed to the wrong set of marks and overstood by 150 to 200 metres. In the poor visibility the red gate marks of the next course along, which was not being used at the time, looked very similar to the dark orange windward marks of the Finn course.

Zsombor Berecz briefly took the lead at the downwind gate, but then Jonathan Lobert, who had rounded the top mark third, moved ahead on the second upwind to lead back into the finish.

Scott had led up the first beat, but had also slightly overstood the top mark and lost his lead to round in sixth. He climbed back up to second on the second upwind leg, to follow Lobert downwind and across the finish. Mitakis sailed well to cross in third.

Scott completed an almost perfect day in the next race, to lead at every mark and win by 50 seconds. Mitakis again produced an outstanding performance in the challenging conditions to cross second, while Caleb Paine, from the USA, made up for the first race mistake with a third place finish. In contrast to the earlier race, there were fewer place changes, though again some boats overstood the first mark, heading for those unused marks on the Laser course area and giving away valuable distance.

Three sailors, Paine, Giorgio Poggi from Italy and Tapio Nirkko from Finland, filed protests for redress. The red marks were found to be approximately 100 metres to windward and 350 metres to the right of the Finn windward marks, but no redress was given. The jury determined that there was no improper action or omission from the Race Committee to justify redress.

COMPARED WITH TUESDAY, Scott was more upbeat, having now taken a lead he would never relinquish.

"Much better than yesterday. It was incredibly windy, top end that we would be in, 20-25 knots, big seas, made for really full on racing, but to come away with a second and a first is a lot more pleasing than my day yesterday for sure."

"It couldn't have been more different today. It was a big change in racing and approach and fortunately for me it came good today. The reason we race such long series is to do away with those particularly fickle races and tricky conditions."

After a poor start to his first Olympics, he said it was important not to panic.

"Going into the week you knew the difficult course would be on Sugarloaf and if you get that southerly condition it is incredibly tricky. I think I could have read too much into it, but it was nice to get into it today and have some different conditions and get away from the thoughts of yesterday. One of the things to remember is that the conditions inside the bay and outside were very different. Racing was a bit more predictable."

One of the other pre-regatta favourites who had struggled in the early races was Pieter-Jan Postma, but he said he thinks he could be back "in the game".

"It was a bit better than yesterday. I had a 12th and a fourth. I was near the front in the first one, and I was struggling a bit with speed but also with placing. You need to be in the shift, and in the gust. With the last race I was in the game, I need to build on that."

"The results are all over the place. It is hard but it doesn't matter if it's hard, as if it's hard it's challenging and that's good."

"But it was windy. Big waves. I even sailed three to one today. Most did I think. A tough day," he added, referring to holding the mainsheet through the three purchases instead of straight from the boom, as Finn sailors do in most conditions.

Mitakis's performance moved him up to fourth overall.

"It was a nice breeze for the Finns, and I think we had better weather conditions than the guys on the inside courses. I had two really good races. I had two good starts so I tried to play the shifts and find the clouds. Normally I am not in the top three in these conditions but I knew that I had good speed, so I knew I had to have good starts and then you are out of the pack."

Lobert, the 2012 Olympic bronze medalist struggled on the first day, but on the Wednesday he had followed his race win with a seventh, but he was still unhappy with himself.

"I was happy with the first race. My speed was good and I managed to sail well and I won. The second race I was leading again and expecting wind from the right hand side like happened in the first race. I had Giles behind me but I didn't look enough and a lot went to the left and we got this left shift and I lost everything. So a little mixed feelings today because I think I could have had a much better day. A seventh is not that good with the speed I had when you look at the beginning of the race. But it's part of the game and I look forward to tomorrow to try to come back."

Sailing in his first Olympics Jake Lilley, from Australia, had a better day.

"Two keepers. I didn't really have my best groove on and got a little bit of the phasing wrong early in both races but managed to grind away and get two keepers."

"I think the four races so far show two things, the level of the fleet and how difficult the conditions are here. It's pretty easy to make a mistake and then you lose 10-15 points. But it's a really long week and I liken it to racing the Tour de France as opposed to the 100 metres, and we're not even a third of the way through yet with a lot of racing to go, and a lot of things can happen."

On his first Olympic experience, "It's been really good so far, a really enjoyable experience, but in terms of racing it's tough as everyone is on peak form and racing really well. That's provides its challenges but it's really enjoyable and there's nothing else you'd rather be doing."

After making a great recovery in the first race from 12th to fourth, Jonas Høgh-Christensen had to pull out of the second race of the day just after the second windward mark because of a damaged sail.

"I pulled the clew ring out of the back of my sail so the sail is destroyed, which is a bit unfortunate. So I had to retire. We do have a spare but we have to figure out what went wrong and check all the sails. It was pretty crazy out there, 25-30 knots and big waves. It was great for the Finn, awesome conditions; I wish this were what was on TV. We had tonnes of wind."

THE CAPRICIOUSNESS OF Rio was clearly evident as the fleet was towed back inside Guanabara Bay towards the marina. The classes set to race inside had been plagued all day by very light and fickle winds leading to postponements and some dubious races.

Scott said, "It was quite nice to get some windy conditions to grunt up, it was really full-on racing. Rio was kind to us on the outside courses. When we towed in past in the races inside the bay it looked like a completely different world. It was quite surreal."

"It's incredibly changeable. We've spent an awful lot of days here, so to get conditions you've never seen before, like today, is pretty unlikely. I guess that's just Rio."

It was probably the toughest day on the water that many sailors had experienced for more than four years, but Rio was about to ramp it up one more level.

25

Magical Rio Turns it Up
for Finn Spectacular

Day 3 – Thursday 11 August

Tired and sore from the exertions of Wednesday, the sailors awoke on Thursday morning expecting a nice quiet day on the Escola Naval course area inside Guanabara Bay. However, due to the forecast conditions, the organisers had changed the schedule to put the Finns back out on the ocean again, this time on the Copacabana course area, as it was deemed too dangerous for the multihulls to sail on the sea, and they were kept inside the bay.

For those who struggled in big breeze and big waves, this was not good news. Second placed Vasilij Žbogar has survived Tuesday with a 7, 10, but was now facing the prospect of even tougher conditions. However he wasn't the only one and luckily for him, several of those who should have performed well on Thursday also struggled.

"I knew I would struggle in strong wind, because I just don't have as much strength as the others have. In my mind I knew that I had to get as less points as possible."

"I knew that inside the bay I had a very good chance because my boat speed was always very good, especially in conditions from 8-12 knots, which was the forecast for the inside, and all my results there were top five.

All the races outside I knew we were going to struggle, even if we didn't have strong winds. I was struggling with the big waves with settings of the boat but all I had in my mind was to realise that I am not good in those conditions. I just had to try getting as few points as possible and trying to sail as cleverly as possible. Make as few mistakes as possible."

"And the good thing you have to always understand, in this game you are not alone, so I was lucky that the others were also making mistakes in the strong winds. Some, for example Lobert, was definitely the fastest in the strongest winds and he made two very bad races for him and was out of the top 10 so you have to take account of this as well. I was a bit lucky on my side that the others didn't use their strength in their conditions."

FOR MANY OF the other sailors, dismay soon turned to delight as the conditions proved to be exceptional and allowed the Finn sailors excel at what they do best. The temperatures were back up to normal, and with the wind pushing past 25 knots, 2 to 3 metres waves, on an even larger swell, coming down the course, it was no day to be shy. The day provided all the ingredients for a gladiatorial battle at the extremes of what is sailable.

With the fickleness of Rio, it was also an important day as the following day was a lay day, with the wind forecast to drop. In Rio, when you are relying on the sea breeze, there is always a remote chance that further racing may not happen. So ending Thursday in good shape, ideally in a medal position was uppermost in most sailors' minds

The third day of racing proved to be a spectacular day of sailing with big winds, huge seas and even bigger stakes. Despite a huge, a potentially decisive mistake, Giles Scott moved into a 12-point lead at the top and Žbogar again hung onto second, while Zsombor Berecz, rocketed up the fleet to third after a great performance.

LOCAL SAILOR JORGE Zarif knew where he was going in the first race and headed inshore, to the right side of the course and out of the current to lead round the top mark from Berecz and Tapio Nirkko, of Finland. Berecz passed the Brazilian on the second upwind to take an emphatic win from Zarif and Nirkko.

One of those foiled by the adverse current was Scott, who initially headed offshore to the left before realising something was wrong. When he finally came back to the right the damage had been done and he rounded in 19th, and a very long way behind the leaders who had disappeared downwind on the current. His coach, Matt Howard had later admitted that he had got the current readings wrong, and had missed the weaker adverse current inshore because he hadn't gone far enough to reach the tide line, due to the limited time between arriving on the course area and the start time. Scott, however, was fast in these conditions and used his downwind speed to recover to 11th, but it was still going to be a counter after his 17th in the first race of the series.

The second race followed a similar format with perhaps slightly more wind and slightly larger waves. This time, Scott, got it right and, after passing Jake Lilley on the first downwind, led round the rest of course for an impressive win. Caleb Paine had rounded the first mark third and moved up to second at the finish, while Josh Junior crossed in third.

ZARIF EXPLAINED HIS tactics, "I think the secret today was to find a good line to cross to the right and I had a good line and good boat speed and I was lucky to cross fully to the right. And that's it. Less current, and more wind. And then in the second one I tried to tack as soon as could after the start, but I was too late already." He finished 18th.

Scott, "There was a huge gain on the right hand side of the course all day today and I was pretty slow to realise that on the first leg and let the fleet get to the right of me." After languishing at the back of the fleet for the first lap, he "…managed to come back to 11th which was damage limitation, but then to come back and win the next race was all I could ask for really."

The performer of the day was Junior, with a 5, 2, who was very animated about his performance. "I finally found the front today – far out!"

"It was a really breezy day with big waves out there. I managed to change a few things and finally got my boat going a bit faster and sailed a lot better, so I'm stoked."

One of the pre-regatta favourites, Junior was still down in 14th overall. He said his problems were caused by poor boat speed and bad decision making. "Not very good speed leads to bad decisions and bad decisions lead to more bad decision. But I think we'll just keep trying to turn that around and see what happens."

"A medal is lot on now. I'm just trying to get as much up the fleet as possible, race as many good races as possible and see what happens from there."

One of the first time Olympians in Rio was Tom Ramshaw from Canada. He said he was really enjoying the Olympic experience.

"I just want to do as well as I can but I didn't really have any results expectations. It was a long shot to get here in the first place. I have missed a couple of small things in pretty much every race so hopefully I can just execute a little better and finish each race strong."

"It's awesome being here. I'm just trying to soak everything in and sail as hard as I can. I don't want to leave here with any regrets. For the next quad I am going to have four years of preparation rather than just one so I hope to be on podium, or on top of the podium for the next one so being here is a lot about getting the experience."

"I was happy with my first race." He placed ninth. "In the second race I slowed down a bit but still happy with how I sailed."

On the possibility of lighter days ahead, "I think I have a little potential to do better when it's lighter, but I am enjoying the breeze too. It was a fun day. You can't ask for better sailing conditions really. That was the ultimate conditions for sailing a Finn for sure."

Berecz described the day as, "…the greatest day in my sailing career. I can't be happier than this. I was a bit disappointed in the morning when they moved us from the inside course to the outside. We knew it would be windy and choppy again today as we expected more wind and bigger waves. But as we were on Copacabana we only had the waves coming from one direction so it was more manageable than yesterday."

"I had a great first race. We had a plan. We executed it, and it worked, because I won the race."

"In the second one I didn't have a good start but managed to hang with the guys and I was around seventh all the way, and I am super happy with that."

"We have four more tough races and for sure it's going to be light, which I am happy about because I am quite tired now. So we'll see what this brings for us. My dream is getting close. We will not change anything; we will just keep the routine."

The fleet was being propped up by Allan Julie, from Seychelles, sailing his fifth Olympics and the first in a Finn, after four Olympics in the Laser. "In the Laser I was always having to diet to keep the weight down, in Finn I can eat whatever I want. It's a good feeling when you look back over all of the achievements. I'm enjoying this, but a fifth Olympics is an achievement for myself."

He said that the support from back home was encouraging him. "It's a great feeling because it's the Olympics. I have millions of spectators watching me sail and have everybody from Seychelles cheering for me."

HOWEVER THE DRAMA was not over yet, as Paine was disqualified in Race 6 following a protest by Ivan Kljaković Gašpić, from Croatia, who had finished eighth in the race. The following hearings, requests for redress and the evidence presented, created a drama that would follow both sailors through to the final fateful race.

The substance of Kljaković Gašpić's protest was that he had altered course while on starboard tack at the very start of Race 6, to avoid colliding with Paine. Both boats, along with Junior and Lilley had started right at the pin end, where there was a 10-degree line bias. After tacking, Junior and Lilley had ducked Kljaković Gašpić, but Paine had crossed in front, allegedly causing Kljaković Gašpić to change course, bearing 'away hard' to avoid contact, and then tacking himself to clear the pin end boat. Without witnesses to dispute the Croatian claim, the jury found that Paine had failed to keep clear and disqualified him from the race for breaking Rule 10.

It was a crushing blow for Paine as it dropped him from fourth to 14th overall. Paine maintained his innocence and starting looking for evidence. There were plenty of TV cameras out on the course, so surely someone had filmed the start of the race? It would take two more days before the matter was finally resolved.

THOUGH SCOTT WAS leading the regatta at the half way stage, "I wouldn't say it makes me feel comfortable. I'm pleased to be leading at the half way stage but I'm very much aware of how much further we have to go."

"At the Olympic Games everyone is at their best, it's the one everyone wants to win so it's incredibly hard-fought. The person who manages to do that is certainly going to have to fight for it."

While Scott extended his lead to 12 points, Žbogar survived a second windy day to remain in second. Berecz's brilliant day moved him up to third. With Paine disqualified for the time being, Pieter-Jan Postma was up to fourth, with Jonas Høgh-Christensen in fifth, despite a day of two tenth places. Only 10 points separated third to tenth, so there was still a lot of racing to go.

One downside of the fleet being moved from the Escola Naval course area to Copacabana, was that it lost its live TV slot, something that it would not regain in the days to come. So while the fleet had some spectacular racing at sea, TV viewers had to watch other fleets drifting around the harbour.

With the first half the Olympic competition over, the sailors were rewarded with a day off on Friday 12 August. It was a day of reflection for some, of regrouping for others, and most importantly a day of recovery, after two extreme days of sailing on Rio's stormy waters.

26

A Day to Recover and Reflect
First reserve day – Friday 12 August

The break in racing allowed gear to be checked, bodies to heal and strategies to be re-evaluated. After three days of dramatically contrasting and brutal Finn racing, the results showed a vastly different pattern to normal. Granted, the favourite Giles Scott was where everyone expected him to be, but he knew as well as anyone that it was a precarious position when racing in Rio.

No one had been anywhere near what could be called consistent. All the sailors had scores in the top and bottom half of the fleet. Nine sailors had letter scores already. The only constant was that there was no constant. It was a constantly changing field, with huge place changes following each race.

But, that also meant the podium was still wide open. Some sailors and pundits had already commented that the gold was now Scott's to lose, but he was only 12 points ahead and on Thursday had collected 12 points. If there was a constant it was that he had led for two days, but with the next four races expected to be held in light and tricky conditions, no one was laying any bets.

Scott commented, "I think the important thing to remember is that everyone has big scores now. I don't think there is one person who has been massively consistent so you really have to fight for every single position, no matter where you find yourself. There is still a long way to go and it's going to be tough."

His 17th in Race 1 would haunt him all the way to the end of the opening series, a little bomb waiting to go off should he make any more mistakes.

Second overall Vasilij Žbogar was satisfied with his performance. He knew the windy races would be make or break for him. He survived, almost, though said he would spend the lay day sleeping – all day – to recover. He is at least 10 years older than most of the fleet and is feeling the pain more than most, but he pushed it away with a smile and a joke. He was happy to be in second.

Hungarian rocket Zsombor Berecz was one of the fastest in training two weeks before, and won the training regatta, so his form was no surprise. Except for a start line error in the second race, he would have been only be four points adrift of Scott at this stage, rather than 15.

Interestingly the sentimentalist's favourite, Pieter-Jan Postma had the lowest 'worst score' of a 14th. In the last three races he had started to make his move, find some form and move up. In London he finished fourth, missing a medal by a single error. What he failed to do in 2012, could he manage in 2016?

London silver medalist Jonas Høgh-Christensen had not had the regatta that he imagined so far either. A broken sail in Race 4 meant a retirement, but he remained in fifth. With just four points separating fourth to ninth, he could not afford any more upsets. In fact there were just 11 points between third and 11th. The battle to make the medal race looked likely to be intense and probably quite scrappy.

While many sailors had spent a lot of time in Rio over the past three years, the jury was still out on whether that had actually made their job easier. Of the top three, only Scott had spent excessive time in Rio. But all the training in the world couldn't limit unforeseen random events. Silver medalist at the 2015 test event Tapio Nirkko broke his rudder in Thursday's extreme conditions, while several sailors were sick and unable to sail to their full potential, especially in the brutal conditions over the previous few days.

Four races remained before the medal race cut would be made. Weather forecasts showed light winds for these two days, with the racing originally scheduled for Copacabana and Niterói course areas, both outside the bay, though a change was expected.

THREE DAYS OF crazy racing had taken their toll. The slumped shoulders around the dinghy park told a tale of disappointment about how it can all go wrong so quickly. After just three days, four years of training seemed a high price to pay for such a reversal of fortunes, but there can only ever be one winner.

The gold medal was still a long way off but many dreams were already in tatters at the expense of Rio's extremely tricky and challenging conditions. A lot of the sailors had overused the word 'tricky' to describe the sailing conditions in Rio. Here's what they said that meant in practice.

Scott, who suffered on the first day said, "Very unpredictable, the wind comes and goes and it just makes it incredibly hard for us to predict what move to make next."

It is manageable, but, "With difficultly. Some days you get it right and some days you get it wrong. And that's true from race to race. And that has showed in the results so far."

Jake Lilley commented, "I would say there's no consistency. When you think you've got it figured out God's going to change the plan on you. That's how I'd describe it. It's not straightforward in any way. You have to be constantly adapting to a changing playing field. It's challenging, but it has its rewards and that is what makes this venue so great, and at the end of a long week the best guy is going to stand on top of the podium."

Jonathan Lobert has had his share of ups and downs so far. "Tricky means that you never know what can happen and means that you are never sure of anything. So you should sail more closely to the other guys and try not to get too much distance between them."

While Scott remained the favourite, he remains unassuming. Great Britain had won Olympic gold in the Finn class for the previous 16 years, first with Iain Percy in Sydney in 2000 and then with Ben Ainslie in Athens, Beijing and London.

"It's been in British hands since 2000 and I'd like to keep it that way obviously, but I wouldn't say that gives me any more pressure. I put pressure on myself to win anyway regardless what's gone on before me. If anything it is a good thing. We've had a pathway put in front of us from 2000 from Iain Percy and since then it's been a constant evolution, and especially over the past four years."

Meanwhile the Croatia-USA protest rumbled on with Paine finding new video evidence from footage recorded by the Olympic Broadcasting Service (OBS). David Dellenbaugh, rules advisor for the US team, requested the jury to reopen the hearing and look at the video evidence. The request for reopening was not held until 18.30 on Friday evening, with the jury taking the decision to reopen after the rights holders released the footage, which was not available to the jury the previous day. However, the reopening would not be held until after racing the following day, Saturday, so Paine, while extremely confident that he had enough evidence to refute Kljaković Gašpić's claims, had another 24 hours of uncertainty.

As the sailors prepared for the final four races of the opening series, only one thing was certain, and that was that it would be a tough fight all the way to the finish.

27

Giles Scott Extends After Incredibly Close Racing
Day 4 – Saturday 13 August

Once again, a course area change produced a very different day to what everyone expected. Originally scheduled for the Copacabana course area, everyone expected a change back to the Escola Naval course area and a day of live TV Finn coverage. But instead the fleet was moved to the Ponte course, the furthest course area inside Guanabara Bay.

It produced some of the closest racing possible with packs of boats crossing the finish line together, with barely any air between them. If any day could be said to have demarcated the medal race landscape, then this would be the one. There was little more margin for error. Most fates were sealed on Saturday 13 August.

The day belonged to three sailors, who were the only ones to get two low results all day. Giles Scott extended his lead to 17 points after a clinical performance with a 1,3. Vasilij Žbogar consolidated second overall with a 5, 4, while Jake Lilley rose up to third after a 3, 5.

But the racing was just so incredibly close; the day could have come out very differently. After 50 minutes of full-on racing, these world-class athletes were separated by just seconds. No one gave an inch. Every inch was fought for very hard and there was no let up until the line was crossed.

The right-hand side was clearly the preferred choice, but the reality was subtly different with gains to be made on the left and also in the middle. Lilley led round the top mark in Race 7, but Scott soon took the lead on the first downwind to extend around the course for a 30 second win, the biggest boat-to-boat margin of the day. Behind him it could not have been closer, with the whole fleet no more than 70 seconds apart. There were some big movers within the fleet though with Jorge Zarif coming through from 15th at the top to take second place at the final downwind mark to lead Lilley into the finish by just three seconds.

Žbogar finished a solid fifth, but it looked like Paine's Games were over with a 17th. Perhaps the mental energy expended in fighting the protest had got to him, even though he was bullish on the outside.

Race 8 was almost as close, with all boats finishing within 100 seconds. Jonas Høgh-Christensen found the top mark first after favouring the left side, but it all went horribly wrong from there in, losing 15 places before the finish. He later complained of picking up some debris in the water. Pieter-Jan Postma rounded in second and took the lead on the first downwind, never to be threatened again. Josh Junior was the biggest climber, coming through from 11th at the first mark to second at the finish, while Scott extended his lead overall with a third place finish, just seconds ahead of Žbogar.

Paine did his cause no harm with a seventh, while Ivan Kljaković Gašpić produced a 4,10 to keep the pressure on the top.

SCOTT EXPLAINED THE day. "Rio really delivered some great conditions for us. Nice clear skies, the sea breeze kicked in, the wind funnelled straight down the bay, with a nice and clean 12 knots. Really nice sailing."

"It's nice to put in consistent results at the top of the fleet. I think myself and Vasilij had a good day today and behind that there were a few guys that were up and down."

"Having the points margin is a big confidence booster, but the thing for me to focus on is that it isn't over, you can't get complacent, you need to attack tomorrow, like I've done today. Nothing really changed, but clearly having that margin is the place to be. There's still a lot to play for."

Žbogar was very happy, almost relieved, with two top fives. "To make these two results keeps me alive. I have some chance if it is light tomorrow. First I need to get into the medal race and then the points will be very close. What is incredible is how compact the fleet is, how we are battling for half a metre. Before we were battling for 10 metres, now it is less than one metre. And you cannot make even a small mistake; we all crossed the finish in a minute. This has never happened before in the Finn class. The level is extremely high and to push, you have to push all the time. You make a wrong gybe and two boats go by. It's nice from my side because it really close racing and it's tough, but it's exhausting as well."

While the top two boats remained the same for the third consecutive day, the new owner of third overall was Lilley. He was keeping calm and not taking anything for granted. "It doesn't matter; we will take it one race at a time. Everyone has big scores, so anything can happen."

"We had a different day compared to the last few days. Very tight tactical racing and it was good to put some low scores together. Hopefully more of the same tomorrow. We will just focus on our processes and try to put as few points as possible on the board."

Kljaković Gašpić, a triple European champion, has been steady most of the week, but consistency was now paying dividends as he rose though the ranks. He ended the day in fifth overall.

"It's exciting, and I should say it's not easy to sail as the competition is really fierce. Everyone is performing really well, as expected, and the differences are very minor. We can only see Giles a little bit in front, and Vasilij is showing quite a consistent performance and steady sailing. Everyone else is going up and down a lot, which is showing a good level. Everyone has high expectations and we are all pushing really hard but at such a level you can always make a few mistakes. It's the same for me."

"Since the beginning I have been struggling a bit, but am now on a steady pace and today I was quite consistent. Only in the last race I made a bad choice on a gate and I lost around 150 meters. And this was hard to recover, but I managed to stay in the top 10 by just inches. I am satisfied, but not really happy because I know I could have done the second race better."

"Tomorrow we have two more races in lighter wind, in which I can perform quite well, so let's hope we get some racing."

One place behind was Zarif. "It's been very hard. I live here and I sailed here for 15 years and sometimes I don't know what goes on here. It's hard to predict."

"The races are also very close. Everyone is now good on the downwind, as opposed to a few years ago. Also, except for Giles everyone has a lot of different results. The important thing is to be close to the top guys going into the last day."

After some ups and downs this week, Postma was pretty happy to win the last race. "A better last race. You know it was such hard work and it's so close racing. It's amazingly close racing. It's hard."

"The first downwind I won three or four places, the second downwind I lost 10. And the last two I extended. So for me it's not automatic. I need to work, fight for every place. And at the mark roundings everyone was super close."

"It will be a fight until the last moments. A lot of respect for Vasilij and Giles. There's very little in it."

"But good to get a win in. Happy with the last one."

At the end of the day Caleb Paine was reinstated into his second place in Race 6 after the protest from Kljaković Gašpić was thrown out.

With Kljaković Gašpić failing to turn up to the hearing, the new video evidence submitted showed Paine clearly crossing ahead of the Croatian boat by more than six feet. Kljaković Gašpić, who was heading to just clear the bow of the pin end boat, luffed slightly aiming at Paine's after starboard side quarter to try to prevent him from crossing. He then bore away slightly and tacked to clear the pin boat. The evidence shed new light on the incident from what was heard at the initial hearing and the Croatian protest was dismissed. Paine was reinstated into his second place in Race 6 and moved back up to seventh overall, and within 12 points of the podium.

With just 14 points separating seventh to 14th, there was still some tough racing to be done, and there was just one day left to make a claim on the medal race.

28

Brilliant Scott Assured Gold With Race to Spare

Day 5 – Sunday 14 August

Taking no more time than was strictly needed, it was all over with a day to spare. Giles Scott assured himself of gold after another brilliant performance that left him 24 points clear at the top after the fifth day of racing. Vasilij Žbogar still remained in second, 13 points ahead of the new third-place holder, Ivan Kljaković Gašpić. Once again, on the final day of the opening series, Rio's challenging conditions provided a mixed bag of results, with several sailors picking up high scores.

There had been no clear form through the fleet apart from Scott and Žbogar, but it was always going to be a scrap to the finish, with the points around the medal race cut off very, very close. For the fifth day in a row it was all change once again after perhaps the toughest day on the water, at least mentally, if not physically. It wasn't so much physically tough, as the wind remained light all day, but mentally it was exhausting, even to just watch as the sailors rose and fell through the fleet like snakes and ladders on probably the trickiest day the fleet had to endure. The day began with a long postponement, first ashore and then afloat to wait for the wind to arrive, and when it did, it remained patchy and difficult to predict.

The fleet was back on the Niterói course area, in a vastly different environment to four days earlier.

Despite being frustrated and disappointed about having his protest against Paine thrown out the previous evening, Kljaković Gašpić was determined to make his stance on the water. He started his day well leading round the top mark in Race 9, in very light winds. He was passed on the second upwind by Race 1 winner, Facundo Olezza, who maintained the lead all the way to the finish, to win by just three seconds. Alejandro Foglia, who had rounded the top mark in 12th, finally found his speed to cross in third.

Many sailors were baffled by the new set of conditions. Jake Lilley was third overall going into the day, but he crossed last after never really recovering from a poor first upwind. But he was just sweeping up a long list of sailors who found themselves at the wrong end of the fleet.

The final race for 13 of the sailors, the final opening series race, Race 10, was little better but it was better as the wind started to build and stabilise.

After a pretty shocking week, Foglia then went on to win Race 10. Paine led round the first lap, only for Scott to take the lead on the second upwind. Then Foglia, who had rounded the first mark in seventh found his pace and took the lead on the final downwind to lead across the finish from Scott, while Ioannis Mitakis ended the race where he started, in third.

Meanwhile Olezza followed up his Race 9 win with a seventh to climb back into the top 10 again. The last place for Jake Lilley in Race 9 initially dropped him out of the top 10, after going into the day in third, but then, Pieter-Jan Postma was disqualified from Race 10 following a protest from Olezza, after an incident on the start line when they had touched. This meant Lilley gained one point to overtake Mitakis, and the Australian was back in the top 10 and could sail in the medal race.

In addition, both Paine and Max Salminen, of Sweden had closed on the top and were now within striking distance of the podium.

TO MAKE SURE of the gold with a day to spare, Scott had to gain three points on Žbogar during the day. In Race 9, Scott looked to have opened out a nice margin, only to lose ground on the second upwind and finish just one place ahead of his main rival. But the points margin had increased to 18 points and most of his other rivals had picked up high scores.

So in the final race, Scott just had to finish more than two boats ahead of Žbogar to win the gold with a race to spare. For a while Žbogar was right behind Scott, but he made a few errors on the second upwind, let Scott escape, and the gold was gone.

Scott crossed the line with his head in his hands, in a highly emotional state after having a small blub after realising what he had achieved. The press boats were crowded round the finish line, waiting expectantly, waiting for him to do something, anything, a display of emotion that would encapsulate the last four years; coming back from the huge disappointment for him of losing the trials for 2012; the mammoth effort since then to be almost unbeatable.

For a while everyone thought it was business as usual and he wasn't going to react. He made the press wait so long – it was probably only a minute or so – they actually started calling to him to do something. They wanted their photo opportunity.

Finally he stood up, threw his arms in the air and let out a huge, unexpected, pent up roar, releasing all the nervous energy of the previous few days. It shattered the tranquil waters off Niterói as the sun was beginning to set behind Sugarloaf, throwing a golden veil over the fleet as they began the long tow back to the Marina da Glória. He had sealed his place in Olympic history; the job was done and the interviews with the circling TV boats could begin.

ASKED WHAT IT meant to him to win the Olympic title, a normally unemotional Scott said, "I know what it meant to me because of the way it made me feel towards the last stages of that final race. I just found myself welling up and in tingles as it slowly dawned on me what I'd done. I wouldn't put myself down as the emotional sort but I had a little cry to myself, which I like to think I don't do that often. Just the emotions that come out of you in that situation, you can't prepare yourself for. It's been amazing."

"When we put the campaign together after London, Matt [Howard], my coach and I we decided that we wanted to campaign flat out. We weren't going to go soft in any regattas and everything we went to, we wanted to win and win it in style."

"That approach is great but it does put a target on your back, especially two or three years out. That target inevitably gets closer as everybody ups their game. To have been able to maintain that gap to win the Olympics with a race to spare – it gives great justification to those decisions earlier on."

A clearly exhausted Žbogar commented, "It was a really difficult day, really stressful because the wind was up and down. Puffs of wind were all over the race area and it was impossible to predict, so very tough mentally. I tried to be conservative playing the middle, and I lost a few places there in both races. But at the end I think I managed to have two good races, which was really good in these conditions."

"In the first race if there were not the big waves, it would have been easy sailable, but the waves made it almost impossible. It was up and down and was a bit of a lottery at the end. And many guys were ahead and in a few moments lost everything."

For the first time in the regatta, Kljaković Gašpić had moved into a podium position. "The first race was quite light, but for me was regular. There were big differences on the downwind in pressure and positions so it was not easy to sail. I was lucky being extended on the front so I didn't have this headache, but for other guys it was quite tough."

"The second one was tragic for me. I was just getting extra points for nothing and making my life more complicated that it should have been. Right from the start everything started to get complicated and when racing gets complicated it's never good. And then the wind picked up and distances got that much bigger and it got harder to recover. On the second beat I went on the left side to get more pressure and it didn't come, and I lost even more places." He finished 13th.

"But at the end of the day I am still in a good position. I need to sleep and relax and get ready for Tuesday."

Scott still had to sail, and finish, Tuesday's medal race, but the result would be irrelevant. He could not be beaten. Mathematically, any boat in the top 10 could win a medal, but that would need some letter scores. Žbogar was almost secure for a medal. To lose a medal, he would have had to be last, with Paine or Salminen winning. Kljaković Gašpić in third, was just five points ahead of Paine and Salminen, so the question on everyone's lips was would the Croatian attack for silver or try to defend the bronze?

WHILE TUESDAY'S MEDAL race, would decide where the silver and bronze medals will go, Giles Scott had the privilege to enjoy the occasion, and savour the moment.

"If you'd have asked me, would I have won the Olympic Games before the medal race, I'd have said absolutely not because of the venue that it is. It's such a privileged situation to be in because for everybody else who is going to be fighting it out for those medals; it's going to be incredibly stressful and to be able to say I'm not going to have to go through that is pretty nice."

"The venue that it is," has proved tricky and unpredictable in the extremes and even caught out Scott on a number of occasions, most notably in the opening race when he had a fight on just to finish in 17th place. After that it was been sublime sailing from the four-time world champion, with just one more race outside the top 10, and seven times in the top three.

Even if all the predictions were for him to win, it was still a surprise, even to him, to have managed to achieve it in quite that manner. Even his predecessor, Ben Ainslie, always managed to spin it out to the final moments before claiming victory. Perhaps this was an accurate reflection of Scott's usually calm and casual style: no stress, no drama, just get the job done in the most efficient way.

Vasilij Žbogar's dream was to end his remarkable Olympic career with a third medal. Žbogar was the oldest Finn sailor in Rio and was the oldest in the medal race by some six years. He had felt the demands of Rio on his body more than most of the fleet, but his experience paid off and he would go into the medal race with an 18 point buffer on fourth place.

After two medals in the Laser class, a third medal in Rio seemed almost certain, but, "You know about medal races, anything can happen and we need to keep our eyes open and fight as much as possible. I cannot go into a match race; that would be impossible, so I need to talk with the team how I will manage the race."

Perhaps more than anyone else, Žbogar is a fighter. He never gives up. He had stood on the podium in numerous events over the previous four years since finishing sixth at London 2012, and the conditions in Rio, while taxing him physically, had suited his sailing style, proven by the fact that he had been in first or second overall all week long.

Third placed Ivan Kljaković Gašpić was at his third Games and was still without a medal. He had won three European Championships between 2009 and 2015 and countless medals at other events, but an Olympic medal continued to elude him. Consistency was always going to be key in Rio, and after 10 races he was in the bronze medal position with only one top-three race result. That was something unusual, however even Žbogar had only finished in the top three in two races.

After a reasonably consistent start, Gašpić started to rack up a few top places, more than his main rivals, to put himself into a great position for the medal race. While he would have one eye on silver, he would also be looking out for the sailors very close behind him and challenging for the bronze.

That included Caleb Paine, who was just five points back. Paine had a very inconsistent week, counting results from second to 17th, but after a strong finish on Sunday he had put himself back into contention for a medal.

"There have been a lot of ups and downs but it's always good to finish on a great day. There is still a lot of racing to be had in the medal race and I'm just looking forward to finishing it off and hopefully getting a medal in the end."

On the importance of getting reinstated into Race 6, "It's huge. It was one of those things, but it was great that it got righted and I got the position that I earned."

He felt he had a good shot at a medal. "I feel great. I always come from behind and I never stop fighting regardless of the situation I am in. I've thought it through and know how to deal with it and hopefully we'll get it done."

Max Salminen was on equal points with Paine. Like many, he started slowly and then began to make ground mid-regatta to finish strongly to make the medal race cut.

"Slow start and catching up? Yes, that's me unfortunately. They call me the diesel engine."

"We expected mixed conditions and we got very mixed conditions. Maybe surprisingly mixed actually but all in all, a little bit like we expected."

"I am happy with my progress through the week. It took a while to get into it and really find a focus and drive in the boat. Since then it's only gone better and better. The years training here have certainly helped, especially on Saturday and Sunday where we got conditions that we were more expecting."

On his chances in the medal race, "The first thing to say is that I am really happy just to be here and competing for a medal after a quite long way, and progressing after four years. It's cool to be here. I just need to tie the bag up [apparently that's a Swedish expression for wrap it up] and finish on a good note."

One of the sailors who had been notably quiet all week was Josh Junior. Predicted by many to be a certain medal prospect, and perhaps even topple Scott, he struggled all week, but a late surge left him in the medal race with an outside chance of medalling.

"I'm pretty stoked to make the medal race. A few days ago it was going to be a struggle just to make the medal race and now I am in the medal race with a shot at a medal. It's just a great opportunity."

"It was very frustrating not to be able to hit my groove from the start, but you live and you learn." He added that it was not so much about getting to grips with the conditions, but "I think it's just me sailing better and executing what I knew how to do."

Junior was in seventh, 15 points off bronze. A medal was perhaps a bit of a stretch, but not impossible. Of the others in with a chance of the medal, Jorge Zarif was sixth, 11 points from bronze. A former world champion, and sailing on his home waters, he had been flummoxed by the conditions as much as his competitors.

At the bottom of the top 10, Facundo Olezza, Pieter-Jan Postma and Jake Lilley were all 18 points off bronze. While mathematically possible, a medal was pretty unlikely.

Olezza was at his first Olympics and the youngest sailor in the fleet. He excelled in the lighter winds, winning two races, but struggled in the big breeze and big waves outside Guanabara Bay.

"It feels weird. I work a lot but I'm new to the class so I was not expecting too much from this. I don't know how I'm feeling. This is new for me. This feels great, but it's weird."

It had not been a good week at all for Postma, another of the pre-regatta favourites and the reigning European champion. He had opened his week by hitting the pin end boat after a risky start in Race 1. In Race 10 he infringed Olezza, who was overlapped and to leeward, when he bore away at the start to speed up. When Postma luffed, the port side of his boat touched Olezza's body. After a 19th in Race 9 and a disqualification in Race 10, his medal hopes had disappeared in the fickle Rio breeze. His flamboyant, risk-taking style had cost him dearly, and we went on to pick up another starting error in the medal race, causing him to return and restart the race in last place.

GILES SCOTT HAD been through a lot to get to this point and in the eyes of the fleet deserved this medal more than most. Any other result would have been a travesty. His elation and relief was palpable, a testimony to the hard hours that preceded an amazing victory.

"It's been a dream of mine for so long. I can't quite believe that I've managed to put together the regatta I have, to come away and win the Olympics with a race to spare."

"It's been a long road. I campaigned properly for London, missed out on the qualification for that, and that was bitterly disappointing. Watching all of my friends racing at the Olympics and get medals wasn't easy, but the amazing thing that came off the back of it was a desire to right the wrongs I felt I made, and to put together a campaign I could be proud of."

"Coming down the last reach in that last race, I didn't quite know what to make of it. I'm not the emotional sort, but I started crying. It's such a weird, but amazing thing to go through."

"It's incredible."

29

Sugar Coated Ending for Žbogar and Paine

Day 6 – Tuesday 16 August

The Sugarloaf course in Guanabara Bay was where the Finns had started racing one week previously, and it was where the 2016 Olympic Sailing Competition would end, with the silver and bronze medals being decided over a 30 minute race. The area was renowned for its tricky, unpredictable conditions, and the medal race was no different, though perhaps slightly less unpredictable than normal.

With Giles Scott's gold medal already secure, he was able to sail round and enjoy the race without worrying about his position, almost a lap of honour.

Second overall, Vasilij Žbogar had a 13-point cushion to third, and an 18-point cushion to fourth. The only way he could lose a medal would be to finish last with Caleb Paine or Max Salminen winning the race.

Ivan Kljaković Gašpić went into the medal race in third overall, but both Paine and Salminen were only five points behind. Paine and Salminen needed to put two boats between themselves and Kljaković Gašpić and beat the other over the water to win a medal.

Before the Finn medal race, both Laser fleets sailed their medal races, so the sailors had plenty of opportunity to analyse the course area off Flamengo Beach and see what the wind was doing.

The sea breeze, blowing from out of the south, had filled in at around 10-12 knots. As was usual for this direction the left side of the course was paying, but as the fleet had found out in Race 1, the right can sometimes pay later in the day, especially if the wind direction is further west of south. The towering peak of Sugarloaf Mountain stood behind the windward mark, a 400-metre high granite monolith directly in the path of the sea breeze.

As the medal race began, Pieter-Jan Postma was called back after starting early at the pin. Some commentators also judged Žbogar over the line, but he was confident, clear and away. Kljaković Gašpić also started near the pin while Paine started in the middle.

Most of the fleet favoured the left, as expected. Paine was forced to bail out and ducked several boats and ended up heading towards the right. He took several hitches back towards the middle before ending up close to the starboard layline. His fate was sealed and, for a while it looked like he was trailing behind the pack on the left, but he only needed one break to capitalise on the leverage he had created and it came along at just the right moment. It was a risky strategy but it paid off handsomely. He had seen some pressure over on the right side and working towards it, he was eventually rewarded with a monster shift, which he tacked into and was lifted into the first mark with a 30 second jump on the fleet.

The chase was soon on with the chasing pack being led by Jorge Zarif and Jake Lilley. Scott was fourth and had moved up to second by the first gate. Salminen had rounded sixth, Kljaković Gašpić in seventh and Žbogar in eighth. It was all still on.

With Paine leading the race, Žbogar had to make sure he was not last, otherwise he would drop to bronze position. He rounded the top mark close on Gašpić's stern, but gybed early and passed him downwind, before taking another boat on the following beat to eventually cross the finish in sixth to take the silver with ease.

Trying to recover from the first upwind, when he was stranded on the left, Salminen again went looking for a favourable shift on the left side, and never found anything to be able to get back into the race. He ended up a very disappointed eighth.

Kljaković Gašpić dropped two places on the first downwind and another on the second beat to cross the line in last place, his Olympic medal dreams in tatters once again.

At the front, Paine cruised away to an easy victory. With both Gašpić and Salminen in the second half of the fleet, he had one hand on the bronze by the first mark. On the second upwind, he maintained his lead, covering the fleet to the right. Several boats tried the left again, and if a serious wind shift had come in from the left, he could have been threatened, but he looked to have everything under control.

As he came into the finish, looking back for the first time to count the places, the realisation of what he had done dawned on him and his smile got bigger and bigger, until he crossed the finish with a whoop of joy, fist in the air.

Ninety seconds later, Žbogar's emotion was equally intense. As he crossed the finish line in sixth he looked as if he was not quite sure what he had achieved and how to react. But soon the emotion, relief and joy overcame him, with his arms held aloft. His Dinghy Academy teammate, Facundo Olezza, who finished seventh in the medal race, soon joined him on board his Finn to congratulate the new silver medalist.

In all the excitement it was easy to forget about Scott. For him the medal race was largely a formality. He had chased down the leaders and given a master class in downwind sailing, crossing just 20 seconds after Paine in the 23-minute race.

With Oscar flag flying to signify free pumping, allowing the competitors to rock, pump and ooch, the aerial cameras illustrated the acrobatics of the Finn fleet perfectly, the powerful and yet acutely graceful manoeuvres to catch and surf the waves, with the 100 kg sailors pushing around 140kg of Finn through the water with extreme skills and finesse. In these conditions, Scott schooled the fleet in a downwind demonstration that was pure poetry in motion. His dominance of the boat was a joy to behold as he slid past Lilley and Zarif and set off after Paine. Scott closed the gap, but perhaps it was fitting that the final race victory went to Paine.

AFTERWARDS, PAINE EXPLAINED how he felt at that moment.

"It's pretty awesome, it's been a pretty tough regatta and to be able to come away with a medal at the end is a great feeling. It was a tough push and a hard medal race but fortunately enough it makes it easier when you hit the right shifts off the bat and I just had to make sure I didn't mess it up."

"I knew if I got ahead and won the race, things would become a lot easier. I was fortunate to establish a lead right ahead of time and let everyone else make mistakes and I sailed the best race I could."

"My initial plan was actually to go a bit left but I but saw quite a bit of pressure coming down the right side of the course so I looked for the duck on Giles and hitched up and was fortunate to catch the pressure all the way and was continuously playing that right side up the beat. I would sail out of it and then tack to sail back into it. On a couple of the courses here in Rio it actually pays to overstand just because it shifts so much and being in the pressure pays so much."

"It's been a tough battle for me even to get to the Olympics. We never stopped fighting until the end and we're fortunate enough to get a medal and I think my past experiences have got me here."

"I've worked on this a long time, I've been sailing for a very long time so being able to get things to come together at the right time is what it's all about. I'm just happy to come away with a third, but I look forward to maybe down the line coming back again and going for gold."

IN WINNING THE Finn silver medal in Rio, Žbogar joined a select group of sailors who had won three or more Olympic medals.

He commented, "I feel relieved. I feel relieved that it's over. It just went well. I was only dreaming of it one week ago. I feel very happy because it's in a different class. The first two were in a Laser, this is in Finn. I am by far the oldest sailor in the Finn and this result is even more meaningful. My body is a bit old and I was struggling over the last few years but I continued pushing all the time. Fortunately, my mind is still 20 years old and I pushed every race as much as I could."

"I managed to survive the week and I just wanted to be in with a chance of a medal. I had nothing to gain in the race; I had everything to lose, as Giles had gold. There was a small chance I could lose it. I knew I couldn't push too much but I did anyway. Second place for me is something unbelievable."

"I'm just very tired. The week was very hard and of course I'm very happy that everything is finished in a good way with second place, which for me is a dream. I'm extremely proud and happy to be able to sail very consistently all week, to get a medal. That's my last one, I'm finished now."

"There were a lot of sacrifices, especially the last two years. I didn't do anything except focus on sailing and try to improve day by day and I left everything; my family, and things I would like to do, because when you focus on training and achievement you need to rest and train. I've been doing that for the past two years and to be able to come out of that with a good result of course is extremely rewarding."

He said the key to surviving the week was to sail as smart as possible. "I was trying to just survive. I did survive and on the last day I just wanted to challenge for the medals. I knew I had to be careful on the starting line, I could only lose, I had nothing to gain."

Speaking about the spectators cheering from the beach. He added, "It was good for the public to see that the Finn is a really tough class."

234 | Between a Rock and a Hard Race

SCOTT WAS BACK to his normal, casual, largely unemotional self. He rounded the top mark fourth, was soon up to third, then second and was chasing, and catching, Paine down the final run. A wave of acknowledgement as he crossed the finish line marked the end of his Olympics and the affirmation of the gold medal. The job was done.

"It was great to be able to go out and enjoy that race today. The 17th place in Race 1 on the Sugarloaf course was not the way I wanted to start the regatta and it wasn't until day three or four that I started to believe that the gold was in my grasp. Winning four world championships is great, but this is one that everyone wants and everyone remembers, so now to have an Olympic gold is a great feeling."

"I've been trying to get to the Olympic Games for at least two cycles so to qualify for Rio firstly was a huge deal for me and then obviously to come here and win is just fantastic and I'm just so thankful for all the decisions that were made early on in the campaign."

"A lot of people say that there's a lot of sacrifices, but in all honesty we all very much enjoy what we do and they're not seen as sacrifices. Yes it's hard work, but there's a lot of enjoyment in there so it doesn't feel like I've sacrificed a great deal."

He had lived with the fact that he would be Olympic champion for the two days before the medal race.

"It's been a huge luxury. There's not many people that can say, 'I've won the Olympics before the medal race'. The end of Race 10 was really the big moment where it really hit me hard, especially then, I had time to stop and think about what I'd done, and look back over the last three years."

30

Rio Reflections

Looking Back and Looking Forward

Sailing a Finn is a demanding occupation. Every one of the 23 Finn sailors who made it to Rio made huge sacrifices to be there and many went home with unrealised goals and unfulfilled ambition. Some will be back, some won't, but all will have created a unique bond with a sporting event that played out as one of the tightest, closest, and most challenging Olympic regattas ever.

The line-up of Finn superstars included two of the medalists from the London 2012 Games and surprisingly neither even made it as far as the medal race.

Jonathan Lobert, who took bronze in London, was disappointed about his own performance, but was philosophical about the week.

"The racing has been good, we've been able to do all the races, but they have been very tricky. For me I am of course very disappointed. I think I had the speed, I was training very hard, I had the fitness, even winning one race and I think could have done much better but sometimes in sailing it's not always going the right way and I have to accept that and move forward."

"I am not depressed, just disappointed, and I think it's time for me to look forward and find a new challenge."

He said it was a very different challenge and competition to four years previously in Weymouth.

"I think compared to London this week has been very, very tight. The fleet was always very compact in almost all races and it has been very hard to come back when you made a mistake. I think it has been a really good competition in terms of the level of sailing. Everyone was very well trained and strong; it has been a very challenging week."

He was not particularly surprised at the conditions. "I think it has been more or less always like this in Rio, nothing very surprising, you think you know the place and then something else is happening. When we have been training here with Max [Salminen] and Tapio [Nirkko] we have always tried to stay open and look around at what could happen, but sometimes you need to be at the right place at the right time. There is no explanation and when you look at the results and the big scores, no one was always able to be in the right place all the time, except maybe Giles who was the most impressive sailor here this week. For the rest of the fleet it was always up and down."

LOBERT SAID HE will be back, but understandably needed a break. "I don't think it will be the end of Finn sailing for me but for sure I need quite a long break to digest all that has happened. And there is a lot of stuff happening now in sailing, foiling and stuff like that and I really want to try that and see what I can do and use my knowledge and experience in Finn sailing and Olympic sailing to join some team and try some different things. I know a lot about the Finn now and I think you never should close any doors, so we'll see how it goes and maybe I'll come back for Tokyo."

Even home favourite, Jorge Zarif, had commented earlier in the week that he had been frequently caught out by the conditions. However he bettered his 2012 result by 16 places to end up fourth overall, the joint highest place that a Brazilian has ever finished in the Finn, after Claudio Bierkarck placed fourth in 1976 and 1980. His coach Rafa Trujillo predicted he could finish fourth or fifth and proved coaches are sometimes right.

Zarif also felt encouraged by the support from the home crowd. "It's nice. We are not practising in a sports arena so we are not used to having people behind us. Here I feel a little bit more of that. A lot of people talk to me after the race and it's great. It's great to feel the energy of the people."

Zarif is expected to continue in the Finn, while also trying to complete his college studies. Like his father before him, he has now sailed in two Olympics, but still as one of the youngest Finn sailors on the circuit he surely has a bright career ahead of him.

For fifth placed Ivan Kljaković Gašpić, he repeated his result from London, at his third Olympics. He is considering his options about whether to carry on to Tokyo.

While first and second places overall were occupied by the same sailors since the second day, Giles Scott and Vasilij Žbogar, third place became a moving target with first Alican Kaynar, then Zsombor Berecz, then Jake Lilley and then Gašpić. It seems none of them could find the consistency to stay there until the end.

Lilley finally ended up eighth, after a quirk of scoring first dropped him out of the medal race, only to be reinstated later after his final race score improved following a protest and disqualification of another boat.

The tall Australian had lost weight for the Olympics, expecting it to be mainly light conditions, so on the lay day before the medal race he tried to prepare as only a Finn sailor would. "I had two steaks. A two steak day is a good day for a Finn sailor."

To add to the occasion of the medal race, his father had arrived just in time. "My father flew in and that was bit of a surprise. It was pretty funny because he was in Argentina and he sent me a text and said 'I'm in Argentina', and I responded with 'I'm not in the medal race', and so that was a bit of a heartbreaker. So he got back on the plane to Rio and he must have had a tough few hours up in the air and when he landed he got another text from me saying 'I am back in'. That was pretty emotional."

He paid credit to Scott, "All credit to Giles. He's had a fantastic week and he's truly one of the greats. But it was great that the rest of the medals were open to the end."

For the future, "I am pretty hungry after this week so I'll keep going and am looking forward to getting into the next quad and working towards the next Games. It just builds the hunger on the motivation after this week." His immediate plans, "Put some weight back on and some gym work, as well as some more two steak days, so it's going to be a good few months."

"It's been a fantastic Olympics but I can't wait to go home."

Lei Gong of China was sailing his second Olympics in the Finn and felt he had made great improvements since London 2012, even though, as he pointed out, his score was similar.

"I feel really relaxed now. Compared to the last Olympics my score was almost the same but I made progress since the last one. But all my rivals also had great improvements. When I sail in China I am more used to the weather and the wind. It feels really good to be involved in the Olympics, but I think this is my last time as a sailor. I'll see after I go back to China, but maybe for next time I will move into coaching."

Deniss Karpak, from Estonia, fell a long way short of his goals. "It was a super hard and tricky week, and I was unexpectedly unlucky."

He fell ill just before the Games with some breathing problems and a heavy cough and remained weak throughout the event. "Weakness and too strong winds for me didn't help to achieve my goals. All my goals were left unachieved."

"But I hope to fulfil my expectations next time in Tokyo 2020."

Josh Junior ended on a high note, after a difficult start to the regatta that left him with, perhaps, too much work to do. On the medal race he said, "I sailed a really great race. I gave myself heaps of opportunities to make a few places, so really happy with that. It was an amazing experience, being around here and coming down to the water front and everyone cheering you on, shouting out and the New Zealand flags flying."

"Apart from the first two days of the regatta I have sailed a really good event and, you know, I am happy with that."

On the future, "I don't know what I am going to do next. I am not going to sell the Finn, so I will definitely keep it." For Tokyo, "We'll see how things go but I'd love to be there as well."

THE OTHER SAILORS in the top 10 had their chances and let them slip away. Max Salminen had the same chances as Paine to take the bronze, but went the opposite side on the first beat and that was that.

Salminen said, "In the end it was a race that got decided already after 4-7 minutes and not many chances for me to catch up. After the first lap the American that I had to beat for bronze was so far ahead that I needed as big a wind shift as on the first upwind to come back. I wasn't interested in the positions between four and nine. I was willing to risk it all for a medal. So I went out to get it but ended up empty handed. I had a plan, I executed it and I was wrong. I made this plan after what I have experienced on that course in 150 days of training in Rio, which means that if I would to sail the same conditions again my plan would have stayed the same."

"My goal going into this Olympics was winning a medal. Not achieving this goal must be considered nothing but a failure. Not even after my wonky start the first two days I ever doubted that it was possible for me to win that medal. I got my sailing back on track and I forced myself to deliver the best sailing I ever have performed."

"With this confidence boost I went into the medal race and I was going for a medal. I was fast compared to my main competitors around the course and I had spent more time in Rio than most. I knew I had to perform at my very best since there were a bunch to beat before the finishing line. I usually perform at my very best when it matters and the small margins somehow often went my way at important times – so in my head I had to win this bronze if not silver."

"The ones to take the glory are the ones who sail fastest around that 25 minutes race track in the end. And I knew that you had to do everything right at the exact time to make it happen."

"Margins, coincidences, luck some said. I can't believe in that. I am the first to defend the sport of sailing on this point. If there is a game of chance there must be some odds, there must be a track record and if you've done your homework you should know the probability. Besides irregularity in the probability should be equalised after six days and eleven races."

"During the race I didn't give up. So I said to myself, maybe someone was over the line at the start, maybe there still is a chance. I was thinking, it couldn't end like this. I can't have fought for this for four years and everything gets decided on this kind of a race. I have met every goal on the way. Everything has been going according to the very ambitious plan towards this medal. It came to me as a complete shock in the moment I realised I was not going to get one of those medals."

"Maybe the lesson is what I heard one of our Swedish coaches saying, we have to be good enough to achieve our goal even on a bad day. Me, I didn't have the time for that. I wouldn't ever lower my goal and I cannot see myself accomplishing that much more in my four years."

"I really struggle to put my name to that sixth place. I see myself as the guy who had the chance on a medal and went for it. And I am really proud of the fact that I had a chance. My chances of winning a medal were far better than for myself and Fredrik Lööf winning gold in 2012. Those four years had been going so well and I have learned so much that I quite got used to accomplishing my goals. It really amazes me how far I've come but this Olympics still has to be considered a failure since my goal was a medal. Some say that it feels better failing when you know you have done your very best. Right now I doubt it. I did my best, I worked as hard as I could for four years and I know there is nothing more I could have done and I don't feel my goal was set to high. But still I fell short. As the Swedish proverb goes, it is fairer to listen to the string that broke than to never strain a bow."

Probably the biggest shock was the poor performance of Jonas Høgh-Christensen, the London 2012 silver medalist. He said his result in Rio was the biggest disappointment of his career. However, in an interview in 2017 he said he did not regret trying for Rio, however far short he fell of his goals.

He was hit by equipment damage before and during the Games, and had more than his fair share of bad luck on the water. He also later revealed he fell sick just before racing started, with tiredness and cramps. At the time, he was unaware what was wrong, but after returning home was diagnosed with meningitis.

At the start of the medal race, Pieter-Jan Postma compounded a disqualification on the final day of the opening series with a starting line error that left him having to restart and trail the fleet. By the medal race, his only route to a medal was to win the race, and as in London, he perhaps risked too much, especially on the starts – including hitting the pin end boat in Race 1 – to make it happen. Before the final day of the opening series he had risen to fourth overall, but those two races on Sunday cost him dearly and once again he left the Olympics empty handed.

And then there is young Facundo Olezza, the youngest, the lightest and the most inexperienced sailor in the fleet. To make the medal race was a huge achievement in itself, but to win two races along the way shows an unbridled talent that will surely rear its head again in the not too distant future.

31

Three Medals

Gold, Silver and Bronze

To conclude the reports from Rio, these interviews with the three medalists were carried out shortly after the Games.

HAVING ONLY LOST two regattas in the previous five years, Giles Scott went into his first Olympics as the absolute favourite, but was still surprised by his decisive victory. After a difficult first day, he moved into the lead on the second day to dominate and extend his points lead to take the gold medal with a day to spare.

He said the first race was the most critical.

"From that point on I knew I had to be as close to flawless as possible."

In the tenth race when he began to sail away from Žbogar to claim the early gold.

"I was desperate to get the 20 points before the medal race. The Sugarloaf course really wasn't where I wanted my medal decided. Race 10 was such a weird 50 minute race; everything over the past 10 years had been geared towards trying to claim a gold. To have it dawn on you that you achieved that during a race is an amazing feeling."

Was he surprised so many favourites failed to make the medal race?

"I was a little surprised yes, however I think it just highlights the difficulties of racing in Rio. It really was a brutal place to go racing."

"Rio was an intense place to be. Off the water I spent all my time before the regatta desperate to be on it. I loved my time there but with the amount of days I spent there I'm OK with not going back in the near future. On the water it was a dogfight and a place to keep a cool head. The racing was predictably tricky, however as a class I think we had a really good week of racing on the whole."

After returning back to the UK, "It's been a bit of a blur really."

He had a few media commitments but then went full tilt into the America's Cup programme with BAR.

"I couldn't resist the temptation of getting back into some racing straight away with the AC World Series event in Toulon shortly after we returned. Having said that, you really do get a bit of a feeling how much the win means to people that are alien to sailing. The Olympics really does bring our sport into the limelight."

At the time, there was much uncertainty about the choice of the Olympic classes for Tokyo, following an overturning of prior arrangements made by World Sailing.

"The uncertainty around [the Games] is troubling. I really feel for the new guys coming into the Finn with this uncertainty looming over them. I think the Finn is perfect for the Games and has served its place as the men's heavyweight division very well and in my opinion should continue to do so for many Games to come. I think that Olympic sailing has to be careful not to play around with its identity too much. It's never going to be like the AC or big ocean races and shouldn't try to be. It's Olympic sailing and should hold its core values and image close."

On his own plans, "I'm not going to sail the Finn over the next year at all. After that we will see."

His win makes it five Finn class Olympic gold medals in a row for Great Britain.

"The feeling I'm left with now is huge satisfaction."

VASILIJ ŽBOGAR ACHIEVED his goal of a dream ending to his Olympic career with another silver medal to add to the bronze and silver won in the Laser class in 2004 and 2008.

"To get the medal with so many good sailors was really tough and stressful. I still wake up every morning and look at the medal to see if it is real or it was just a dream."

Leading the regatta after the first tricky day was no real surprise, but his biggest challenge, and success, was holding onto silver for the rest of the Games, surviving two huge days at sea.

"The racing outside in strong wind was the most critical for me. My boat speed was very poor as it was physically very demanding, but I tried to make as few mistakes as possible and I survived."

Despite being the oldest sailor in the fleet, his experience paid off as he skillfully maintained his consistency right to the end. With three medals after five Olympics he had sealed his place in Olympic sailing history.

He said one of his best memories was, "entering the stadium at the opening ceremony as flag bearer for Slovenia", but otherwise, "definitely the medal race and the prizegiving. In the medal race I had a lot of Slovenians cheering for me on the beach."

"The welcome home was just incredible. More than 10,000 people just in my home town made me speechless. The pictures speak for themselves."

"It was a really difficult regatta. I think many of the favourites tried to beat Giles and they ended up making a lot of mistakes."

What does the future hold?

"The Finn is just a fantastic boat and it has everything. It is physically very demanding, technical, adjustable, tactically demanding, nice to watch on TV. It has a bright future ahead."

"At the moment I am working on a project with Esimit Europa. I hope it goes well because it will help a lot of Finn sailors. From the Finn I will take a break until the New Year, and then I will start to plan my last regatta."

Summing up his Olympic experience, he said, "I think everybody expected the Rio Olympic Games to be a bit of a disaster. But in the end the organisers tried really hard and everything went quite smoothly. The sailing had great TV coverage and a lot of viewers had much more than expected which is the most important for sailing."

CALEB PAINE NEVER gave up – and was rewarded with the bronze medal. He produced at least one good race each day, although often combined with a high score. He survived a protest that at first disqualified him, though he was later reinstated after video evidence was found. His best day was the fifth day of racing where he rose to fourth overall while many others fell by the wayside.

His big chance came in the medal race where, just five points off a medal, he chose the right side and was gifted a shift that allowed him to lead the race at every mark while his main opponents languished at the back, unable to recover.

"I knew I had a good chance of securing the medal after the first weather mark rounding but sailboat racing is a wild sport so I only knew I had done it after crossing the finish line."

While Paine was tipped for top 10 and a possible medal, was he surprised many favourites didn't even make the medal race?

"No not at all. Sailing is a wild sport and who can predict who will be in the medals in a fleet that is so strong?"

"The Olympics was an event I will remember for the rest of my life. Over 200 counties competed at the Olympic Games and the fact the Games can bring them all together in the name of sport and compete peacefully on the World stage is something truly magical."

"The Olympics fully deserves the hype it is given and represents all the best aspects of the human race. I personally have grown from the experience and will encourage young athletes to follow their dreams of going to the Games."

He said returning home after the Games was really special.

"It takes an army to get someone to an Olympic medal and being able to share that with the people that helped me get there is really special. Besides that I have had some downtime, which is exactly what I needed."

A lot of people have worn his medal, both in Rio and back in the USA. How many?

"I have no idea. Let's just say I haven't kept it in the box and it has some scratches."

He described the high points of the Games.

"One of the moments that really stood out for me was the day before the medal race. On the reserve day before the medal race, and I went up Sugarloaf with my family and it was a grounding before the biggest race of my life. That and being a member of Team USA and more specifically my sailing team mates. I think with each passing day it starts to slowly set in. Telling the stories of the Games and the experience of the event helps me come to realise what has happened."

"The Finn is a great Olympic Class. It has a great balance of tradition, sailing and the modern physical demand of the Olympic Games."

And the future?

"No idea. I am in the processes of figuring that out."

GILES SCOTT, COMPLETELY focused on the job he had to do, showing hardly any emotion whatever happened, and then exploding when he finally achieved his goal under the shadow of the Sugarloaf Mountain.

Vasilij Žbogar, the oldest Finn sailor in Rio achieving the near impossible in very tricky conditions, but at the end looking more surprised than anyone watching him. His vast experience and his professional campaign finally paid off.

And Caleb Paine, the young guy who had a dream and put the hours in to make it happen. Despite some ups and downs along the way, he maintained focus and won the bronze in a dramatic and decisive manner, perhaps helped by the intricacies of sailing under the rock that is the Sugarloaf.

Three great medalists – three great stories.

32

Gold Medal Partnership
Matt Howard on Coaching the Olympic Champion

Behind every great sailor, there is a great coach. For Giles Scott, this person was Matt Howard. As coach to Scott, Howard became one of the most successful Finn coaches of all time, with two European titles, four World titles, one Olympic gold medal and more major regatta wins than anyone can remember.

Howard's Finn career ended in 2007 following a career best tenth place at the 2006 Finn Gold Cup in Split, Croatia. His last event was the 2007 Finn Gold Cup in Cascais, Portugal. "I had decided I was going to retire before I went; in fact, several months before I went. I still approached it professionally but my mind I had just switched off. I don't really know why I went, but decided months before that I felt I had gone as far as I was going to go, I had reached my ceiling and I think as soon as you feel that, even it its not true, it's very hard to carry on. Perception is reality and my perception was that I had got as good as I was going to get."

So he turned to coaching and immediately became coach to the younger element of the British team, including Giles Scott, whose first international event was that same Finn Gold Cup in Cascais. As one career ended, another one was born. The rest, as they say, is history.

Soon after the gold medal was won, Scott was quoted as saying their

Rio programme was aimed at winning every event during the campaign. Howard explained what he meant, "I have done two cycles coaching Giles. In the quad leading up to London we certainly didn't have the goal of winning every regatta. You can only set that goal if you know you can win regattas and coming out of the back of that cycle we knew he could win regattas. But the goal wasn't so much to win every regatta between then and Rio, it was to go to every regatta with the goal of winning. Maybe that's just semantics but it was more of a mindset thing. We treated every regatta like it really meant something."

"Some people will say before a regatta, or when they are doing badly 'it is just a training event.' Some people will even say before a regatta, 'I am just practicing my starts and if I achieve that, then I am happy', and that has its place. We had a variety of different little work-ons that we would go into regattas to try and refine. But we wanted to go into every regatta without an 'out' and treating it absolutely properly, and that was hard work because the level of preparation and everything else to do that is huge. You can't just turn up with some settings that are not quite right or your second favourite mast. It puts a lot of pressure on getting everything in the right place logistically and putting that pressure on you, and I genuinely believe that it helped Giles deal with the pressure better because we had done it so many times before."

He explained that putting that much pressure on both of them at every event they went to would eventually pay off. "Giles just got better and better and better at it; and at some regattas he came back from huge setbacks – think about that first race in Rio – but we had been there before. While you can never compare the pressure the Olympics brings we had done a really good job in bringing enough pressure on ourselves at the other events."

"A little bit of it was about training everyone else's mind to see you as the winner, although I think the Olympic Games changes that mindset for other people a bit as it's the kind of event that can overturn dominance or pecking order. But we said we wanted to approach every regatta with the intention of winning it and we wanted to go into the Olympics after having dominated the top step of the podium. To dominate doesn't necessarily mean you have to win everything, but we did put a very high emphasis on winning in the venue."

Another big part of Howard's influence was to implant low risk strategies onto Scott's race management. "Always, our mantra was low risk, low risk, low risk. And it's been quite an interesting journey with Giles on that. When I first started coaching him in 2007 he was a by-the-seat-of-your-pants sailor. He'd say, 'I think right is going to pay' and he'd send it. So I worked with him quite hard on all that positioning stuff and being conservative, as well as spending a lot of time working on his downwind so he didn't have to take so many risks upwind."

"That ended up quite interesting really as then we went to San Francisco [for the 2010 Finn Gold Cup], which was a right side favoured venue, and by that stage he was sailing nice and conservatively, so I was like, 'no, you're just having to go all the way Giles'. Actually it turned out that sending it to a side sailing, when that did happen, ended up being was one of the things he found hardest in the end."

HOWARD EXPLAINED THAT as far as equipment was concerned, they placed an emphasis on being consistent across the whole cycle.

"We worked really hard on getting masts with the same numbers, similar hulls so that when you went to an event when the boat went in a container and you had to sail with a different boat at another regatta, that there was consistency, but the downside of that is that is does make it harder to do a proper testing programme. And also if your goal is to go to every regatta with the intention to win it, you are not going to turn up with a trial sail or a trial mast."

"We did play around with numbers a little bit in testing. We did quite a lot of development work and I would probably say, 50 per cent of it was unsuccessful in that we didn't use it. But I don't believe there is anything unsuccessful about a development programme where you come away with not using that bit of kit because you are always learning, and ideally you would come away with a bit of kit that is faster, but quite a lot of our testing was looking at what other people were doing and testing a bit of their kit and saying, no we're happy that ours is faster."

It was all about collecting information. "For example, if you try a softer mast, and it's a little bit slower, you can extrapolate where going even softer will take you. In general we were reasonably limited where we could go, but we did spend a lot of effort on making everything as good as it could possibly be, going into the detail on the hull, the rudder, the mast and sails and so on. We didn't do any huge changes to shape or anything, just chasing the small gains that we felt were there, even though they were small enough that you often couldn't even measure them. It was mainly standard gear that was fine-tuned."

"I wouldn't say that our gear was any more bespoke than anyone else's, but a big part of the Finn is the stiffness of your boat and your rig so everyone is trying to do the same thing, trying to get the best combination, so in that regard it was bespoke."

As far as sails go, Scott's sails were standard sails, with his modifications.

"The way it normally works is that a sail designer works with a sailor and the sailor has an agreement with the sailmaker that it won't go on the market until after the Games, and what's in it for them is that if they can come up with something that's going to win the Olympics then they will make their money after it, but the only way they are going to get that to happen is with the help of that sailor, so they are happy to give that sailor those rights."

This is what Ainslie did in London. "There were plenty of other sailors who were using sails at both Olympics that were not on the market, such as Jonas [Høgh-Christensen] who used a sail in London, which was not available to anyone else. The interesting thing about Ben's sails was that when they became available after the Olympics, no one was using them in the next two years. Lots of people tried them and thought they were not any better."

"Ben could get an exclusivity deal on those sails going into the Olympics, but it's wrong to say that is one of the reasons he won the Games. After the exclusivity deal ended, no one used them, so if they were better everyone would have been using them and they didn't."

With the diverse conditions in Rio he revealed there was never any programme to specifically tailor a sail to just the Olympics.

"We looked at what we thought was going to happen in Rio weather wise and from the kind of the sailing we had done and the conditions, we thought it was likely to be a light sea breeze venue or windy south-westerly when the cold fronts come over. Unless there is good heating, there is just no wind, so you probably wouldn't race. If it was hot enough you'd get a light sea breeze of 7-11 knots, and then if it was windy it was 18-25 knots and that is pretty much what we got."

"But I know if we had been on different course areas it might have been a different Olympics, but we only sailed in light sea breezes, or wind. So we got that right, but on the equipment, that is a pretty big range, so we never went too specific with stuff, just all round on our equipment choices."

The ideas and technical development was joint effort between the two of them.

"We have worked together since 2007 and our relationship has changed a lot in that time, as most coaching relationships do. It started off with me being a lot more experienced and being more me-led I guess and then over the years it evolved into more of partnership. We would both come up with different ideas. We would have some pretty honest conversations and that was something we always talked about: that we needed to be honest and ask whether we were doing the right thing. Always asking those difficult questions. And that was very, very much both of us in the last three years."

"I would tend to mange the process, whoever came up with the idea, although he did quite a lot of the legwork. Not to the level of shore crew; they'd laugh if he told them he was good at that stuff. But as far as a Finn sailor goes, he's pretty handy."

"I think, like a lot of people, Giles became a lot more obsessive about his equipment. But he wasn't any more overtly stressed about that than about anything and we did what we always do really. And we had plenty of practice at that over the nine years."

IN TERMS OF physical training, Matt explained that keeping fitness, and ensuring that Giles carried out enough training was always a juggling act, and sometimes a compromise.

"If you say your goal is the Olympic Games, then all the regattas you do in between, to some extent, you should carry on doing your physical training. Because one of the problems you get in sailing, is that you de-train during events, which is not dissimilar from many sports. In cycling they do the one-day classic, and they obviously taper it to the classic and then if it's a flat one or no attacks it's a pretty comfortable ride for the elite cyclists, and then they go into recovery. So they lose a few days of training, and don't get the stimulus. It's the same with sailing. I am not going to do any gym or cycling before a regatta and then you get a six day regatta at less than 12 knots and then two days travelling afterwards and then suddenly you can find that you haven't done anything for two weeks."

"So one approach is just to say, 'what's your goal' and prepare for that, but we didn't say that, we said we wanted to try and win every regatta we went to, so we had to juggle everything a bit. If your goal is to try and win, you don't go in tired and you don't train during the regatta, but it meant we had to train harder between regattas."

"And physically Giles is a responder, meaning that he responds well to training stimulus. Some people are and some are not and everyone is on a scale. So he benefits more quickly than others."

The role of the coach is also to be there when things go wrong and to maintain the balance when the pressure is on the sailor. This took on a special relevance during the Olympics when external distractions and additional pressures can destroy concentration.

"We never talked about the pressure. We never discussed any articles about him or the pressure. We just totally ignored it and we didn't discuss whether that was the correct strategy or not. I don't think I actually read much during the Games, though I suspect that Giles probably did read them as he generally reads everything. I tried to pretend as much as possible that it wasn't the Games. I didn't even watch any of the other sports on TV, which I think is a bit easier to do in sailing than in other sports. Of course you can go for a media blackout, but equally if you have never done that before that is something a bit different, so you might want to avoid. But I am sure if you have had a bad day then reading about how stupid you have been afterwards, when you are trying to move on, is not great."

One of the major things Howard said he brought to the campaign was being asked for his opinion and giving it; sometimes it was taken and sometimes it wasn't.

"I've always been a coach who will give my opinion if it is based on observations and facts. I will rarely go 'left is going to pay', but I will go 'I think there is more breeze left', or 'I think these are long phase shifts right', or 'there's a tidal feature here', or 'historically this course in this direction has been this', and that was no different in Rio."

"He'd always ask for my opinion on what was going to pay and he'd disregard it sometimes."

"Rio is an incredibly difficult venue and, as Giles once described it, when it comes to tide over a course, a bit of a coaches race in some regards, because they can get information that the sailors can't. You can see them all going up the course to measure the current and so in Rio, on all the course areas, I had quite a big role to play gathering information, and interpreting it and giving it to him."

ON SCOTT'S CHARACTER, Howard said, "Giles has always had a leash on himself, so I think that's one of his strengths, he genuinely does have a strong self-belief in what he is doing. He is always calm, and a very good learner, one of the best learners I have ever worked with, and a very growth orientated mindset. He will have a crack at anything, there's no trying to safeguard his ego, which made it quite easy to go through that regatta winning goal. And of course he is fiercely competitive." The pair got on well as a team. "On a few occasions we had some difficult conversations, but never any clashes."

The pressure and the expectations on both of them were huge, but Howard tried to block it as much as possible.

"For myself, it was go down and get the job done. It's only afterwards you realise how much pressure there was, because you are trying desperately, the whole time, not to think of the pressure and what it means. You are just not engaging with it. It's only afterwards that you, well probably not on day one, but that pressure just goes whooooaaaa…!"

He found it very hard to cope with the expectation that Scott was assured the gold medal. The final day: "That was big. You had the British Olympic Association and UK Sport actually naming Giles as the most likely medalist in the entire British team. And people talking dead certs, even within our team, I always found quite difficult. It's not accounting for the sport and there's no such thing as a dead cert. If you look a the results from Rio, it was far from being a dead cert."

"When he won [his third Finn Gold Cup] in New Zealand, without having to do the last race or the medal race, afterwards the write up was, 'wow, never in doubt', but it never feels like that at the time, because you know you are one OCS away from losing your discard and the pressure is back on and you are one gear failure away. So you are never a dead cert, and it never feels like that. So you come away from a regatta with a decent points margin, but the results or numbers don't reflect how hard the regatta was, how close you always are to the precipice."

"We identified three years before that the danger of the Games would be if you had a shortened series. We always felt that if there was a range of conditions, and a full series then Giles would have a very good chance, but if we only got five races in and then went to medal race, it would be a much harder regatta, therefore you had to make a good start. And we always said you needed to be in a bib by the end of day two and ideally that would be a yellow bib, just to make sure because you never know. You could do one race on day three and not do another race. So that was one of our threats."

However it didn't start the way they hoped with Scott collecting a 17th in the first race after a very light wind and random race under the shadow of Sugarloaf. He came back out fighting the next day for a 2, 1, but there was not much room for further errors.

And, so on day three in Rio, the Finn fleet was out on the course area off Copacabana. It was sunny, blowing 20-25 knots with huge rolling waves running past the spectacular shoreline. It was also quite tidal.

"We arrived late because it was so far out. We were late not as far as other boats were concerned, but the whole fleet arrived close to the start time, so we didn't have much time. It was blowing 25 knots and I went and did my usual left and right tidal rates. This gave no gradient, no difference in tide, though there was a lot coming against us but no difference left to right, and I only kind of just got that done in time. I got back to Giles and gave him that information and some other observations, and then he started the race and he ended up to the left of the group. And it wasn't until we were going up the course that I realised my right-hand reading wasn't over a tide line. It was the wrong side of the tide line that I hadn't got to, and there was a sudden drop off of 0.5 knots. I measured it later. So he was still out in a half a knot more foul tide than the guys to the right of him. And I could see that happening. It was a pretty horrible time in the coach boat I can tell you. He was almost last at the top mark and the distance was huge as they went round on the tide."

"He obviously realised there was something going on and went right on the next beat and had a phenomenal race and came back to 11th. He was hugely rapid."

"It tarred my brushes somewhat, but equally it was a potential disaster. He already had a 17th and now he had an 11th. He was running out of discards. As it happened he won the next race but a lot of the guys you would have expected to dominate that day didn't. The disappointing thing from my point of view was that he was so much faster than anyone else in that breeze that it should have been a two-bullet day and at that venue when you don't know what the next day is going to bring, you can't give up the days like that."

"He came alongside [the coach boat] after that race and said, something like 'don't tell me there isn't something tidal going on', and I said, 'I'm not going to tell you that because there is, there's a point five of a knot gradient and it's my mistake, but it's a no brainer. You've got to go that side.' Which he did next time obviously."

On the first day of racing. "We had an interesting conversation between Race 1 and Race 2." After finishing 17th, "He came alongside and said, "well that's not how you start an Olympic Games' and I said something like, 'that is how we started it. So today we just need to move on and take whatever we learned from that race into the next one.'"

Though of course there was disappointment and frustration, it did not affect Scott's approach. "If you look at the results it didn't. He was straight back into it."

But they were not the only problems for Scott. "On the second day he went to the wrong mark, which was a bit annoying. And he was leading three quarters of the way up the beat, but then overstood and rounded fourth. Interestingly the people who made that mistake in the first race, knew about it for the next race and it was a different set of people overstanding in the second not realising there were other marks up there that were difficult to see."

It was a day of appalling weather, with bad visibility, rain, huge waves and 25 knots. Around six or seven boats headed to the wrong set of marks and ended up reaching into the first mark.

"There is very little difference between orange and red in 25 knots in a big sea and bad visibility. Our windward marks 1 and 1A look exactly like gate marks. But it was the outer loop gate of the Laser or 470, which wasn't being used at the time. That was quite annoying."

"So we generally gathered a few extra points here and there, but obviously less than anyone else. And back to my mistake with the tide, you could say will that haunt me for the rest of my life? Well I thought it might at the time but actually I was really proud how I dealt with that for the rest of the regatta. I could have just said, I am not going to give him any more information or not give him my opinion any more, having made that error but I didn't, so I was pretty happy. Obviously he won, so that helps, but I am happy I didn't let it affect me, but I also think the role I have played over the years in that regard has been part of, or had a contributing factor, to his success over the years, and therefore if I had done that for the past seven years I couldn't not do it at the Games. It kind of worked out. You have to get it wrong sometimes."

"He had a juddery start to the pre-Olympics the year before as well, and at some other events he's been on the back foot initially. We had certainly been there before."

THE GAMES FOR Howard ended on a note of hilarity as he nearly caused the shutdown of the entire venue.

"They shut down the Finn boat park on the last day because I had left Giles' dry bag on the dock, and they thought it was a bomb. On the day he won, after the last fleet race, it was getting dark. I unloaded his bags and sail onto the dock and carried his sail to his boat to join in the celebrations. By the time I went back to the dock – it was two trips – I had totally forgotten about his black drybag that I had left there and it was so dark I just didn't see it."

"So the next day I get a phone call from the team manager asking if I had left a bag on the dock so I said 'no' and he said, 'well they're saying there is a bag on the dock belonging to Matt Howard that they are about to blow up'. So they secured the area and the boat parks had been closed down and all the rest of it, and it was the bag with Giles' sailing kit in it. So I said, 'that might be mine actually', and wandered down as they reviewed the CCTV footage until they found somebody getting out of a Team GB Rib having just towed a Finn in, so I was like 'don't blow that up!'"

"I AM NOT a terribly reflective person. It's interesting because it almost feels like I wasn't there. Real life comes back so it all feels like a bit of a dream."

"Obviously it was fantastic experience and we came away with what we went there for and looking back on that campaign, I think I am very proud of what we did and how hard we worked. It was gruelling. We worked so hard over those three years, so that's my reflection, and thankfully we got rewarded for it."

33

When Experience Counts

An Unbelievable Dream Come True
for Vasilij Žbogar

Not for one moment during the six days of racing in Rio did Vasilij Žbogar let himself believe that he would be leaving with a third Olympic medal. And yet he was the only sailor in the entire fleet to stay in a podium position from the first day until the last. From the look on his face even after having the medal in his hands, he still didn't quite believe it. His dream was to finish his Olympic career with a third medal and everything conspired around him to make that happen.

He was completely surprised to be in first or second position all the way through the Games. "It was incredible how I managed to do that but I was also surprised that Giles could recover from that first day. He was really bad, with an 17th and a yellow flag, so it was hard for him to sail all the week. I started really well and I thought that he would make another mistake."

"We were talking with Trevor [Millar] before the racing that the only thing I can count on is the experience. It was my fifth Olympics, so I said if the conditions will allow me to be in the top, for sure I will take advantage of it and I was seeing day by day people falling out of the top three and I said I have to be patient and not try to make a big mistake and bide my time. Maybe I never thought I would beat Giles, but a lot of sailors had in mind just to beat Giles, but I admitted to myself that he was unbeatable and not focussing on him; I was focussing to be second and putting a series together, which was for me like a win."

"The goal was to have a counter at the end of each day."

He knew that inside the bay he had a good chance of some good races because he was fast in the 7-12 knot range, and physically it would be a lot easier. He also knew that he would struggle on the outside courses, whether it was windy or not because his speed through waves was not so good. So he just told himself to get as few points as possible.

Then, "After the strong wind days, I told myself I had survived this, and I saw the forecast for the coming days. I am not saying I was thinking about the medal, because I never think about the medal. I just thought, I survived this, good, so I have a chance."

He also believes that luck played on his side with many sailors who should have excelled in the windy conditions picking up one or two high scores. During the week there were many ups and downs. "Facu [Olezza], Jake [Lilley], and Zsombor [Berecz] all went up and then all went down."

"I think that the good thing was that no one was pushing the rules, everyone was sailing cleanly, very few collisions, because there were very difficult sailing conditions inside and outside. If you remember the day we all finished the racing inside one behind the other, it is almost impossible to imagine that there were no collisions, but I was not aware of any."

He went into the medal race with a very good chance of a medal as long as he sailed a clean race, kept out of trouble and was not at the back.

At the start, "I remember that PJ [Postma, who was over the line at the start]] was just going ahead of me a little bit. Everyone was scared about the starting line. They told me you have to start carefully. I said I cannot sail with the handbrake on. I need to go for it otherwise I won't do it. I was still relieved when the flag came down but I never thought I was OCS. It was close, but not near an OCS."

He also thinks the Games in the Finn class went very smoothly and fairly. "Of course there were sailing battles but not in a personal way. I think there were very few protests, one or two only and apart from some sailors disappointed from the racing, I felt a really good atmosphere, even if the Olympics were very intense and a lot of good sailors were hoping for a medal. But at the end before the prizegiving they all came and offered congratulations, no matter what, in spite of their disappointment."

SAILING THE FINN was never the plan when he stopped sailing the Laser after the Beijing Olympics. "I thought I would finish in the Laser."

"But then after finishing the Laser and my career in 2008, after about six months off, I realised I wanted to sail some more but in a different boat. I had spent so much time in the Laser, and I thought two Olympic medals was enough and I felt comfortable to sail by myself so thought I would try the Finn."

"I met Luca [Devoti] just before London. I was training two years by myself a little bit with Trevor, a little bit in Split, with Bambi [Ivan Kljaković Gašpić], and then I met Luca and I met the Italian guys and we trained together for London."

"And then after London we agreed with Luca that we would train and sail together and we just needed a formula on how it will work out. Because up until London Luca was working for the Italian federation and after he wanted to stay more in Valencia and I arranged we would bring some more sailors and divide the costs and this is how it all happened. Then we started with the Dinghy Academy."

"And as with the Laser it was mainly young guys starting in the Finn like Zsombor and Alejandro [Foglia]."

"I knew I couldn't learn anything from them but I knew they would learn quickly and they would push me at the end before the Olympics."

Through his Laser days and his first Finn campaign his coach was Trevor Millar.

Millar remembers, "When I first met Vasilij he didn't speak English. So that was the challenge to start with. But we had a nice training group in the Lasers and he enjoyed training with us and kept coming back and his English improved, very quickly. I think at the beginning he was very, very good in light winds, so when we had the light wind races he was always in the top in the Laser and I think if you can sail in light winds that shows you have ability, because it is a lot easier to grunt in the strong stuff."

"We had the South African with us, Gareth Blanckenberg, who was very good in the strong winds, and I think the two of them learned off each other. Blanckenberg became a much better light wind sailor and Vasilij became much stronger in the strong winds, and I think that group worked quite well."

"We had Allan Julie from Seychelles and one or two others and I always try as a coach to make a nice environment. For me the environment is very important and if you have people that you enjoy spending time with on the campaign trail then it makes campaigning much easier."

"Vasilij was obviously very eager to learn. You could see he was getting stronger all the time. The first year I met him, even the second year, you wouldn't say he was an outstanding talent, but he was a hard worker and intelligent, and he can put all the pieces of the jigsaw together. And at the end of the day people would look back and say he was very talented, but maybe he was very smart."

"I think what he said about Rio was a combination of all that. When you are young you think you can do everything, you take more risk, but at the end of the day an old head is better than a young one."

Žbogar continued, "You don't need to be a big sailing nation to have a lot of strength. You can be a small nation and succeed quite easily in your sports. When I started sailing I had to adapt. I still had to acknowledge other sailors; my goal was to become a good sailor. I never thought I couldn't be as good as the sailors from bigger countries. So I just started travelling Europe first and then round the world and trying to train with the best."

"Being outside Slovenia was important because there was basically no one from Slovenia who knew much about the Laser and it was hard to improve. So I had to get into a training group and try to get better. At that stage just to get to the Olympics was a big thing. We never thought about medals, probably not even for Athens. We knew we were close but we never thought about it."

COMING FROM A small country such as Slovenia affects the way he approached his campaigns.

"Our federation is very small, with a small budget. There is no programme to develop a sailor, even these days. All sailors have to develop their own programmes. I want to try and change this a little bit but it's hard because the resources are very limited."

He said the major turning point was winning the Laser Europeans in Split in 2003. "Of course the results always give you a lot of confidence that you are on the right way. No major drastic changes, Trevor was with me all these years. I also had a fitness coach for 17-18 years. We knew it was going to take time, but with the results we knew it was the right way."

"In other classes it may be easier to get into the top ten but in the single handed classes the top 10 is really difficult, so already when you are 20th or 30th, it is a good result. And especially in the Laser. After getting the first medal I got a lot of confidence. Of course I got a lot of support from the federation, and that started to move everything in the right direction and I could afford more training and everything else I needed."

"I felt very good with SailCoach and with Trevor. I knew I had to try to have as much training as possible with them as a group because I saw it was the only way to actually improve and get some good results in the future. We were just working day by day and had a small dream and it came true."

"I stayed with SailCoach until 2008 and we were all the time together. Then I swapped to the Finn and Trevor was with me at the beginning, helping me. And then I used Trevor at the major regattas, at the Olympics, and so we always had this relationship, he was more focussed on the Laser so didn't have much time to learn the Finn."

"It's probably one of the longest coaching relationships in sport – coaches don't usually last very long. Trevor was with me in London and was Slovenian team manager in Rio."

"Every group that I was training in no matter whether the sailors were good or bad, I was never thinking 'OK I am here to train with some bad sailor'. From every sailor, no matter who they were, or if they were worse than me, I could always find something that was good and to learn from him. In Beijing, during the training before I was using the guy from Abu Dhabi, Adil, he was not a good sailor but he was 65 kg, and with Beijing being really light conditions no one wanted to train with him so we organised training with him and taught him how to sail in a straight line and for me it was very good trying to keep up with him. At the end he was sailing very well, and he helped me a lot, and probably with a better sailor who was heavier, I wouldn't have learned so much."

"I learn from every sailor. I always take something out it."

Millar said, "In Athens they brought out the new kicking strap arrangement, but both Vasco and Robert sailed with the old system. I think that's a good mentality. It was very difficult but you were both used to that system and felt comfortable with it. Whilst everyone else changed straight away to the new system and I think that shows Vasilij considers things and a lot of people would complain their training partners are not good enough but he is able to get into a training group and take the positives out of it rather than look on the negatives. A lot of people look at the negatives too much and not enough at the positives."

"I think also one of Vasilij's good points, is that he is able to fight hard on the water, even within our training groups, and come ashore and what happened on the water is left there and there are friendships. You are back to where you are on shore again and I think that's really important that they can fight hard in competition and in training but when you come ashore you have to leave what happened on the water and get on with life."

In 2015 he took on his younger brother, Jure, as his administrator and coach.

"Actually it was a good decision, and of course it worked out well. Definitely it was a really hard decision to get my brother involved. I knew I had some gaps I had to fill because the Olympics were getting closer and I had lost a lot of time on the small details in my programme and I needed somebody who would help me out."

"It was Santander that was the turning point and getting Jure involved."

At the end he was doing more and more. "At the beginning he was given a few tasks but by the end he was dealing with the sailmakers, with transport and payments, so I didn't have to think about anything. It was just a privilege to be able to sail like this."

"It was the small things. At that stage I was with Luca [Devoti] at the Dinghy Academy and Luca had 6-7 sailors and they were all much younger than me and he couldn't focus just on me. To survive and get a good a salary he had to focus on all of them but I was at a different stage in my development. I had different necessities than the younger sailors. I needed more time, I needed a swimming pool and to have a massage, and it was hard to ask Luca to fill all these gaps, so I rang my brother and said can you help me when I go to events, I need this and can you organise all these things so I have the right food, can you be in contact with Wilke for the masts and everything, transport, hotels, and my brother was slowly taking over all this."

"Not so much on the water because Luca was on the water, but all the other things. You know when you need to move the boat, who is going to take the boat, who needs to fix this. Jure was taking over all this so I could have my 2-3 hours of regeneration per day, which I needed at my age, and all normal training. I have minimum 2-3 hours regeneration, because if I skip that for 2-3 days I will be unable to walk."

One of the most important parts of his programme was the recovery process. "In the last year I couldn't be without a swimming pool so I'd do a minimum of 30-40 minutes light swimming in the pool each day. I felt a huge recovery because your body is so light in the water. It helps your joints and back to recover – like a small massage and you really feel relaxed after 30-40 minutes swimming."

"And then I did a little bit of stretching, and then a massage, every day. I couldn't go through a day without this, but you know, when I was with the other guys, we took an apartment and I was looking around for a pool and it took time. In the end my brother just went to an event before, found a good apartment with a swimming pool close by, so I didn't have to waste time on the small things. He filled the gap on these small things."

"Then I was able to sail which for me at this stage was the most important."

"For the last year and a half I had same recovery process. I didn't even change it for the Games. Come home, eat, cycling, swimming pool, stretching and massage. Every day the same. All really light stuff. It gets out the stiffness of the muscles, and loses the lactic acid. You get stiff muscles and break a lot of muscle fibres, so you need to regenerate as fast as possible."

"Of course at the Olympics you don't only get tired physically but also psychologically, so it's a combination of both, and at the end you get more and more tired and when you are 41 years old it is hard to be less tired than the others."

Of his three Olympic medals, Žbogar said the first was the most important to him. "Definitely the first was most important and it changed my life. I went from nobody to sporting hero. It was the first medal in sailing ever in Slovenia. I had much better conditions afterwards. I remember it was a very stressful final race, with three of us fighting for the bronze."

Žbogar carried the Slovenian flag at the opening ceremony at the Rio Games. Looking back at the 2016 Games he said, "It was just a dream come true. Unbelievable. I look back at the last few days in Rio, and it was really something special. Finishing my sport career like this is what all sportsmen want. I even had a phone call from Prime Minister of Slovenia offering congratulations."

For the future, "I have come to a point in my career when I want to help sailing grow as a sport. I have quite a lot of knowledge, not just sailing, but how it could be run, and how to help sailors to have better future in sailing; that's why I applied to the Athlete's Commission." During the Rio Games he was appointed to the Athlete's Commission within World Sailing.

"We have a lot of knowledge. We went through so many things, good and bad, and I made so many mistakes in my sailing career and over the next few years we would like to give this knowledge to some other sailors so they don't make the same mistakes and can learn faster."

34

Tokyo Dreams
The Greatest Show on Earth

Following the end of the Rio 2016 Olympic Games, most of the sailors announced the intention to try again for Tokyo 2020, while several announced their retirement. It had been a tough campaign, and a tough Olympics, and many sailors had now done three or more campaigns.

Giles Scott's return was largely dependent on the future of the America's Cup. However within a few months of the end of the 2017 America's Cup in Bermuda, and with the next Cup being announced for 2021, he was back in the Finn training in Tokyo. Later in the year he won the Enoshima Olympic Week. It was the first event for Finns at the 2020 Olympic venue and the first win for Scott on the long road to defending his title.

Silver medalist, Vasilij Žbogar, stated that Rio was his last Olympics, but in early 2017 commented that he might try to qualify Slovenia for the Tokyo Olympics, even if he didn't expect to go himself. Caleb Paine took an extended break after Rio and didn't race at all in 2017, but was expected back to the class in 2018.

Jonathan Lobert took time out after returning home unsure about his future, and said he was close to quitting sailing altogether. Then, when he was home in La Rochelle looking at the sea, he realised how much he missed sailing, and wanted to come back. But first he had a much needed operation on his knee, and then was back in the boat training for the 2017 season, where has was on top form, winning the European Championship in Marseille, in 2017, the venue for the sailing events of 2024 Olympic Games.

As well as Scott, several other sailors were tied up with the America's Cup during 2017, notably Josh Junior, who was a cyclor on the winning New Zealand boat. Jake Lilley also did some time with Artemis.

Max Salminen put the disappointment of the Games behind him and went back to training. He came back to have a fantastic 2017 season, winning the Trofeo Princesa Sofia in March, before claiming the Finn Gold Cup on Lake Balaton in September.

And then by mid-2017, rumours were rife that Jonas Høgh-Christensen was considering a comeback and a potential fifth campaign. With the first qualifier for Tokyo in Denmark in 2018, could he do it again? He declared after London that his Olympic career was over. His body would be a further four years old, and broken because of the years campaigning. He said he has so many injuries that he can no longer cycle or run properly, and has trouble with his knees, back and hips after two decades of elite competition. He feels the injuries every day and he went into Rio having cortisone treatments and pain relief to cope with his injuries.

Of the others, many were straight back into training after a short break. Ambition runs high in the Finn class, and many still have unrealised ambitions, but also still have the enthusiasm and commitment to see through another Olympic campaign.

The class never stands still, and whoever decides to campaign for Tokyo 2020 will have to match up against the continual stream of talented youngsters moving up the ranks. The transformation of the athleticism of the fleet that started in London and continued in Rio, will be even more prevalent in Tokyo. Anyone thinking about a medal will have to raise his game to new heights to be close to winning a medal. And no one is expecting Scott to give up his crown very easily.

To win in the Finn class takes tenacity and hard work. It remains a tough challenge for both the body and the mind. Those who make the decision to come back for Tokyo will be sharper, stronger and better prepared then ever before, but will also have to train harder and longer. Gold in Tokyo is the goal and it is already shining brightly in the distance. Many will try, but only one will succeed.

THE OLYMPIC GAMES is often called the Five Ring Circus. It is a sporting event that captures the imagination of sports fans and media more than any other competition in the world. Sailing has been part of the Olympics since the beginning of the modern Games, and the Finn has been part of the Olympics since 1952. Of all dinghy classes, the Finn has been used as Olympic equipment for the longest amount of time.

The 'circus' is also an apt way to describe what goes on between each Games, with political manoeuvring, lobbying and vast restructuring of the sport to cater for what the governing authorities decide is in the best interests of the sport to remain a viable and attractive Olympic sport. For justification, the media, the classes and sailors are told the changes are necessary to preserve sailing in the Olympics. Of course the flip side to that is that sailing derives a lot of its income from the Olympics. Much of the development work done by sailing bodies would disappear if sailing were no longer in the Olympics, including many jobs.

In terms of sailing's attractiveness, London 2012 changed everything. Here was proof that sailing could be engaging, that the public could be interested. The conditions, the location and the story were all attractive and brought in bigger spectator numbers than any prior Olympic sailing event. How many spectators actually understood what was going on is another issue, but that didn't really matter. The images that went round the world and across the general media of thousands of people cheering for dinghy sailors was almost unheard of prior to London 2012.

Sailing has always suffered through an under appreciative public and press who didn't really understand what the sport was all about. Perhaps it took the publicity and human story surrounding Ben Ainslie to finally bring sailing coverage to an indifferent audience with the energy and fanfare that had been needed for so long.

In many ways, Rio offered even better opportunities to showcase sailing as the most attractive sport of the Olympics. The natural amphitheatre of Guanabara Bay made it almost impossible not to succeed. But that is what happened and the hoped for live coverage from Rio was sadly lacking.

Much of the changes in the sport revolve around modifying the format and scoring systems so that the public and the general media can better understand and follow the sport. Of course, more spectators equates to more advertising revenue.

But as people's attention span gets shorter and shorter, it is not just affecting the media but also the nature of the sport. The call for faster boats, shorter races, smaller fleets and more sensationalist news, will come at a cost.

The traditional format of sailing has always been a series of equally weighted races, with either none, one or sometimes two or more discards. Sailors could discard their worst result, which might end up being a starting penalty, equipment failure or an accident that was no fault of their own, but more often than not the ability to survive a random quirk of nature that affects all sailing races. It accounted for the randomness and outside influences that were an integral part of the sport, and which the sailors often have no, or little, control over. The rationale for this is very simple and embodies the fundamental principles of sailing: the best sailor should be the one who is the more consistent over a wide range of conditions.

REVIEWING AND CHANGING Olympic formats and scoring goes back a long way. While many sports have had the same rules for generations, sailing seems to feel a need for continual change and reinvention to try and make the sport more popular or understandable. The concept of radical change focussed on the media first appeared in the early 1990s with a lot of experimentation at events to try and make sailing more interesting for TV and spectators, especially at the then SPA Regatta in Medemblik, which became famous for trying out new ideas. However most of the experiments failed, and were largely unpopular with sailors. Some of the arguments being used a quarter of a century ago are the same arguments being used today to justify change.

It's probably fair to say that, despite all the trials, experiments and changes, little has really improved over the past 25 years in terms of the sport's popularity. If anything, this constant tampering and adjustment has reduced confidence and interest and numbers on the water are down at many events that were highly successful in the past.

One of the stated problems with the traditional format and scoring was that the winner was often decided before the final race, or even the final day. This was no good for TV. How do you sell advertising at an event where the winner is already in the shower while the last race is still ongoing?

So formats were developed to try and minimise this scenario and force the competition to play out until the final moment; force every sailor, however dominant they had been to take part in the final act.

One new idea that did stick, from around 2007, was the controversial medal race, a short, double points, non-discardable final race for the top 10. It was part of the rules that non-attendance was not an option, even with an insurmountable points lead. Non-attendance would mean finishing tenth, whatever the scoreboard actually read.

It was controversial because it was designed, not only to draw out the competition to the final short race, but also to create drama and emotion. With 20 points on offer in one 10 boat race, mistakes were severely punished, and as happened many times, the best sailor of the week would fall short at the final, artificial hurdle. For creating dramatic, emotional out-comes and sporting TV, it worked. For rewarding the best sailor, it didn't always work.

It is really hard making sailing look good live, while also keeping some degree of fairness in the racing. Medal races were often very close to shore for spectators and media coverage. Taking the spectators to the sailing is not easy, but bringing the sailing to the crowd, will, more often than not produce an unfair arena because of the influence of the land on the wind.

However, despite the medal race format, the very best sailors still man-aged to amass a 20 point or more lead going into the medal race, so in effect had still won before the medal race, even if they were forced to sail round the course to complete the event. So further changes were discussed and the argument still rumbles on. In general sailors dislike medal races because they lose control of the situation, and too many times, one shift can make the difference between going home with a medal, or going home with nothing. Rio proved that without a doubt.

To try and provide some structure to the season, in 2008 the then ISAF came up with the idea of the troubled Sailing World Cup. It took a series of well functioning, high attendance, traditional and popular regattas and included them in a worldwide series. For the first four years the structure was the same, but then it was evolved into an elite series with limited num-bers that restricted the calendar. It is still being developed.

Through the early part of the quadrennium, a series of format trials and scoring trials were held to try and simplify and 'improve' the events and make them more media-worthy. Each event was slightly different, and each had it's own problems. In general the sailors did not like the changes because, as is often heard, it changed the sport from being one of sailing consistently, to one more based on random chance. In addition, not only were the sailors confused, the media were even more confused than ever before, so it was back to the drawing board.

There were many calls before and after Rio for a format that was easier for the public and media to understand. Not just shorter, simpler races that were easier to televise, but also a final deciding race where the winner was the first across the line – just like the 100 metres sprint – so that specta-tors did not have to have an in-depth knowledge of the points and scoring systems, but could see with their own eyes who had won.

There are many inherent problems with this approach.

Fundamentally it was widely contentious because it goes against all yacht racing tradition where the best sailors over a series of races and over a range of conditions is the winner, and perhaps leads to the question: do we want sailing to be sport or entertainment?

Sailing is not like other sports in the Olympics. It is largely dependent on weather conditions, and therefore weighting any part of the regatta, can unduly favour particular sailors. Ending a regatta with a 25-minute race in flat water and light winds, when the previous five days have been sailed in 25 knots and big seas, may not produce a winner who is the best sailor across the week, only the one who is best at flat water and light winds.

Sailing also suffers from having one of the most complicated and often changed set of rules in any sport. Not only do the rules change year to year, they also change event to event. Imagine turning up to a football match and receiving a set of rules for the game that is different from the match played the previous week?

Another viewpoint is that sailing is a participation sport, and not a spectator sport, so all this change is just undermining the integrity of a great sport. There are those who sincerely believe that sailing can never be tennis, or Formula 1, or Ryder Cup, or Tour de France, because it is sailing. It can never be guaranteed to start and finish on time. In fact it can never be guaranteed to start at all.

THE YEARS SINCE London 2012 were not only tough for the sailors, but also for the class. The politics and lobbying surrounding the choice of Olympic classes is the subject of much deliberation between sailing officials, sailors and media. Every four years there is a heated debate about the classes for the next Games.

Despite being one of the most physical, progressive, attractive and reliable classes ever used as Olympic equipment, the Finn has always had to fight for its place on the Olympic programme. These quadrennial battles became known as the Finn Nightmare, so it was with some relief that after London 2012, ISAF Regulations allowed for selection for two Olympic Games in a row. The class looked secure for at least 2016 and 2020 and could focus on growing sailing rather than politics.

But it wasn't going to be so easy. Suddenly in early 2016, the whole slate of classes was opened up again because of IOC directives for gender equality and the demand from some quarters for more modern and 'exciting' classes. All the classes were reviewed, but in the end nothing changed apart from a reduction in the number of athletes, from 23 in Rio to perhaps just 19 in Tokyo. But the process had created a lack of confidence in all the Olympic classes, as no one knew what would happen. This negative impact stymied class development for nine months. Sailors put their careers on hold while the decisions were taken.

How do you categorise what is 'exciting'; and to whom? Speed is exciting, but then so is close competition. In Rio the most exciting races were the two days in big winds on the ocean, conditions deemed too dangerous for most of the other classes. It was exciting racing that very few people got to see.

The racing on these days could have produced some of the best coverage ever shown of the Finn class: huge waves, high winds, with big, strong sailors conquering the extreme conditions, all set against a spectacular backdrop. It was the perfect combination of conditions for showcasing the Finn and Olympic sailing at its best.

Inside the bay, the racing was often so tight that after an hour of tough competition, the fleet would all cross the finish line in less than two minutes, many of them overlapped. They were fighting for every metre.

Media also has its part to play. After another round of format trials in early 2017, the comment came back from the sailors that the perceived problems with making sailing more attractive and exciting were more to do with the media coverage, and how sailing is delivered to the audience, than anything to do with the format.

Great venues, great conditions and great winds are the prerequisites for any successful sailing media package, but the story – the challenges faced by the sailors to get to the start line, and then to the finish line – is often far more important to general spectators than any specific racing action, whatever the format.

THERE WERE MANY stories coming out of Rio, but this was the story of the Finn class. Most of the favourites failed to live up to expectations and many had failed to even make the medal race. This spoke volumes both about Rio as a venue, but more importantly about the competitive depth within the Finn class.

The racing was as tight as the class had ever seen, the complex conditions stretching every sailor through the light days and the epic, monumental days at sea with monster waves. But all along, one man was perhaps destined to dominate and come away with the gold medal.

The Rio 2016 Olympic Sailing Competition for the Finn class was an absorbing battle of wits, skill, strength and mental stamina. The three worthy medalists highlighted the diversity of sailors and the skill sets required to conquer Rio's challenging conditions. Caleb Paine, brimming with young ambition, hard work and a sense of optimism; Vasilij Žbogar, the veteran of five Olympics, with huge experience and skill, and still never quite believing he had achieved his dream ending; and Giles Scott, the undisputed king of Finn sailing in the quadrennium.

Postscript

A Finn Photographer in Rio

Capturing the Finn class on camera at the Rio Olympics was an extraordinary experience. The work was not without its problems and challenges, both logistical and physical, but it was an incredible privilege to watch the Finn class racing close up every day.

Having worked with Olympic Finn sailors for the best part of 25 years it was an eye-opener to see what it takes to make it to that level, how the sailors coped with the constant media attention, and how they dealt with unexpected success or failure with the whole world watching closely.

Like the sailors, the week for me had its ups and downs, but the photos in the books are testament to the fact that Rio has many moods. Every day was different, the backdrops changed, the light changed. On one day the weather was so bad, the only bright points were the lights along Copacabana twinkling through the murk.

Each day was first spent trying to get a place on board one of the photo boats provided by the organisers, and then making sure the driver got to the right place at the right time to get the photos. Some boats were clearly not up to the job, especially offshore, with everything getting a thorough soaking.

As well as the normal yachting journalists there were also journalists from news agencies assigned to sailing for the odd day, who had no idea what to expect. Most went blithely out to sea in all conditions with little or no protection for either themselves or their expensive camera equipment.

The second and third days afloat were unforgettable days, standing out from many hundreds of days afloat, like big Wednesday at the 2012 Finn Gold Cup in Falmouth or Big Saturday at the 2007 Finn Gold Cup in Cascais.

The second day was wet and uncomfortable with bad visibility and relentless rain. Everything got wet. I never expected to be that cold in Rio, with fingers so numb that operating the camera and the iPhone became quite difficult while also trying to hold on to the wildly churning media boat, as it rose and fell and swirled around in the confused seas.

Many of the other non-sailing photographers spent these days in misery with seasickness, and on the third day, on the Copacabana course area, one was even knocked unconscious when he fell over after the boat launched off a big wave.

Like a true professional he apologised to the other photographers because we had missed a mark rounding while trying to raise his lifeless body from the deck. Afterwards, on the way in he asked me how I would grade the day in terms of how tough it was as a day covering sailing. He offered 8/10 or 9/10. I said it was more like 3/10. He seemed disconcerted with my assessment, but it had been the kind of day that sailing photographers dream about. It doesn't get much better than 20-25 knots, sunshine, great visibility and light, with a three metre swell with two metre waves on top, all rolling past Copacabana beach with Corcovado and Sugarloaf as perfect backdrops.

Most days went smoothly, but on the last day of the opening series there was nearly a diplomatic incident over the flags for the media boat. As usual we were allocated a media boat, marched to the pontoons and sent afloat.

We had been there 30 minutes or so waiting for the wind when an official boat arrived alongside and started talking in an increasingly heated tone with the driver. It turned out our media flag was missing. Despite all having accreditations and wearing the photographer bibs, we had to go back to the marina and get a flag. That was 20-30 minutes away, and the wind was slowly appearing so it would mean we would most likely miss the race.

Couldn't they bring one out?

"No, we must go in."

We were stopped on the way in by another security boat and had to explain what we were doing, before being escorted back to the marina.

Once there, a 30-minute wait ensued while we waited for a flag to arrive.

A man was standing there holding three flags. They were not for us.

We persuaded him to give us one and tied it on the boat. Someone else came along and took it off. One of the photographers saw someone else with a flag and ran round to get it and tied it on the boat. The same official comes and took it off. Three times we acquired a flag and three times we lost it.

Finally we were given a flag, but there were no ties, so the man goes off and comes back 10 minutes later with ties to attach the flag to the pole.

The photographers were now getting anxious. We had been at the dock over 45 minutes and the racing had started.

But finally we were off. We got stopped at the marina entrance for a security check, were marshalled across the first section of open water, and then another security check before leaving the bay for the ocean where the Finns were now coming downwind on the Niterói course area.

And that is why there are no photos of the first lap in Race 9.

Another part of the Rio experience was that I wasn't in the media bus that got attacked by stones (when everyone thought it was bullets), I wasn't on the so-called mugger's bridge outside the marina at the wrong times, I wasn't in the media tent when it started coming down around the journalist's heads when the wind came in hard one day, and I definitely wasn't in the media tent (not at the sailing venue) that gained a new hole at each end one day when a stray bullet came passing through – "at a low velocity" we were comfortingly told. I also didn't see much in the way of pollution. The horrid smells and debris in the water from the test event in 2015 were all but gone, and though I suffered numerous mosquito bites, I did not seem to have too many Zika symptoms.

Ever since the 2016 Olympics had been awarded to Rio, the doom merchants had been out in force predicting unsailable, light winds. What actually happened was that there was almost too much wind at times. There was also a huge disparity between the wind outside and inside Guanabara Bay. One day we came in from the offshore course, having survived huge seas and strong winds to be greeted by a mirror like bay with bad visibility. In fact, it had been that way all day and the live TV had been postponed for several hours because there was nothing to show – while the conditions outside had produced some of the best sailing ever filmed. But because it was not on the 'live' course, very few people saw anything.

It was a vastly different experience from London in many ways, much more low-key and laid back, as you would expect in Brazil. While almost all of Weymouth was decked out in Olympic banners and bunting, in Rio, it was easy to escape the Olympic mania and in some areas it was hard to know the Olympics was even happening.

Two things were expected out of the Rio Olympics, that Giles Scott would win and that the unexpected would happen. Well both happened and it made covering the event all the more interesting. Perhaps Scott's destiny was set while sitting on the Nothe in Weymouth watching Ainslie win gold in 2012 and knowing that it could have been him. Ever since then he has had one goal – gold in Rio. Having watched Giles calmly, and almost unemotionally, win four world championships, this gold was different: the culmination of nine years hard work.

Acknowledgements

THANKS TO EVERYONE who helped with the material for this book, especially of course all the Finn sailors who put up with interminable interviews and questions.

To Matt Howard and Trevor Millar for background information.

To Pat Healy for the initial inspiration and encouragement.

To the Finn Class Executive Committee, past and present, for both providing the pathway and the opportunity to spend my life watching Finn sailing, and also letting me generally having free reign to explore creative avenues.

To my long-suffering and understanding family.

Chapter 2 has been edited, abridged and amended from an article by David Leach, Richard Creagh-Osborne, Georg Siebeck and Robert Deaves and originally published in FINNLOG and FINNatics by the International Finn Association.

Parts of many chapters have also appeared in FINNFARE and in yachting magazines and websites worldwide. Some parts of Chapter 17 originally appeared in Sailing World.

Thanks to input from Prof. Jan Bourgois, Professor of Exercise Physiology at Ghent University, for some of the material in Chapter 3, originally published in FINNFARE.

For more information on the Finn Class see: finnclass.org

APPENDIX A

Profiles of Olympic Sailors

ARG – Facundo Olezza

Age: 21 • World Ranking (highest): 64 (61) • Previous Olympics: None
Results: 2016 SWC Miami (10), 2016 Europeans (69), 2016 Palma 2016 (58), 2015 Silver Cup (8)
Facundo Olezza was the youngest of the Finn sailors competing in Rio. He started sailing the Finn in February 2015, when he grew too big to sail the Laser, also after some 49er sailing in Argentina. When he switched to the Finn he joined the Dinghy Academy in Valencia. He had only competed in six major events in his Finn career prior to Rio, but his coach, Luca Devoti, saw enormous potential in the young sailor. Having spent most of 2016 recovering from injury, he sailed the Sailing World Cup Miami with a partially healed broken hand to qualify Argentina for the South American place in Rio.

AUS – Jake Lilley

Age: 23 • World Ranking (highest): 5 (2) • Previous Olympics: None
Results: 2016 Finn Gold Cup (4), 2016 Hyères (1), 2016 Europeans (37), 2016 Palma (4), 2016 Miami (4)
Jake Lilley was beginning to show a lot of potential on the race course with several top results during the year before the Rio Games. He qualified Australia for Rio in 2014 but then had an extended trials against Oliver Tweddell that only ended after the 2016 Finn Gold Cup. An intensely physical sailor Lilley started sailing Finns in 2012, when at 2 metres tall and 96 kg he had outgrown the Laser. He soon found his way in the Finn and early on set himself some very high goals, and with his then coach, John Bertrand, won the 2014 Junior European title.

BRA – Jorge Zarif

Age: 23 • World Ranking (highest): 7 (6) • Previous Olympics: 2012 (20)
Results: 2013 Finn Gold Cup (1), 2016 Finn Gold Cup (17), 2016 Hyères (7), 2016 Palma (9), 2016 Europeans (7), 2015 Finn Gold Cup (7)
Jorge Zarif was the youngest sailor in the Finn fleet at 2012 Olympics, just 19, but one year later went on to win the world title in Tallinn, Estonia. Mainly coached by Rafa Trujillo during this cycle, he had moderate success at some regattas, notably winning the Miami World Cup in 2016 against a top class field. Zarif has been competing in the Finn since 2008 when he was just 15. Though he sails from the late Clube do Rio de Janeiro, his hometown is São Paulo. His late father, Jorge Zarif Zeto, competed in the Finn in the 1984 and 1988 Olympics.

CAN - Tom Ramshaw

Age: 24 • World Ranking (highest): 27 (27) • Previous Olympics: None
Results: 2016 Finn Gold Cup (8), 2016 Europeans (10), 2016 Miami (13), 2016 Palma (31)
Tom Ramshaw only took up Finn sailing at the end of 2015 after taking a break from the Laser, when it was suggested he try out the boat. He immediately knew it was the boat for him, qualified Canada for Rio in Miami in January 2016 and then produced an outstanding tenth place at his first overseas Finn event at the Europeans in Barcelona. He followed that with six weeks training at the Dinghy Academy in Valencia before placing eighth at the Finn Gold Cup in Gaeta, to be selected shortly after. His progress after just nine months in the boat was nothing short of astonishing.

CHN - Lei Gong

Age: 33 • World Ranking (highest): 56 (56) • Previous Olympics: 2012 (24)
Recent results: 2016 Miami (7), 2015 Finn Gold Cup (52), 2015 Qingdao (1), 2015 Rio Test Event (17)
Lei Gong was sailing his third Olympic campaign and Rio was his second Olympics. His best result of this cycle was a seventh at the 2016 Miami World Cup, including a string of top seven places. While China does have a strong fleet of Finn sailors, they rarely appear at international events. Gong is no exception having sailed only eight ranking events since 2012. He went into the Olympics as one of the lowest ranked sailors, but three places higher than in 2012. His first international event was the Europeans in 2004 where he picked up the bronze medal in the Junior European championship.

CRO - Ivan Kljakovic Gaspic

Age: 32 • World Ranking (highest): 12 (1) • Previous Olympics: 2008 (8), 2012 (5)
Results: European Champion 2009, 2010, 2015; 2009 Finn Gold Cup (3), 2016 Europeans (8), 2016 Finn Gold Cup (20), Hyères (9), 2015 Finn Gold Cup (20)
Ivan Kljakovic Gaspic was one of the most experienced sailors in the fleet with an excellent record of regatta wins and top finishes. However since claiming his third European title in 2015 he had failed to live up to expectations, as seen in his drop from world No 1 in October 2015 to 12th. This was perhaps largely due to a tense and often heated Olympic trials against Milan Vujasinovic, which was only settled at the Finn Gold Cup three months before the Games.

DEN - Jonas Høgh-Christensen

Age: 35 • World Ranking (highest): 6 (1) • Previous Olympics: 2004 (9), 2008 (6), 2012 (2)
Results: World Champion 2006, 2009, 2016 Finn Gold Cup (2), 2016 Hyères (6), 2016 Palma (16), 2016 Europeans (12), Miami (2)
One of the smartest sailors on the circuit, Jonas Høgh-Christensen had the knack of peaking at just the right time. After a disappointing 2008 Olympics where he was one of the favourites he took several years off. He won his second Finn Gold Cup in 2009 after a year out of the boat, before coming back a year later with a superb campaign for London 2012. After that he went back to the music industry in Denmark before coming out of retirement for a second time in 2014. His results leading up to Rio showed a familiar upward trend as he headed into his fourth Olympics in the Finn.

EST - Deniss Karpak

Age: 30 • World Ranking (highest): 19 (1) • Previous Olympics: 2008 Laser (24), 2012 (11)
Results: 2011 Finn Gold Cup (8), 2016 Finn Gold Cup (13), Europeans (40), 2015 Finn Gold Cup (11), Kiel 2015 (1), Kiel 2016 (4)
Deniss Karpak moved into the Finn after the 2008 Olympics after he got too big for the Laser and has been a regular in the top 20, occasionally top 10 ever since, including winning races at all levels. He led the 2016 Finn Gold Cup early on before suffering on the windier days at the end. Despite being one of the tallest and biggest sailors in the fleet he seemed to produce his best in the lighter trickier winds. Karpak won the Sailor of the Year in Estonia on numerous occasions and was the Best Young Athlete of the Year in Estonia in 2007.

FIN - Tapio Nirkko

Age: 31 • World Ranking (highest): 13 (7) • Previous Olympics: 2008 (18), 2012 (10)
Results: 2015 Test Event (2), 2009 Europeans (2), 2016 Palma (3), 2015 Finn Gold Cup (10), Weymouth (4)
Tapio Nirkko is a very tall and strong sailor, as well as a very hard to predict sailor. Clearly capable of beating everyone on his day he often struggles with consistency when it counts, and for many years, the only competitive Finn sailor in Finland. On the occasions when he can put it all together he is a force to be reckoned with, and picking up the silver medal at the 2015 Test Event in Rio was not only the best regatta he had ever sailed, but also perhaps a sign of his true potential. He spent a lot of time training in Rio.

FRA - Jonathan Lobert

Age: 31 • World Ranking (highest): 2 (2) • Previous Olympics: 2012 (3)
Results: 2015 Finn Gold Cup (3), 2015 Test Event (4), 2016 Palma (8), 2016 Hyères (3), 2016 Weymouth (2)
Jonathan's Lobert's bronze medal at the 2012 Olympics was until late in 2015 his only major medal in the Finn class. For many years he failed to convert his potential into a medal, except at Weymouth. He has a very athletic style in the boat, especially downwind. Since he overcame his medal shortage with a silver at the 2015 Finn Gold Cup, his confidence blossomed and he was one of the top favourites in Rio. His selection for Rio was almost assured after long time training partner Thomas Le Breton dropped out of the race, allowing Lobert to focus on training in Rio, and he did a lot of that.

GBR - Giles Scott

Age: 29 • World Ranking (highest): 1 (1) • Previous Olympics: None
Best results: Finn Gold Cup 2016 (1), 2015 (1), 2014 (1), 2011 (1), Europeans 2014 (1), 2011 (1), 2015 Test Event (1), Weymouth (1), Palma (2)
Giles Scott went into the Olympics as the absolute favourite after only being beaten twice in the previous five years. Apart from gear failure in Palma 2016 he remained unbeaten since April 2013. He spent considerable time in Rio training and only competed in four major regattas since the 2015 test event. Many thought he would have won gold at London 2012 given the chance, but he lost out to Ben Ainslie for selection. Following his win at the Weymouth World Cup he went go into the Games as reigning world champion and World No. 1.

GRE - Ioannis Mitakis

Age: 26 • World Ranking (highest): 10 (6) • Previous Olympics: 2012 (14)
Results: Europeans (1), 2016 Finn Gold Cup (6), Hyères (11), Palma (6), 2016 Europeans (9), 2015 Finn Gold Cup (9), 2015 Test Event (16)
Ioannis Mitakis first appeared in a Finn in 2009 and took the Junior European title twice before winning the 2012 senior European title in very light and shifty winds. A clearly talented sailor, he had upped his game since London 2012, regularly placing in the top ten at major events, including winning many races but was yet to take a medal at a major event since the 2012 win. Though historically better in lighter winds, he had also improved in a breeze to become a great all round sailor.

HUN - Zsombor Berecz

Age: 30 • World Ranking (highest): 38 (14) • Previous Olympics: 2008 Laser (29), 2012 Laser (21)
Results: 2016 Europeans (2), 2015 Finn Gold Cup (23), Palma (7), 2015 Test Event (11)
Zsombor Berecz moved into the Finn after two Olympics in the Laser. Coming from Lake Balaton, he made the decision early on to join the Dinghy Academy in Valencia and clearly benefitted from training there. Going into the Games he perhaps lacked regatta practice, preferring to train in his Valencia group, and only competed in three events since the 2015 test event, but picked up silver at the 2016 Europeans, the highest placed Hungarian ever at an International Finn championship.

ITA - Giorgio Poggi

Age: 34 • World Ranking (highest): 16 (6) • Previous Olympics: 2008 (11)
Results: 2016 Finn Gold Cup (5), 2016 Europeans (33), 2016 Miami (11), 2015 Finn Gold Cup (24)
Giorgio Poggi won perhaps the most intense of all the Olympic trials to earn his space in Rio, fighting all the way to the end of the 2016 Finn Gold Cup when a fifth place earned him his ticket. After sailing in 2008 and narrowly missing the medal race, he lost a close 2012 trials. For Rio he was coached by Emilios Papathanasiou, and was sailing as well as he had ever done. He certainly raised his game for the selections, producing his best ever result at the Finn Gold Cup. Between 2002 and 2008 Poggi won six gold medals in different classes at the Italian national championships.

NED - Pieter-Jan Postma

Age: 34 • World Ranking (highest): 3 (2) • Previous Olympics: 2008 (14), 2012 (4)
Results: 2016 Europeans (1), 2011 Finn Gold Cup (2), 2016 Finn Gold Cup (3), 2015 Test Event (3), Palma (5), 2015 Finn Gold Cup (6)
Pieter-Jan Postma was undoubtedly the most popular sailor on the circuit with a very positive and introspective outlook, but this had been as much a hindrance as a help, as he was prone to taking unnecessary risks. He was heading for a medal in London 2012, but for a last minute rash move. Since then he had refocused, and was more calm than ever before. His 2016 European title win came amid a string of podium performances over the previous 12 months, including leading the 2015 Test Event every day, only losing gold on the punishing medal race.

NOR - Anders Pedersen

Age: 24 • World Ranking (highest): 11 (10) • Previous Olympics: None
Results: 2014 Finn Silver Cup (1), 2014 Finn Gold Cup (8), Hyères (5), Palma (14), 2016 Europeans (14), Miami (8), 2015 Test Event (1)
Anders Pedersen was one of the rising stars of the Finn fleet. After a seminal 2014 season in which he won the Junior Worlds and qualified Norway for the Olympics at the ISAF Worlds in Santander, he improved to the point where he was regularly at the top of big fleets and challenging the big names. Coached by Peer Moberg, since 2015 he also trained alongside Jonas Høgh-Christensen to learn from the Dane's experience. Pedersen started in the Optimist aged six and found he could overcome a fear of sailing by himself by practicing, so has been practicing for this ever since.

NZL - Josh Junior

Age: 26 • World Ranking (highest): 3 (1) • Previous Olympics: None
Results: Palma 2016 (1), 2015 Europeans (2), Hyères (4), 2015 Finn Gold Cup (14), 2015 Test Event (5), 2016 Europeans (4)
Josh Junior is from Wellington and has been sailing since he was five years old. He won selection for Rio against Andrew Murdoch, to whom he lost selection to in the Laser class in 2012. Junior was one of the brightest talents in the fleet and was the only sailor in Rio to have bragging rights that he had beaten Giles Scott since 2012. His win in Palma 2016 was a career highlight and his first major win in the class. A former New Zealand match racing champion, he went into Rio as a firm favourite for a medal. Junior was coached by John Cutler, who took bronze in the Finn at Seoul 1988.

SEY - Allan Julie

Age: 39 • World Ranking (highest): 89 (89) • Previous Olympics: Laser: 1996 (37), 2000 (28), 2004 (20), 2008 (32) • Results: 2016 Finn Gold Cup (45), Palma (56), Hyères (32), 2016 Europeans (62)
Allan Julie sailed four Olympics in the Laser and is a national sporting hero in his native Seychelles. He was tempted back to the Olympics by the opportunity of winning the African nation place and duly qualified in Palma in 2016. A product of the SailCoach programme he has been helped by his good friend Vasilij Žbogar, from their days training together in Lasers. Julie won gold in the Laser at the 2011 All-Africa Games in Maputo, Mozambique. At the 2004 Olympics, as the most experienced member of the Seychelles team, Julie was the flag bearer for Seychelles at the opening ceremony. He has also been Seychelles Sportsman of the Year five times.

SLO – Vasilij Žbogar
Age: 40 • World Ranking (highest): 35 (4) • Previous Olympics: Laser: 2000 (19), 2004 (3), 2008 (2); Finn: 2012 (6)
Results: 2013 Europeans (1), 2015 Finn Gold Cup (3), 2015 Europeans (3), 2016 Europeans (6), 20916 Test Event (13)
Vasilij Žbogar was a four time Olympian already and had the dubious honour of being the oldest Finn sailor in Rio. After a tough trials for 2012, he was selected early for 2016 and like many focussed on training in Valencia rather than travelling, and only competed in three events in the year before Rio. He lost much of the 2015 season after a cycling accident, but recovered to take his first world championship medal at the 2015 Finn Gold Cup. He is one of the most famous sportsmen in Slovenia and his first Olympic medal in 2004 also won him Slovenian Sportsman of the Year.

SWE – Max Salminen
Age: 27 • World Ranking (highest): 4 (4) • Previous Olympics: 2012 Star (1)
Results: 2015 Finn Gold Cup (5), 2013 Europeans (7), Weymouth (3), Hyères (10), Palma (10), La Rochelle 2015 (1), 2015 Test Event (6)
Max Salminen moved into the Finn class after winning the gold in the Star class at the London 2012 Olympics, along with his helm Fredrik Lööf. For Rio he won a fairly tense and close trials against Björn Allansson and improved year on year to the point where he was regularly qualifying for medal races. He spent more time training in Rio than most of the fleet – he said 150 days – and less time at regattas. A quick and tactically astute sailor, he was coached by Dayne Sharp, and stood a good chance at claiming a medal to add to his London gold.

TUR – Alican Kaynar
Age: 27 • World Ranking (highest): 20 (17) • Previous Olympics: 2012 (18)
Results: 2013 Europeans (10), 2016 Finn Gold Cup (21), Palma (18), 2016 Europeans (27), 2016 Miami (17), 2015 Finn Gold Cup (34)
Alican Kaynar was the only internationally competitive Finn sailor in Turkey this cycle and was based at the Dinghy Academy since 2012, but later was training alongside Giorgio Poggi. He qualified Turkey for the Olympics at the last possible chance, in Palma 2016. He has always shown far more promise than he has delivered, winning races at major events, but rarely finishing inside the top 10 at the end. However he is a skilled and intelligent sailor who is more than capable of being in the medal race.

URU – Alejandro Foglia
Age: 32 • World Ranking (highest): 45 (36) • Previous Olympics: Laser: 2004 (34), 2008 (17), 2012 (8)
Results: 2016 Europeans (12), Palma (22), 2015 Finn Gold Cup (17), 2016 Europeans (13)
Alejandro Foglia was the first Uruguay Finn sailor to compete at the Olympics since 1968 and only the second athlete in the history of Uruguay to qualify for four Olympics. In 2008 he was the flag bearer for the Uruguay team. He qualified for the final open spot at the Rio Olympics during the 2015 Finn Gold Cup in Takapuna. Since he joined the Finn class in 2013 he was been supported by the Finn class development programme, FIDeS, and moved to Valencia to train at the Dinghy Academy. In spite of a series of injuries setting back his campaign he remained one of the fittest Finn sailors in the fleet.

USA – Caleb Paine
Age: 25 • World Ranking (highest): 9 (1) • Previous Olympics: None
Results: 2012 Delta Lloyd Regatta (1), 2014 Finn Gold Cup (7), 2015 Finn Gold Cup (12), Hyères (8), Palma (13), 2016 Europeans (24), Miami (6), 2015 Test Event (15)
Described as the most hard working sailor on the circuit, Caleb Paine said it was because he needed to train to make up for lack of talent. At the 2016 Europeans in Barcelona he overcame double Olympian Zach Railey to earn his chance to represent the USA in Rio. That regatta of course included the famous mark trap incident from Railey that so nearly cost Paine his Olympic dream. Paine was introduced to the Finn in 2008 and was briefly World No. 1 in 2012, when he won two World Cup events.

APPENDIX B

Map of race areas

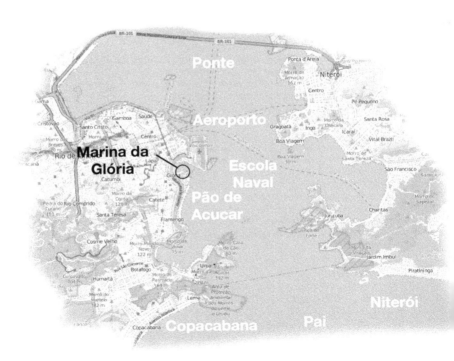

APPENDIX C

Olympic Medalists

Year and venue	Gold	Silver	Bronze
1952 Helsinki Finland	Paul Elvstrøm *Denmark*	Charles Currey *Great Britain*	Rickard Sarby *Sweden*
1956 Melbourne Australia	Paul Elvstrøm *Denmark*	André Nelis *Belgium*	John Marvin *USA*
1960 Naples Italy	Paul Elvstrøm *Denmark*	Alexandr Chuchelov *USSR*	André Nelis *Belgium*
1964 Enoshima Japan	Willy Kuhweide *Germany*	Peter Barrett *USA*	Henning Wind *Denmark*
1968 Acapulco Mexico	Valentin Mankin *USSR*	Hubert Raudaschl *Austria*	Fabio Albarelli *Italy*
1972 Kiel West Germany	Serge Maury *France*	Elias Hatzipavlis *Greece*	Victor Potapov *USSR*
1976 Kingston Canada	Jochen Schumann *DDR*	Andrei Balashov *USSR*	John Bertrand *Australia*
1980 Tallinn USSR	Esko Rechardt *Finland*	Wolfgang Mayrhofer *Austria*	Andrei Balashov *USSR*
1984 Long Beach USA	Russell Coutts *New Zealand*	John Bertrand *USA*	Terry Neilson *Canada*

1988 Pusan Korea	Jose Luis Doreste *Spain*	Peter Holmberg *US Virgin Islands*	John Cutler *New Zealand*
1992 Barcelona Spain	José Maria van der Ploeg *Spain*	Brian Ledbetter *USA*	Craig Monk *New Zealand*
1996 Savannah USA	Mateusz Kusnierewicz *Poland*	Sebastien Godefroid *Belgium*	Roy Heiner *Netherlands*
2000 Sydney Australia	Iain Percy *Great Britain*	Luca Devoti *Italy*	Fredrik Lööf *Sweden*
2004 Athens Greece	Ben Ainslie *Great Britain*	Rafael Trujillo *Spain*	Mateusz Kusznierewicz *Poland*
2008 Qingdao China	Ben Ainslie *Great Britain*	Zach Railey *USA*	Guillaume Florent *France*
2012 Weymouth & Portland UK	Ben Ainslie *Great Britian*	Jonas Høgh Christensen *Denmark*	Jonathan Lobert *France*
2016 Rio de Janiero Brazil	Giles Scott *Great Britain*	Vasilij Žbogar *Slovenia*	Caleb Paine *USA*

Medals by nation

Nation	Gold	Silver	Bronze	Total
Great Britain	5	1	-	6
USA	-	4	2	6
Denmark	3	1	1	5
USSR	1	2	2	5
Spain	2	1	-	3
France	1	-	2	3
New Zealand	1	-	2	3
Belgium	-	2	1	3
Germany/DDR	2	-	-	2
Poland	1	-	1	2
Austria	-	2	-	2
Italy	-	1	1	2
Sweden	-	-	2	2
Finland	1	-	-	1
Greece	-	1	-	1
Slovenia	-	1	-	1
US Virgin Islands	-	1	-	1
Australia	-	-	1	1
Canada	-	-	1	1
Netherlands	-	-	1	1

Also available:

BETWEEN A ROCK AND A CAMERA LENS

BETWEEN A ROCK AND A HARD RACE has an
accompanying photobook with more than
400 photos of the Finn Class
at the Rio Olympic Games.

BETWEEN A ROCK AND A CAMERA LENS is initially only
available as a limited edition hardback

80 pages • 210 x 210 mm • Full colour
ISBN: 978-0-9559001-6-7
Price £21

Available through Amazon

By the same author

Finntastic Games

The story of the Finn Class at the 2012 Olympic Games

64 pages; Size: 210 x 210 mm; full colour throughout; US trade paper; softcover; perfect bound; ISBN: 9780955900136; published: 3 Dec 2012.

£11.99

Only available through Amazon

Photo FINNish

60 Years of Finn Sailing

224 pages; Size: 297 x 210 mm; partial colour; silk paper; softcover; perfect bound; ISBN: 9780988900112; published: 2009.

£25 plus shipping

finnclass.org/shop

Completely OK

The History, Techniques and Sailors of the OK Dinghy

208 pages; Size: 297 x 210 mm; black and white; silk paper; softcover; perfect bound; ISBN: 9780955900105; published: 2008.

£20 plus shipping

okdia.org/completelyok.php

FINNatics – The History and Techniques of Finn Sailing

First published in 1999, now available again through Amazon.

208 pages; 297 x 210 mm; US trade paper; black and white; soft cover; perfect bound; ISBN 9780955900143.

£16.95

Only available through Amazon

Lightning Source UK Ltd.
Milton Keynes UK
UKHW010617071119
353079UK00002B/315/P